Postmodernism in a
Global Perspective

Postmodernism in a Global Perspective

Edited by
Samir Dasgupta
Peter Kivisto

www.sagepublications.com
Los Angeles • London • New Delhi • Singapore • Washington DC

First published in 2014 by

SAGE Publications India Pvt Ltd
B1/I-1 Mohan Cooperative Industrial Area
Mathura Road, New Delhi 110 044, India
www.sagepub.in

SAGE Publications Inc
2455 Teller Road
Thousand Oaks, California 91320, USA

SAGE Publications Ltd
1 Oliver's Yard, 55 City Road
London EC1Y 1SP, United Kingdom

SAGE Publications Asia-Pacific Pte Ltd
3 Church Street
#10-04 Samsung Hub
Singapore 049483

Published by Vivek Mehra for SAGE Publications India Pvt Ltd, typeset in 10.5/12.5pt Adobe Caslon Pro by Diligent Typesetter, Delhi and printed at De-Unique, New Delhi.

Library of Congress Cataloging-in-Publication Data

Postmodernism in a global perspective / edited by Samir Dasgupta, Peter Kivisto.
    pages cm
    Includes bibliographical references and index.
    1. Postmodernism. 2. Sociology—Philosophy. I. Dasgupta, Samir, 1949– editor of compilation.
    HM449.P726   301.01—dc23   2014   2013050692

ISBN: 978-81-321-1318-8 (HB)

The SAGE Team: Supriya Das, Archa Bhatnagar, Nand Kumar Jha, and
                Dally Verghese

Dedicated to Our Wives

Contents

Acknowledgments

Edited books are, by their very nature, collaborative undertakings. The fact that this book has been coedited by two people who live half the world away from each other is testimony to the fact that we truly do live in a global world, for if there is one thing we discovered during this joint undertaking, it is that the ease of communication made possible a remarkably smooth process from the initial inception of this project up to its completion.

This being said, the project could not have come together as it did, had it not been for the cooperative spirit of our contributors. We would like to extend our heartfelt thanks to the authors of this book: Ananda Das Gupta, Gabe Ignatow, Lindsey Johnson, Douglas Kellner, Jason Mast, Murray Milner, Jr., Mahbuba Nasreen, Jan Nederveen Pieterse, Andy Scerri, Nico Stehr, Rosalind Sydie, Imre Szeman, and Immanuel Wallerstein.

Any number of colleagues from around the world have proven to be supportive and encouraging over the years and have assisted in explicit or implicit ways to this endeavor. Peter Kivisto appreciates in particular his collegial relationships with Jeffrey C. Alexander, Nancy Berns, Paolo Boccagni, Paul Croll, Martina Cvajner, Thomas Faist, Inger Furseth, Douglas Hartmann, Auvo Kostianen, Lauren Langman, Kevin Leicht, Linda Lindsey, Ewa Morawska, Chris Prendergast, George Ritzer, Giuseppe Sciortino, William H. Swatos, Jr., Bryan Turner, Östen Wahlbeck, R. Stephen Warner, and Mary Zimmerman. Likewise, Samir Dasgupta would like to extend his appreciation to Rajat Subhra Mukhopadhaya, Pujan Kumar Sen, Swapan Kumar Bhattacharyay, Basabi Chakraborty, Robyn Driskell, Julia Sylvia Guivant, Yvonne Braun, Ruby Sain, Sheila Steinberg, Steven Steinberg, Ismail Siriner, Gulten Dursun, Md. Mizanuddin, Ray Kiely, Arzu Ozsoy Ozmen, Abbas Mehdi, Sing Chew, and Joy Alemazung. Finally, both the editors would like to offer a special recognition to their wives, Sumitra Dasgupta and Susan Kivisto. It is commonplace in acknowledgments to say that one's life partner made it all both possible and worthwhile. And, as we know full well, in our cases it also happens to be the simple truth.

Introduction

Postmodernism in Global Perspective

SAMIR DASGUPTA AND PETER KIVISTO

During the past three decades or so, two highly contested terms have entered not only academic discourse, but everyday discourse outside the groves of academe: postmodernism and globalization. Over the course of this period, despite many attempts to sort out with some precision exactly what each term means, they both remain highly contested—as concepts that are meant to specify something distinctive about the contemporary social world and as normative evaluations of that world. This collection of essays is assembled with a conviction that both postmodernism and globalization have the potential to be valuable tools for social analysts, this despite the uncertainties and ambiguities that persist.

The editors (and the authors) make no claim to have found a solution that would overcome the uncertainties and ambiguities. Indeed, it is our conviction that setting such a goal would amount to a fool's errand. Rather, it is assumed that at some level both concepts will remain contested. That being said, the task at hand is twofold. First, all of the essays are expressions of efforts to employ one or both of the concepts in terms of empirically grounded topics, and secondly, to add further precision or clarity to the concepts themselves in order to assist in the task of enhancing their utility in making sense of the dynamics of social change.

Postmodernism and Globalization

As with all such terms, there is a history that always predates the recent past. Thus, one can find uses of the terms "postmodernism" and "globalization" at least as early as the middle of the 20th century.

However, it was more recently that the terms came into far more general usage and only in the past two decades that they have taken on a life of their own. Books, articles, conferences, and other staples of academic life have been devoted to aspects of each concept, and it is fair to say that academic careers have been made by proponents of one or the other who were astute enough to see the potential for widespread interest—and, indeed, enthusiasm—in their application in various disciplinary contexts.

From the vantage of the sociology of knowledge, postmodernism, the main focus of this collection, arose at a moment when modernity itself was in various ways called into question. Thus, the idea that progress was inevitable—a view found in both orthodox Marxist thought and in modernization theory—was questioned. In part, this was due to the growing realization of the unintended consequences of the application of science and technology to solve a wide array of problems existing in both the natural and social worlds. The discovery that DDT, a chemical developed with the honorable intention of eradicating malaria from the world, was not only killing the mosquitoes responsible for the disease, but was working its way through the food chain. Rachel Carson's (1962) famous account, *Silent Spring*, was one of the harbingers of a new awareness that science and technology were mixed blessings. The ripple effect of this awareness regarding human efforts to control the natural world has grown over time. It is likewise with our capacity to employ the social sciences to remedy social problems. Emblematic of this parallel awareness was the famous comment made by architectural critic Charles Jencks that the destruction of a public housing project in St. Louis, Missouri in 1972 represented the dawn of the postmodern age. Once seen as a solution to urban poverty, it had become defined as part of the problem.

Meanwhile, globalization—a phenomenon that Marx was well aware of in the 19th century—accelerated and intensified during this same period. The developed industrial nations witnessed the constriction of the manufacturing sector, leading to a process that became known as deindustrialization or the beginning of a post-Fordist economic order, while the developing world experienced the relocation of manufacturing plants in their countries. This shift gave way to theoretical accounts of the advent of postindustrial society (Touraine, 1971; Bell, 1973). The idea that automation would result in the reduction of workers needed in basic industries, while no doubt partially correct, was only part of the story, the larger part being the relocation of manufacturing and the resultant substitution of workers in wealthy countries with workers from poor countries. More recently, a counterpart to deindustrialization took off in earnest, the phenomenon of downsizing the size of the white collar workforce, outsourcing the work to "offshore" locations, which meant the same places that manufacturing jobs had ended up earlier. But economic globalization was about more than this. It involved the creation of global markets and the expansion of powerful transnational corporations no longer rooted in or with allegiances to particular nations or their respective citizens.

Economic globalization was intimately connected to both political and cultural globalization. Much of the focus of the former has been on the emergence of an international human rights regime and the expanded significance of trans-state institutions. However, the darker side of the equation concerns the militarization of the globe. During the Cold War this entailed the struggle between the American and Soviet empires for hegemony. After the collapse of the Soviet Union, it resulted in a uni-polar world in which American military might had no counterpart (which is not to say, as insurgencies have amply proven, that it is all-powerful). American consumer culture has a parallel impact on global culture. It has exhibited an enormous influence on the world, but it has not been a one-way street resulting in the destruction of local cultures. On the contrary, one can find homogenization American-style existing side-by-side with efforts to shore up and strengthen local cultures. Moreover, one can find ample evidence of the interplay between the two, the growing hybridity of cultures.

Postmodernism, in its most general sense, is often seen as offering an attempt to account for temporal change: the move from premodern to modern to postmodern. Globalization, meanwhile, is depicted as an effort to account for the way in which spatial definitions of reality are being transformed in the era of fast capitalism. In attempting to frame all of this theoretically in a manner that can account for both postmodernism and globalization and for the ways they are necessarily implicated in and help to define each other, we turn briefly to one particular theoretical approach that we find compelling. Time-space compression is a concept developed by the Marxist geographer David Harvey to describe contemporary developments in capitalism which have led to the speeding up of the circulation of capital and with it a speeding up of social life in general while simultaneously reducing the significance of place. Harvey's concept derives from his consideration of Marx's claim that capitalism leads to the annihilation of space by time, and from Heidegger's foreboding about the implications of the shrinking of both time and space. For Heidegger (1971: 165), this shrinking produces a "uniform distancelessness," which he views as both unsettling and terrifying because it does not promote what he refers to as "nearness" by which he means a sense of identity rooted in the particularities associated with specific places—which he considers to be "the locale of the truth of Being." Harvey appropriates this general orientation while rejecting the reactionary political implications of Heidegger's anti-cosmopolitanism. He sees in Heidegger's thought a convincing articulation of the dislocation of identity from place that is a consequence of the penetration of the modern capitalist economy predicated on the ceaseless expansion of industrialization and ever-changing technological developments.

Harvey contends that space-time has been significantly reconfig-ured since the 1970s as a consequence of the accelerated pace of the globalization of capital accumulation during this time. This temporal framing signals the end of the alliance between labor and capital that had been forged in the most developed capitalist economies during the quarter of a century after World War II and the beginning of the neoliberal epoch. Described somewhat differently, the 1970s witnessed the end of the Fordist age of industrialization and the beginning of the post-Fordist era. The result of this shift is that some urban centers that were key to the success of Fordism—cities such as Detroit in the United States, Liverpool in the United Kingdom, Lille in France, and Duisburg in Germany—have had their place-specific identities as centers of industry undermined. The increasing mobility of capital has led to the deindustrialization of these and similar industrial centers in capitalism's quest for ever-new sources of cheap labor. Aiding such mobility are developments that have resulted in improved transporta-tion systems and the revolution in communication technologies. In combination, Harvey (1996: 297) contends, they have undermined the "monopoly of power inherent in place."

Marx's relevance is seen in Harvey's discussion of the shift from Fordist production methods of the industrial era to the post-Fordist emphasis of contemporary capitalism. Capitalism, as Marx under-stood it, was restless and rootless, and the modern consciousness that it engenders is one wherein "all that is solid melts into air." Part of capitalism's contradictory character is evident in the fact that it needs, on the one hand, to create fixed structures in particular places in order to permit accumulation but, on the other hand, it must be perpetually prepared to be mobile. Schumpeter's (1942) notion of "creative destruction" captures well the character of this inherent tension between fixity in place and mobility in space. While for Schumpeter this tension represented the creative dynamic inherent in capitalism that made it a force for progress, Harvey—the Marxist and the geographer—emphasizes the dialectical character reflected in the space of flows and the fixity of place. He is also attentive, in a way that Schumpeter was not, to the human and social costs of time-space compression, as space increasingly trumps place.

Harvey's concept bears a family resemblance to two other concepts, Manuel Castells' (2000) "network society" and Anthony Giddens' (1990) "time-space distanciation." The former is described in terms of the "space of flows," flows being understood as meaningful and routinized exchanges and interactions in the dominant social structures of society. Castells (2000: 443) writes that places get absorbed by the network, the result being that "the space of flows is not placeless, although its structural logic is." Thus, for example, global cities become crucial hubs in financial and commercial networks, places where the managerial elites critical to the functioning of the network society reside and operate. However, there is nothing intrinsically distinctive about New York's Wall Street and London's City that necessitate that they remain centers of finance. The central difference between Harvey and Castells is reflected in two diametrically opposed career shifts: whereas Harvey began his career as a positivist geographer, over time he abandoned his earlier work as a consequence of his intellectual encounter with Marx; in contrast, Castells' early work as an urban sociologist was shaped by Marxist thought, but by the time he developed the idea of network society, Marx had in significant ways became less central to his thought. Thus, it is not surprising that time-space compression is defined as part of the logic of capital accumulation, while Castells' analysis of "the new economy" is more likely to frame its contours in terms of information technologies, markets, and the like without overly stressing the capitalist character of the economy.

While Giddens was never a Marxist, his early work focused attention on capitalism in a way that his later work on globalization does not. The term "distanciation" refers to the stretching of social relations across space and time, allowing for the expansion of social relations that are not predicated on co-presence. The focus of this concept is on social interaction, not on the changing face of capitalism. As with Castells, Giddens places primary emphasis on communication and transportation technologies, and not on capitalism per se as a cause of distanciation. The contrast between Harvey and both Castells and Giddens serves to highlight that which is distinctive about the concept of time-space compression, which has to do with its theoretical rootedness in orthodox Marxism's historical materialism, or as Harvey would prefer to specify the theory's explanatory logic, in "historical-geographical materialism."

Overview of Chapters

With this theoretical outline of how to connect postmodernism and globalization in mind, we turn to the contents of this volume. The first three chapters in this collection, by Douglas Kellner (Chapter 1), Immanuel Wallerstein (Chapter 2), and Jan Nederveen Pieterse (Chapter 3) do not directly take up the topic of postmodernism; rather, they serve to frame the issues that are addressed in subsequent chapters by highlighting the fact that postmodernism must be understood in terms of a global framework and not simply within the confines of nation states. Thus, they appear in a section of the book titled "Framing Postmodernism in Global Terms." Kellner's contribution expands on his earlier work on the subject by treating globalization as contested, stressing that there is a dialectical tension between capitalism and democracy. This critical theory of globalization can, in effect, serve to frame all that follows. Wallerstein, using the language of globalization rather than world systems, links it to the discourse on developmentalism that, as he notes, was in its heyday from 1945–1970. He seeks to explore what might be seen as inherent economic limits to capitalism's capacity to accumulate, and with that in mind, he examines the potential openings for opposition to capitalist hegemony and sketches out what the foreseeable future might look like. Jan Nederveen Pieterse's chapter parallels Wallerstein's. He is intent on exploring the contours of variations of both capitalism (capitalisms, in his terminology) and globalization. His empirically rich account focuses on East Asia,

China, and India, seeking to see how developments in this general part of the globe are being shaped by neoliberalism. He concludes by examining new potential fissures and conflicts resulting from the new international division of labor.

The next five chapters, in a section titled "Explicating Postmodernism," turn explicitly to postmodernism, beginning with Andrew Scerri's (Chapter 4) examination of the origins of postmodernism in sociology—where, it should be noted, it arrived somewhat later than in the humanities. He locates the deeper and often unexplored connections between classic figures in the discipline and the late 20th century postmodern turn, and concludes with a defense of what he calls the "weak postmodern thesis." Peter Kivisto's (Chapter 5) entry can be read as a parallel contribution, for he, too, seeks to locate the deeper roots of postmodern thought in the history of sociology. In this case, it is in particular Simmel who is viewed as a precursor to subsequent postmodern sociology. Kivisto also contends that, in contrast to more radical versions of postmodernism that postulate a dramatic rupture between the modern and postmodern, it is best to read postmodernity as a critique of modernity—or in other words, as residing in modernity, whether or not one prefers to quality that by defining modernity today as advanced, late, or some other designation intended to indicate that modernity has a history. This line of analysis continues with the following chapter by Nico Stehr and Jason Mast (Chapter 6), which differs from the preceding two chapters insofar as it analyzes postmodernism from the sociology of knowledge perspective. Offering a more critical and skeptical assessment of postmodernism than one finds in Scerri and Kivisto, Stehr and Mast are inclined to treat postmodernism more as a symptom of an unsettled epoch than a cogent account of the present.

Samir Dasgupta's (Chapter 7) contribution constitutes a vigorous defense of the sociological imagination and a meditation on what it means to do "good sociology." As such, his chapter is very much, to borrow from Alvin Gouldner (1973), "for sociology." And, like Gouldner, Dasgupta is intent on seeking avenues for promoting "renewal and critique in sociology today." To that end, he is less interested in exploring the adequacy of postmodernism's philosophical underpinning, its ethical implications, and so forth; rather, he wants to determine to what extent postmodernism can assist in the task of advancing the discipline of sociology. Though quite different in approach, Murray

Milner's (Chapter 8) selection, too, seeks to analyze the implications of postmodernism for sociology. He is quite critical of many proponents of postmodernism, challenging in particular those who are intent on forging an anti-foundational yet morally relevant theory. However, rather than writing postmodernism off as irredeemable, he urges the articulation of a "constructive postmodernism" that is more tempered and moderate, and as such is prepared to meet sociology halfway, at a place where one is prepared to see the virtues of "generalizations, objectivity, grand narratives, and transcendent categories."

The remaining four chapters of the book constitute case studies entailing applying postmodernism to various facets of social life. The first two chapters in the section address the connection between postmodernism and feminism. R. A. Sydie (Chapter 9) does so in a broad ranging and theoretically sophisticated analysis. Viewing, as she says at the outset, postmodern theory as both constraining and liberating for feminism, Sydie seeks to explore those avenues in postmodern theorizing that can contribute to emancipatory politics. In making her case, she also takes up the issue of multiculturalism, as is evident in her discussion of figures such as Charles Taylor and Tariq Modood. In effect, she enters the territory framed by Susan Moller Okin's (1999) question, namely, "is multiculturalism bad for women?" Sydie asks the same of postmodernism, and does so by locating the issues at hand squarely in a global perspective. Mahbuba Nasreen (Chapter 10) takes up a far more specific topic, which is the contribution of Julia Kristeva to a postmodern variant of feminism. Kristeva's work is difficult to summarize or locate in terms of various theoretical traditions, not least because of her desire to distance herself from various sources of influence and labels. Given the challenge, Nasreen offers an evenhanded, sympathetic yet critical assessment of her work, which includes discussions of some of Kristeva's most significant critics, such as Nancy Fraser and Gayatri Spivak.

The following chapter, by Gabe Ignatow and Lindsey Johnson (Chapter 11), very explicitly links postmodernism and globalization theory. The authors are intent on indicating the potential for postmodern concepts to inform and shape empirical research. More specifically, Ignatow and Johnson contend that the idea of "market religion" can be construed as a postmodern concept, and after a discussion of recent work on market Islam, they attempt to illustrate the usefulness of the more general idea of market religion in non-Islamic settings, in this instance focusing on Guatemalan neo-Pentecostalism. The collection shifts to a very different, but equally grounded analysis of critical management studies, authored by Ananda Das Gupta (Chapter 12). The argument advanced is that the growing interest in this alternative to traditional management theories is a consequence of what are described as "postmodernist movements," in particular feminism and environmentalism. These movements, so it is argued, have led to the emergence of a critical epistemology that serves as the philosophical underpinning of this new alternative approach to management studies.

The volume concludes with Imre Szeman's "Globalization, Postmodernism, and Literary Criticism" (Chapter 13). In effect, this contribution takes us full circle, for Szeman begins by offering an analysis of the different characteristics of postmodernism and globalization, in the process indicating in what ways both terms, however different, serve as coordinates that map our contemporary condition. The specific focus—and thus the case study nature—of his contribution is on the place of literary criticism in a globalized world where transnational connections take on heightened significance. But in this regard, literary critics are but one manifestation of a broader concern, which might be succinctly summarized as calling into question the future of intellectuals.

Taken as a whole, this volume has in a variety of ways helped to develop and clarify our theoretical understanding of both postmodernism and globalization. Moreover, it has stressed and sought to indicate the necessity of locating postmodernism in a global framework. Finally, as some of the chapters have illustrated, there is a payoff for sociological research in taking up the challenges presented by these new developments in theory in a critical and constructive way.

References

Bell, D. 1973. *The Coming of Post-Industrial Society.* New York: Basic Books.
Carson, R. 1962. *Silent Spring.* New York: Houghton Mifflin.
Castells, M. 2000. *The Rise of Network Society, Vol. I: The Information Age: Economy, Society, and Culture,* 2nd ed. Malden, MA: Blackwell.

Gouldner, A. 1973. *For Sociology: Renewal and Critique in Sociology Today.* New York: Basic Books.

Giddens, A. 1990. *The Consequences of Modernity.* Cambridge: Polity.

Harvey, D. 1996. *The Condition of Postmodernity.* Oxford: Blackwell.

Harvey, D. 1996. *Justice, Nature, and the Geography of Difference.* Malden, MA: Blackwell.

Harvey, D. 2007. *A Brief History of Neoliberalism.* New York: Oxford University Press.

Harvey, D. 2010. *The Enigma of Capital and the Crises of Capitalism.* New York: Oxford University Press.

Marx, K. and F. Engels. [1848] 1967. *The Communist Manifesto.* NewYork: Penguin Books.

Okin, S.M. 1999. *Is Multiculturalism Bad for Women?* Princeton, NJ: Princeton University Press.

Schumpeter, J. 1942. *Capitalism, Socialism, and Democracy.* New York: Harper & Brothers.

Touraine, A. 1971. *The Post-Industrial Society.* New York: Random House.

Waters, M. 2001. *Globalization,* 2nd ed. London: Routledge.

PART I

Framing Postmodernism in Global Terms

1

Dialectics of Globalization
From Theory to Practice

Douglas Kellner

Globalization continues to be one of the most hotly debated and contested phenomenon of the past two decades. A wide and diverse range of social theorists have argued that today's world is organized by accelerating globalization, which is strengthening the dominance of a world capitalist economic system, supplanting the primacy of the nation-state by transnational corporations and organizations, and eroding local cultures and traditions through a global culture. Contemporary theorists from a wide range of political and theoretical positions are converging on the position that globalization is a distinguishing trend of the present moment, but there are ongoing debates concerning its origins, nature, effects, and future.[1]

For its defenders, globalization marks the triumph of capitalism and its market economy (see apologists such as Fukuyama, 1992; Friedman, 1999 and 2005 who perceive this process as positive), while its critics portray globalization as destructive and negative (see Mander and Goldsmith, 1996; Eisenstein, 1998; Robins and Webster, 1999). Some theorists highlight the emergence of a new transnational ruling elite and the universalization of consumerism (Sklair, 2001), while others stress global fragmentation of "the clash of civilizations" (Huntington, 1996). While some argue for the novelties of globalization and even claim it constitutes a rupture in history, others stress continuities with modernity and play down differences and novelties (see Rossi, 2007). Driving "post" discourses into novel realms of theory and politics, Hardt and Negri (2000, 2004, and 2009 present the emergence of "Empire" as producing evolving forms of sovereignty, economy, and

---

[1] This chapter draws on my previous studies of globalization, especially Cvetkovich and Kellner, 1997; Kellner, 1998; Best and Kellner, 2001; and Kellner, 2007.

culture that clash with a "multitude" of disparate groups, unleashing political struggle and an unpredictable flow of novelties, surprises, and upheavals.

Discourses of globalization initially were polarized into pro or con with a "globophilia" that celebrates globalization contrasted to globophobia that attacks it.[2] For critics, "globophilia" provides a cover concept for global capitalism and imperialism, and is accordingly condemned as another form of the imposition of the logic of capital and the market on ever more regions of the world and spheres of life. For defenders, globalization is the continuation of modernization and a force of progress, increased wealth, freedom, democracy, and happiness. Its "globophilic" champions thus present globalization as beneficial, generating fresh economic opportunities, political democratization, cultural diversity, and the opening to an exciting new world. Its "globophobic" detractors see globalization as harmful, bringing about increased domination and control by the wealthier overdeveloped nations over the poor underdeveloped countries, thus increasing the hegemony of the "haves" over the "have-nots." In addition, supplementing the negative view, globalization critics assert that it produces an undermining of democracy, a cultural homogenization, hyperexploitation of workers, and increased destruction of natural species and the environment.

There was also a tendency in some theorists to exaggerate the novelties of globalization and others to dismiss these claims by arguing that globalization has been going on for centuries and there is not that much that is new and different. Some imagine the globalization project—whether viewed positively or negatively—as inevitable and beyond human control and intervention, whereas others view globalization as generating new conflicts and new spaces for struggle, distinguishing between globalization from above and globalization from below (see Brecher, Costello, and Smith, 2000).

---

[2] What now appears at the first stage of academic and popular discourses of globalization in the 1990s tended to be dichotomized into celebratory globophilia and dismissive globophobia. There was also a tendency in some theorists to exaggerate the novelties of globalization and others to dismiss these claims by arguing that globalization has been going on for centuries and there is not much that is new and different. For an excellent delineation and critique of academic discourses on globalization, see Steger, 2002.

Engaging the "dialectics of globalization," I sketch aspects of a critical theory of globalization that will undercut the opposing globophobic and globophilia discourses in order to discuss the fundamental transformations in the world economy, politics, and culture in a dialectical framework that distinguishes between progressive and emancipatory features and oppressive and negative attributes. This also requires articulations of the contradictions and ambiguities of globalization and the ways that globalization is both imposed from above and yet can be contested and reconfigured from below in ways that promote democracy and social justice. Theorizing globalization critically and dialectically involves contextualizing it at once as a product of technological revolution and the global restructuring of capitalism in which economic, technological, political, and cultural features are intertwined (Best and Kellner, 2001; Kellner, 2002). From this perspective, one should avoid both technological and economic determinism and all one-sided optics of globalization in favor of a view that theorizes globalization as a highly complex, contradictory, and thus ambiguous set of institutions and social relations, which takes economic, political, social, and cultural forms. Finally, I focus on the politics of globalization, stressing resistance and oppositional movements to corporate and neoliberal globalization from "the Battle of Seattle" to "Occupy Wall Street" and "the Arab Uprisings," concluding with a sketch of a "militant cosmopolitan globalization" as an alternative model.

Toward a Critical Theory of Globalization

As the ever-proliferating literature on the topic indicates, the term "globalization" is often used as a code word that stands for a tremendous diversity of issues and problems and that serves as a front for a variety of theoretical and political positions. While it can serve as a legitimating ideology to cover over and sanitize ugly realities, a critical globalization theory can inflect the discourse to point precisely to these phenomena and can elucidate a series of contemporary problems and conflicts. In view of the different concepts and functions of globalization discourse, it is important to note that the concept is a theoretical construct that varies according to the assumptions and commitments of the theory in question. Seeing the term globalization as a construct helps rob it of its force of nature, as a sign of an inexorable triumph of market forces and the hegemony of capital, or, as the extreme right fears, of a rapidly encroaching world government. While the term can both describe and legitimate capitalist transnationalism and supranational government institutions, a critical theory of globalization does not buy into ideological valorizations and affirms difference, resistance, democratic self-determination, and an alternative cosmopolitan globalization against forms of global domination and subordination.

Viewed dialectically, globalization involves both capitalist markets and sets of social relations and flows of commodities, capital, technology, ideas, forms of culture, and people across national boundaries via a global networked society (see Appadurai, 1996; Castells, 1996, 1997, and 1998; Held et al., 1999). The transmutations of technology and capital work together to create a new globalized and interconnected world. A technological revolution involving the creation of a computerized network of communication, transportation, and exchange is the presupposition of a globalized economy, along with the extension of a world capitalist market system that is absorbing ever more areas of the world and spheres of production, exchange, and consumption into its orbit. From this perspective, globalization cannot be understood without comprehending the scientific and technological revolutions and global restructuring of capital, which are the motor and matrix of globalization. Many theorists of globalization, however, either fail to observe the fundamental importance of scientific and technological revolution and the new technologies that help spawn globalization, or interpret the process in a technological determinist framework that occludes the economic dimensions of the imperatives and institutions of capitalism. Such one-sided optics fail to grasp the coevolution and co-construction of science, technology, and capitalism, and the complex and highly ambiguous system of globalization that combines capitalism and democracy, technological mutations, and a turbulent mixture of costs and benefits, and gains and losses (Best and Kellner, 2001).

In order to theorize the global network economy, one therefore needs to avoid the extremes of technological and economic determinism, and to see how technology and capitalism have contradictory effects, creating both immense wealth, but also conflict and destruction. In addition, globalization is constituted by a complex interconnection between capitalism and democracy, which involves positive and negative features that both empower and disempower individuals and groups, undermining and yet creating potential for fresh types of democracy and struggle. Yet most theories of globalization are either primarily negative, presenting it as a disaster for the human species, or as positive, bringing a wealth of products, ideas, and economic opportunities to a global arena. Hence, I would advocate development of a critical theory of globalization that would dialectically appraise its positive and negative features. A critical theory is sharply critical of globalization's oppressive effects, skeptical of legitimating ideological discourse, but also recognizes the centrality of the phenomenon in the present age. At the same time, it affirms and promotes globalization's progressive features such as global movements of resistance to corporate and neoliberal globalization, which, as I document below, makes possible a reconstruction of society and more democratic polity.

Indeed, a global movement of "Arab Uprisings," to use Al-Jazeera's term, in 2011 expanded struggles for democracy and justice throughout the Middle East targeting oppressive authoritarian regimes that had ruled for decades. A critical theory of globalization thus moves in a dialectic of theory and practice that reconstructs theory and politics through engaging existing democratic movements for democracy and emancipation.

Consequently, I want to argue that in order to properly theorize globalization one needs to conceptualize several sets of contradictions generated by globalization's combination of technological revolution and restructuring of capital, which in turn generate tensions between capitalism and democracy, and haves and have-nots. Within the world economy, globalization involves the proliferation of the logic of capital, but also the spread of democracy in information, finance, investing, and the diffusion of technology (see Friedman, 1999 and 2005; Hardt and Negri, 2000, 2004, and 2009). On one hand, globalization is a contradictory amalgam of capitalism and democracy, in which the logic of capital and the market system enters ever more arenas of global life, even as democracy spreads and more political regions and spaces of everyday life are being contested by democratic demands and forces. But the overall process is contradictory. Sometimes globalizing forces promote democracy and sometimes inhibit it, thus either equating capitalism and democracy, or simply opposing them, is problematical. These tensions are especially evident, as I will argue, in the domain of the Internet and the expansion of new realms of technologically mediated communication, information, and politics.

The processes of globalization are highly turbulent and have generated proliferating conflicts throughout the world. Benjamin Barber (1996) describes the strife between McWorld and Jihad, contrasting the homogenizing, commercialized, and Americanized tendencies of the global economy and culture with traditional cultures which are often resistant to globalization. Thomas Friedman (1999) makes a more benign distinction between what he calls the "Lexus" and the "Olive Tree." The former is a symbol of modernization, of affluence and luxury, and of Westernized consumption, contrasted with the Olive tree that is a symbol of roots, tradition, place, and stable community. Barber (1996), however, is too negative toward McWorld and Jihad, failing to adequately describe the democratic and progressive forces within both. Although Barber recognizes a dialectic of McWorld and Jihad, he opposes both to democracy, failing to perceive how both generate their own democratic forces and tendencies, as well as opposing and undermining democratization. Within the Western democracies, for instance, there is not just top-down homogenization and corporate domination, but also globalization from below and oppositional social movements that desire alternatives to capitalist globalization. Thus, it is not only the traditionalist, non-Western forces of Jihad that oppose McWorld. Likewise, Jihad has its democratizing forces as well as the reactionary Islamic fundamentalists who are now the most demonized elements of the contemporary era, as I discuss in the following paragraph. Jihad, like McWorld, has its contradictions and its potential for democratization, as well as elements of domination and destruction (see Kellner, 2012).

Friedman (1999, 2005), by contrast, is too uncritical of globalization, caught up in his own Lexus high-consumption lifestyle, failing to perceive the depth of the oppressive features of globalization and breadth and extent of resistance and opposition to it. In particular, he fails to articulate contradictions between capitalism and democracy, and the ways that globalization and its economic logic undermines democracy as well as circulates it. Likewise, he does not grasp the virulence of the premodern and Jihadist tendencies that he blithely identifies with the Olive tree, and the reasons why globalization and the West are so strongly resisted in many parts of the world. In *The World is Flat*, he focuses on parts of the world that have to some degree benefited from neoliberal globalization, while ignoring regions and groups where it has no negative and destructive effects documented in cascading stacks of studies and books (Stiglitz, 2002; Hayden and el-Ojeili, 2005; Amoore, 2005).

Hence, it is important to present globalization as an amalgam of both homogenizing forces of sameness and uniformity, and heterogeneity, difference, and hybridity, as well as a contradictory mixture of democratizing and anti-democratizing tendencies. On one hand, globalization unfolds a process of standardization in which a globalized mass culture circulates the globe creating sameness and homogeneity everywhere. But globalized culture makes possible unique appropriations and developments all over the world, thus proliferating hybridity, difference, and heterogeneity.[3] Every local context involves its own appropriation and reworking of global products and signifiers, thus proliferating difference, otherness, diversity, and variety (Luke and Luke, 2000). Grasping that globalization embodies these contradictory tendencies at once, that it can be both a force of homogenization and heterogeneity, is crucial to articulating the contradictions of globalization and avoiding one-sided and reductive conceptions.

The present conjuncture is thus marked by a conflict between growing centralization and organization of power and wealth in the hands of the few contrasted with opposing processes exhibiting a fragmentation of power that is more plural, multiple, and open to contestation than was previously the case. As the following analysis will suggest, both tendencies are observable and it is up to individuals and groups to find openings for political intervention and social transformation. Thus, rather than just denouncing globalization, or engaging in celebration and legitimation, a critical theory of globalization reproaches those aspects that are oppressive, while seizing upon opportunities to fight domination and exploitation and to promote democratization, justice, and a progressive reconstruction of the polity, society, and culture.

---

[3] For example, as Ritzer argues (1993 and 1996), McDonald's imposes not only a similar cuisine all over the world, but circulates processes of what he calls "McDonaldization" that involve a production/consumption model of efficiency, technological rationality, calculability, predictability, and control. Yet as Watson et al. (1988) argue, McDonald's has various cultural meanings in diverse local contexts, as well as different products, organization, and effects. Yet the latter's pluralization of McDonaldization goes too far toward stressing heterogeneity, downplaying the cultural power of McDonald's as a force of a homogenizing globalization and Western corporate logic and system (see Kellner, 1999).

Globalization as a Contested Terrain

It is clear from theoretical debates concerning what globalization is and actual struggles in the world for and against neoliberal globalization, that globalization is a highly contested terrain that is conflictual, contradictory and open to resistance and democratic intervention, and is not just as a monolithic juggernaut of progress or domination as in many discourses. The September 11 terror attacks on the United States and the subsequent era of Terror War show that capitalism, technology, and democracy do not work smoothly together to create a harmonious and increasingly affluent social order, as Friedman (1999) and others have argued. The events of September 11 and their aftermath dramatically disclose the downsides of globalization, the ways that global flows of technology, goods, information, ideologies, and people can have destructive as well as productive effects. The disclosure of powerful anti-Western terrorist networks shows that globalization divides the world as it unifies, that it produces enemies as it incorporates participants. The events disclose explosive contradictions and conflicts at the heart of globalization and that the technologies of information, communication, and transportation that facilitate globalization can also be used to undermine and attack it, and generate instruments of destruction as well as production.[4]

September 11 deflated once and for all the neoliberal and globophilia celebrations of globalization. It was evident that globalization produced intense conflicts, and many Western states, led by the United States, created more repressive and authoritarian forms of state-corporate globalization in which the state promoted neoliberalism and the interests of some corporations while repressing its own citizens and generating a police-state and military surveillance apparatus. Thus if 1990s globalization was a form of "deterritorialization" in which the state ceded power to global corporations and institutions, as well as the power of an increasingly unregulated market, an authoritarian state returned with a vengeance post-9/11—giving rising to another set of conflicts against repressive corporate-state apparatuses.

---

[4] I am not able in the framework of this chapter to theorize the alarming expansion of war and militarism in the post-September 11 environment. On war and militarism in the contemporary era (see Boggs, 2003 and 2005; Bacevich, 2005; Best and Kellner, 2001; Kellner, 2003b, 2005, and 2007).

Seeing globalization as a contested terrain is advanced by distinguishing between globalization from below and globalization from above of corporate capitalism and the authoritarian state, a distinction that should help us to get a better sense of how globalization does or does not promote democratization. Globalization from below refers to the ways in which marginalized individuals and social movements resist globalization and/or use its institutions and instruments to further democratization and social justice. While on one level, globalization significantly increases the supremacy of big corporations and big government, it can also give power to groups and individuals that were previously left out of the democratic dialogue and terrain of political struggle. Such potentially positive effects of globalization include increased access to education for individuals excluded from entry to culture and knowledge and the possibility of oppositional individuals and groups to participate in global culture and politics through gaining access to global communication and media networks and to circulate local struggles and oppositional ideas through these media. The role of new technologies in social movements, political struggle, and everyday life forces social movements to reconsider their political strategies and goals and democratic theory to appraise how new technologies do and do not promote democratization (Kellner, 1997; Best and Kellner, 2001).

In their book *Empire*, Hardt and Negri (2000) present contradictions within globalization in terms of an imperializing logic of Empire and an assortment of struggles by the multitude, creating a contradictory and tension-full situation. As in my conception, Hardt and Negri present globalization as a complex process that involves a multidimensional mixture of expansions of the global economy and capitalist market system, information technologies and media, expanded judicial and legal modes of governance, and emergent modes of power, sovereignty, and resistance.[5] Combining poststructuralism with

---

[5] While I find *Empire* an impressive and productive text, I am not sure, however, what is gained by using the word "Empire" rather than the concepts of global capital and political economy and "multitude" in place of traditional class and sociological categories. While Hardt and Negri combine categories of Marxism and critical social theory with poststructuralist discourse derived from Foucault and Deleuze and Guattari, they frequently favor the latter, often mystifying and obscuring the object of analysis. I am not as confident as Hardt and Negri that the "multitude" replaces traditional concepts of the working class and other modern political subjects, movements, and actors, and find the emphasis on nomads, "New Barbarians," and the poor as replacement categories problematical.

"autonomous Marxism," Hardt and Negri stress political openings and possibilities of struggle within Empire in an optimistic and buoyant text that envisages progressive democratization and self-valorization in the turbulent process of the restructuring of capital and creating of new forms of economy, polity, culture, and subjectivity.

In *Multitude* (2004), Hardt and Negri valorize the struggles of masses of people against Empire. Many theorists, by contrast, have argued that one of the trends of globalization is depoliticization of publics, the decline of the nation-state, and end of traditional politics (Boggs, 2000). While I would agree that globalization is promoted by tremendously powerful economic forces and that it often undermines democratic movements and decision-making, one should also note that there are openings and possibilities for both a globalization from below that inflects globalization for positive and progressive ends, and that globalization can thus help promote as well as destabilize democracy.[6] Globalization involves both a disorganization and reorganization of capitalism, a tremendous restructuring process, which creates openings for progressive social change and intervention as well as highly destructive transformative effects. On the positive ledger, in a more fluid and open economic and political system, oppositional forces can gain concessions, win victories, and effect progressive changes. During the 1970s, new social movements, emergent nongovernmental organizations (NGOs), and novel forms of struggle and solidarity emerged, which have been expanding from anti-capitalist struggles in mostly Western democracies to anti-authoritarian democratic uprisings in North Africa and the Middle East.

[6] I am thus trying to mediate in this chapter between those who claim that globalization simply undermines democracy and those who claim that globalization promotes democratization like Friedman (1999 and 2005). I should also note that in distinguishing between globalization from above and globalization from below, I do not want to say that one is good and the other is bad in relation to democracy. As Friedman shows (1999), capitalist corporations and global forces might very well promote democratization in many arenas of the world, and globalization-from-below might promote special interests or reactionary goals, so I am criticizing theorizing globalization in binary terms as primarily "good" or "bad." While critics of globalization simply see it as the reproduction of capitalism, its champions, like Friedman, do not perceive how globalization undercuts democracy. Likewise, Friedman does not engage the role of new social movements, dissident groups, or the "have-nots" in promoting democratization. Nor do concerns for social justice, equality, and participatory democracy play a role in his book.

From Anti-Corporate Globalization Movements to Alter-Globalization and the Arab Uprisings

Against capitalist globalization from above, from the 1990s to the present, there have been a significant eruption of forces and subcultures of resistance that have attempted to preserve specific forms of culture and society against neoliberal and homogenizing globalization, and to create alternative forces of society and culture, thus exhibiting resistance and globalization from below. Most dramatically, peasant and guerrilla movements in Latin America, labor unions, students, and environmentalists throughout the world, and a variety of other groups and movements have resisted capitalist globalization and attacks on previous rights and benefits.[7] Several dozen people's organizations from around the world have protested World Trade Organization (WTO) policies and a backlash against globalization is visible everywhere. Politicians who once championed trade agreements like GATT and NAFTA are now often quiet about these arrangements.

Since the protests in Seattle and throughout the world against the WTO meeting in December 1999, there has been a mushrooming anti-corporate globalization movement. Behind these actions was a global protest movement using the Internet to organize resistance to the WTO and capitalist globalization, while championing democratization. Many Websites contained anti-WTO material, and numerous mailing lists used the Internet to distribute critical material and to organize the protest. The result was the mobilization of caravans from throughout the United States to take protestors to Seattle, many of whom had never met and were recruited through the Internet. There were also significant numbers of international participants in Seattle that exhibited labor, environmentalist, feminist, anti-capitalist, animal rights, anarchist, and other groups organized to protest aspects of globalization and form new alliances and solidarities for future struggles. In addition, protests occurred throughout the world, and a proliferation of anti-WTO material against the extremely secret group spread throughout the Internet.

[7] On resistance to corporate globalization by labor, see Moody (1988 and 1997); on resistance by environmentalists and other social movements, see the studies in Mander and Goldsmith (1996); the Hardt-Negri trilogy (2000, 2004, and 2009) and Amoore, ed. (2005) document multiple alter globalization movements.

Furthermore, the Internet provided critical coverage of the event, documentation of the various groups' protests, and debate over the WTO and globalization. Whereas the mainstream media presented the protests as "anti-trade," featured the incidents of anarchist violence against property, while minimizing police violence against demonstrators, the Internet provided pictures, eyewitness accounts, and reports of police brutality and the generally peaceful and non-violent nature of the protests. While the mainstream media framed the protests negatively and privileged suspect spokespeople like Patrick Buchanan as critics of globalization, the Internet provided multiple representations of the demonstrations, advanced reflective discussion of the WTO and globalization, and presented a diversity of critical perspectives.

The Seattle protests had some immediate consequences. The day after the demonstrators made good on their promise to shut down the WTO negotiations, Bill Clinton gave a speech endorsing the concept of labor rights enforceable by trade sanctions, thus effectively making impossible any agreement and consensus during the Seattle meetings. In addition, at the World Economic Forum in Davos, a month later, there was much discussion of how concessions were necessary on labor and the environment if consensus over globalization and free trade were to be possible. Importantly, the issue of overcoming divisions between the information-rich and poor, and improving the lot of the disenfranchised and oppressed, bringing these groups the benefits of globalization, were also seriously discussed at the meeting and in the media.

More importantly, many activists were energized by the new alliances, solidarities, and militancy, and continued to cultivate an anti-globalization movement. The Seattle demonstrations were followed by April 2000 struggles in Washington, D.C., to protest the World Bank and IMF, and later in the year against capitalist globalization in Prague and Melbourne; in April 2001, an extremely large militant protest erupted against the Free Trade Area of the Americas summit in Quebec City and in summer 2001 a large demonstration took place in Genoa.

From 2001 to 2008, the anti-corporate globalization movement became increasingly associated with targeting the militarist policies of the Bush/Cheney and Blair administrations as part of a growing anti-war grassroots movement. In May 2002, a surprisingly large demonstration took place in Washington against capitalist globalization and for peace and justice, and it was apparent that a new worldwide movement was in the making that was uniting diverse opponents of capitalist globalization throughout the world. Indeed, on February 15, 2003, an anti-war/globalization protest was convened that brought together an estimated 15 million people in some 60 countries worldwide, which resulted in media outlets such as the *New York Times* referring to the unprecedented resistance as the "other superpower."

The anti-corporate globalization movement favored globalization from below, which would protect the environment, labor rights, national cultures, democratization, and other goods from the ravages of an uncontrolled capitalist globalization (see Falk, 1999; Brecher, Costello, and Smith, 2000; Steger, 2002). Initially, the incipient anti-globalization movement was precisely that—anti-globalization. The movement itself, however, was increasingly global, was linking together a diversity of movements into global solidarity networks, and was using the Internet and then new media and social networking and other global forums to advance its struggles. Moreover, many opponents of capitalist globalization recognized the need for a global movement to have a positive vision and be for such things as social justice, equality, labor, civil liberties and human rights, and a sustainable environmentalism. Accordingly, the anti-capitalist globalization movement began advocating common values and visions.

In particular, the movement against capitalist globalization used the Internet from the 1990s to the present to organize mass demonstrations and to disseminate information to the world concerning the policies of the institutions of capitalist globalization. The events made clear that protestors were not against globalization per se, but were against neoliberal and capitalist globalization, opposing specific policies and institutions that produce intensified exploitation of labor, environmental devastation, growing divisions among the social classes, and the undermining of democracy. The emerging anti-globalization from above movements are contextualizing these problems in the framework of a restructuring of capitalism on a worldwide basis for maximum profit with zero accountability and have made clear the need for democratization, regulation, rules, and globalization in the interests of people and not profit.

The new movements against corporate globalization have thus placed the issues of global justice and environmental destruction squarely in the center of important political concerns of our time. Hence, whereas the mainstream media had failed to vigorously debate acute problems of globalization until the eruption of a vigorous anti-globalization movement, and rarely, if ever, critically discussed the activities of the WTO, World Bank, and IMF, there is now a widely circulating critical discourse and controversy over these institutions. Stung by criticisms, representatives of the World Bank, in particular, have been pledging reform, and pressures are mounting concerning proper and improper roles for the major global institutions, highlighting their limitations and deficiencies, and the need for reforms like debt relief from overburdened developing countries to solve some of their fiscal and social problems.

To capital's globalization from above, members of global social movements and cyber activists have thus been attempting to carry out globalization from below, developing networks of solidarity and propagating oppositional ideas and movements throughout the planet. To the capitalist international of transnational corporate-led globalization, a Fifth International, to use Waterman's phrase (1992), of computer-mediated activism is emerging, which is qualitatively different from the party-based socialist and communist Internationals. Such networking links labor, feminist, ecological, peace, and other anti-capitalist groups, providing the basis for a new politics of alliance and solidarity to overcome the limitations of postmodern identity politics (see Dyer-Witheford, 1999; Burbach, 2001).

And so, to paraphrase Foucault, wherever there is globalization from above, globalization as the imposition of capitalist logic, there can be resistance and struggle. The possibilities of globalization from below result from transnational alliances between groups fighting for better wages and working conditions, social and political justice, environmental protection, and more democracy and freedom worldwide. In addition, a renewed emphasis on local and grassroots movements have put dominant economic forces on the defensive in their own backyard and often the broadcasting media or the Internet have called attention to oppressive and destructive corporate policies on the local level, putting national and even transnational pressure upon major corporations for reform. Moreover, proliferating media and the Internet make possible a greater circulation of struggles and the possibilities of new alliances and solidarities that can connect resistant forces who oppose capitalist and corporate-state elite forms of globalization from above (Dyer-Witheford, 1999; Best and Kellner, 2001).

In a certain sense, the phenomena of globalization replicates the history of the United States and most so-called capitalist democracies in which tension between capitalism and democracy has been the defining feature of the conflicts of the past two hundred years. In analyzing the development of education in the United States, Bowles and Gintis (1986) and Aronowitz and Giroux (1986) have analyzed the conflicts between corporate logic and democracy in schooling; Robert McChesney (1993 and 1999), myself (Kellner, 1990 and 2005), and others have articulated the contradictions between capitalism and democracy in the media and public sphere; while Joshua Cohen and Joel Rogers (1983) have been arguing that contradictions between capitalism and democracy are defining features of the US polity and history.

On a global terrain, Hardt and Negri (2000, 2004, and 2009) have stressed the openings and possibilities for democratic transformative struggle within globalization, or what they call Empire. I am arguing that similar arguments can be made in which globalization is not conceived merely as the triumph of capitalism and democracy working together as it was in the classical theories of Milton Friedman or more recently in Francis Fukuyama. Nor should globalization be depicted solely as the triumph of capital as in many despairing anti-globalization theories. Rather, one should see that globalization unleashes conflicts between capitalism and democracy and, in its restructuring processes, creates new openings for struggle, resistance, and democratic transformation.

I would also suggest that the model of Marx and Engels as deployed in the "Communist Manifesto" could also be usefully employed to analyze the contradictions of globalization (Marx and Engels, 1978: 469ff). From the historical materialist optic, capitalism was interpreted as the greatest, most progressive force in history for Marx and Engels, destroying a backward feudalism, authoritarian patriarchy, backwardness and provincialism in favor of a market society, global cosmopolitanism, and constant revolutionizing of the forces of production. Yet in the Marxian theory too, capitalism was presented as a major disaster for the human race, condemning a large part to alienated labor, regions of the world to colonialist exploitation, and generating conflicts between classes and nations, the consequences of which the contemporary era continues to suffer.

Marx deployed a similar dialectical and historical model in his later analyses of imperialism arguing, for instance, in his writings on British imperialism in India, that British colonialism was a great productive and progressive force in India, and at the same time it was highly destructive (Marx and Engels, 1978: 653ff). A similar dialectical and critical model can be used today that articulates the progressive elements of globalization in conjunction with its more oppressive features, deploying the categories of negation and critique, while sublating (*Aufhebung*) the positive features. Moreover, a dialectical and transdisciplinary model is necessary to capture the complexity and multidimensionality of globalization today that brings together in theorizing globalization, the economy, technology, polity, society and culture, articulating the interplay of these elements and avoiding any form of determinism or reductivism.

Theorizing globalization dialectically and critically requires that we both analyze continuities and discontinuities with the past, specifying what is a continuation of past histories and what is new and original in the present moment.[8] To elucidate the later, I believe that the discourse of the postmodern is useful in dramatizing the changes and novelties of the mode of globalization. The concept of the postmodern can signal that which is fresh and original, calling attention to topics and phenomena that require novel theorization, and intense critical thought and inquiry. Hence, although Manuel Castells has the most detailed analysis of new technologies and the rise of what he calls a networked society, by refusing to link his analyses with the problematic of the

---

[8] On debates over continuity versus discontinuity in globalization theories, see Rossi (2007). Rossi polemicizes against those who claim that contemporary globalization constitutes a radical rupture with the past and that therefore radically new theories are necessary. I argue for a dialectic of continuity and discontinuity in theorizing globalization and thus argue that while past theories can be of use in theorizing globalization, we also need new theories and concepts to theorize its novelties (see Kellner, 2002 and 2007). On the conjunctions between globalization and the postmodern and debates over the latter (see Harvey, 1989; Jameson, 1991; Kellner, 1998; Best and Kellner, 2001).

postmodern, he cuts himself off from theoretical resources that enable theorists to articulate the novelties of the present that are unique and different from the previous mode of social organization.[9]

Consequently, although there is admittedly a lot of mystification in the discourse of the postmodern, it signals emphatically the shifts and ruptures in our era, the novelties and originalities, and dramatizes the mutations in culture, subjectivities, and theory, which Castells and other theorists of globalization or the information society gloss over. The discourse of the postmodern in relation to analysis of contemporary culture and society is just jargon, however, unless it is rooted in analysis of the global restructuring of capitalism and analysis of the scientific-technological revolution that is part and parcel of it (see Best and Kellner, 1997 and 2001).

Globalization should thus be seen as a contested terrain with opposing forces attempting to use its institutions, technologies, media, and forms for their own purposes. There are certainly negative aspects to globalization which strengthen elite economic and political forces over and against the underlying population, but, as I suggested above, there are also positive possibilities. Other beneficial openings include the opportunity for greater democratization, increased education and health care, and new opportunities within the global economy that open entry to members of races, regions, and classes previously excluded from mainstream economics, politics, and culture within the modern corporate order.

In 2011, a new focus has emerged with the Arab Spring Uprisings in which powerful democratic movements erupted to overthrow long-entrenched authoritarian governments. Like the global movement against corporate neoliberalism, militants in the Middle East used the Internet to critique existing institutions and power structures, to mobilize people to demonstrate and resist, and to circulate their

---

[9] Castells claims that Harvey (1989) and Lash (1990) say about as much about the postmodern as needs to be said (Manuel, 1996: 26f). With due respect to their excellent work, I believe that no two theorists or books exhaust the problematic of the postmodern which involves mutations in theory, culture, society, politics, science, philosophy, and almost every other domain of experience, and is thus inexhaustible (Best and Kellner, 1997 and 2001). Yet one should be careful in using postmodern discourse to avoid the mystifying elements, a point made in the books just noted by Best and Kellner as well as by Hardt and Negri (2000).

struggles throughout the world. As we will see in the next section, the Arab Uprisings of 2011 overthrew long-entrenched authoritarian governments and helped generate struggles against oppressive forces globally, making 2011 a potentially iconic year of world global uprisings, as was 1968.

2011: A Year of Global Uprisings and Struggles

With the Spring 2011 North African Arab Uprisings in Tunisia, Egypt, and Libya, we see that political insurgencies and hope for revolutions have been unfolding as global media spectacles that have circulated forms of protest and struggle throughout the world. These insurrections—which erupted in late January 2011, and have continued to shake the world and reconstitute the political landscape of North Africa and the Middle East during Spring and Summer of and into the Fall of 2011 and beyond—may be seen in retrospect as inaugurating a new epoch of history, in which democratic uprisings radicalize entire regions of the world and drive out corrupt and entrenched dictatorships.

To begin, however, I should open with some caveats and cautionary warnings. While Al-Jazeera, CNN, and most US media networks at first repeatedly used the term "revolution" to describe the events in Tunisia, Egypt, and Libya in the "Arab Spring," since we do not know if a thorough transformation of the these societies will take place or not, I'm using the more modest term "Arab Uprisings" to describe the important political insurrections of our time which may yet be looked back upon as world-historical and transformative events.[10] Reflecting upon the dramatic uprisings in North Africa in the Arab Spring, it is, to be sure, "revolutionary" to overthrow military regimes and corrupt dictators who have been oppressing their people for decades.

---

[10] After initially using the discourse of "revolution" to describe the overthrow of dictatorships in Tunisia and Egypt, Al-Jazeera and other global networks then used terms like "Libya's Uprising," "Egypt's New Era," and "Tunisia in Transition," followed by terms like "The Arab Spring," "The Arab Awakening," or "The Arab Uprising." By "revolution," I follow Herbert Marcuse's concept of revolution as a rupture with the previous social order that develops new forms of economy, politics, culture, and social relations (on the Arab Uprisings, see Kellner 2012).

It is revolutionary to put aside a government and political system and to construct another freer and more democratic one. It is tremendous that self-organizing people can produce a democratic upheaval that hopefully will fundamentally alter their political fate and future. These events are clearly astonishing examples of people's power, of the masses becoming a force in history who throw off decades of oppression and fundamentally alter the forces of sovereignty in specific societies.

But we do not yet know if North African Uprisings will produce a revolution proper, as we do not know the form the military government in Egypt, for example, will take in the immediate future, what kind of constitution the Egyptians will produce, the quality and results of their promised elections, the amount of popular participation and other goals that would constitute a fundamentally different social order, and thus a revolutionary break from the Mubarak era. Hence, it is premature to pronounce the 18 Days That Shook the World in Egypt a "revolution" at this time—nor can we predict the form that the insurrections will take in Tunisia, Libya, Yemen, Bahrain, Syria, and other Middle Eastern states that were challenged by their people in the Arab Spring that has blossomed into a Year of Upheaval, 2011.

To be sure, if the Egyptians throw out the corrupt leaders and functionaries of the past three decades, this would be remarkable, but if the same people are governing in similar ways in Egypt the word "revolution" wanes in significance, so I am using the term "Uprising." Yet what is remarkable about the uprisings of 2011 is the global nature of the insurrections in which the media spectacle of people's uprising and overthrow of a corrupt dictatorship in Tunisia was followed by an Uprising and overthrow of the Mubarak regime, followed by an attempt in Libya to overthrow the Qaddafi regime, a struggle that mutated into Civil War now apparently won by the Qaddafi forces by Fall 2011.

Following the North African Arab Uprisings, intense political struggles erupted across the entire Middle East in the spring and then across the Mediterranean in Greece, Italy, and Spain, all of which faced economic crisis and cut backs of social programs. Madison, Wisconsin also participated in the global struggles during the Egyptian Uprising where workers and students fought against cutbacks of their rights and livelihood and occupied the statehouse in Madison; Egyptians declared their solidarity with protestors in Madison and sent them pizzas. For weeks during the summer of 2011, there were also widespread demonstrations in Israel in which demonstrators, like in Tahrir Square in Cairo, occupied and set up a tent city in Tel Aviv to protest against declining living conditions and oppressive government policies in Israel.

In the face of the failures of neoliberalism and a global crisis of capitalism, tremendous economic deficits and debts in these countries enabled and produced by unregulated neoliberal capitalism, there were calls by established conservative political regimes to solve debt crises on the backs of working people by cutting back on government spending and social programs that help people rather than corporations. In all of these struggles, youth played an important role, as youth throughout the world were facing diminishing job possibilities and an uncertain future in an era of global economic crisis.

There were also global revolts against nuclear energy plants, one of the most beloved forms of power in techno-capitalist regimes, where high-tech solutions to energy production was celebrated and promoted. But after the frightening nuclear meltdown and catastrophic leakage of radiation in the Fukushima-Daiichi nuclear plant, demonstrations throughout Japan protested nuclear energy production, leading Japan to cancel some plans for new nuclear power plants, to close down many existing plants for more stringent tests, to demand stricter regulation of nuclear power plants, and to call for development of new renewal and safe energy sources. Dramatic demonstrations in Italy, Germany, and Switzerland led national governments to declare moratoriums on nuclear energy production and to call for new types of energy.

Existing forms of energy and economic production, as well as existing politics and the state, were put in question and contested in 2011, and bankrupt forms were overthrown. In particular, neoliberal economics and authoritarian states were shown to be highly defective and destructive, and the worst examples of the latter were overthrown. Solutions to social problems in the North African Arab Uprisings of 2011 involved citizen participation in democratic protests, calls for social justice and political reform, and redefinitions of relations between people and their social institutions. In Japan after the Fukushima-Daiichi nuclear catastrophe, people and politicians demanded the end of nuclear energy production and the Japanese people demanded a more responsible and accountable government, putting new demands on politicians.

Further, in October 2011, a movement "Occupy Wall Street" emerged in New York as a variety of people began protesting the economic system in the United States, corruption on Wall Street, and a diverse range of other issues. Using social media, more and more people joined the demonstrations which received widespread media attention when police attacked peaceful demonstrators, yielding pictures of young women being pepper-sprayed by police. Mainstream media attention and mobilizing through social media brought more people to demonstrate and by the first weekend in October, there was a massive protest in lower Manhattan that marched across the Brooklyn Bridge and blocked traffic, leading to over 700 arrests.

The idea caught on and during the weekend of October 1–2, similar Occupy Wall Street demonstrations broke out in San Francisco, Los Angeles, Chicago, Boston, Denver, Washington, and several other cities. On October 5 in New York, major unions joined the protest and thousands marched from Foley Square to the Occupy Wall Street encampment in Zuccotti Park. Celebrities, students and professors, and ordinary citizens joined the protest in support, and daily coverage of the movement was appearing in the United States and global media.[11] During the weekend of October 8 and 9, large crowds gathered in Occupy! sites throughout the country, and it appeared that a new protest movement had emerged in the United States that articulated with the global struggles of 2011.

Occupy Wall Street was focused against financial capitalism and the corruption of the political class in the United States, just as the 1990s anti-corporate global capitalism movement focused on the WTO, World Bank, IMF, and other instruments of global capital. In Greece, Spain, and Italy, people were demonstrating against these same institutions of global capitalism, as well as their own national governments. Like the Arab Uprisings, the Occupy Wall Street and other anti-corporate movements were outside of the domain of old-fashioned party politics, embraced diversity and tended to be leaderless, although spokespeople were emerging and participants in Occupy Wall Street, after meeting with Egyptian and other militants, indicated that

[11] As it has come to own many major political stories of 2011, *The Guardian* was the place to go for Occupy Wall Street with a Live Blog documenting news and actions related to the movement, and a web-page collecting their key stories with links to other stories at http://www.guardian.co.uk/world/occupy-wall-street (accessed on October 3, 2011).

they were going to search for specific issues that could lead to action. Activism in these movements was taking place simultaneously on-line and in the streets, and activists circulated information, planned events, and mobilized for action. New politics and subjectivities were thus emerging from specific sites, but they are global in inspiration, tactics, and connections, leading to a new era of global, national, and local politics with unforeseeable outcomes.

For a Militant Cosmopolitan Globalization

The first stage of the anti-corporate globalization movement was largely negative and against corporate globalization and neoliberalism. But pursuing the need for an alternative vision and an answer to TINA (There Is No Alternative, i.e., to corporate globalization), in the past years the search has been for alter or other globalizations, providing positive visions of what a more democratic, just, ecological, and peaceful globalization could be and how to attain it, or at least move beyond the disastrously flawed and largely failed neoliberal vision. In 2011, new forms of struggle emerged on a global level, from the Arab Uprisings through Occupy New York, an idea and strategy that has circulated throughout the United States.

A critical theory of globalization and dialectical emancipatory vision thus needs to not only develop a critique of neoliberal or corporate globalization and analyze its contradictions, but needs to project a positive ideal of alternative globalizations. Resistance and struggle against corporate globalization needs to have a positive ideal of what kind of globalization to struggle for, since we are fated to live in a global world. Different societies and groups will, of course, have different alternative versions and strategies in mind, but in conclusion I want to suggest that corporate and neoliberal globalization could be opposed by alternative globalizations that are multipolar and multi-lateralist, involving autonomous partners and alliances, and that are radically democratic and ecological. Such a cosmopolitan globalization would include NGOs, social movements, popular institutions, and a multiplicity of struggles, as well as states and global institutions like the UN. A democratic and multipolar globalization would be grounded philosophically in Enlightenment cosmopolitanism, democratic theory, human rights and ecology, drawing on notions of a cosmos, eikos, global citizenship, and genuine democracy.[12]

The need for cosmopolitan globalization shows the limitations of one-sided anti-globalization positions that dismiss globalization out of hand as a form of capitalist or US domination. Taking this position is admitting defeat before you've started, conceding globalization to corporate capitalism and not articulating contradictions, forms of resistance, and possibilities of democracy grounded in globalization itself. Rather, a US-dominated or corporate globalization represents a form of neoliberal globalization which, interestingly, Wallerstain claims is "just about passé" (2004: 18). The argument would be that Bush/Cheney administration unilateralism has united the world against US policies, so that the United States can no longer push through whatever trade, economic, or military policies that they wish without serious opposition. Wallerstein points to the widely perceived failures of IMF and WTO policies, the collapse of Cancun and Miami trade meetings that ended with no agreement as strongly united so-called southern countries opposed US trade policy, and, finally, global opposition to the Bush administration Iraq intervention. He also points to the rise of the World Social Forum as a highly influential counterpoint to the Davos World Economic Forum, which has stood as an organizing site for a worldwide anti-neoliberal globalization movement (see Hardt, 2002).

A cosmopolitan globalization would overcome the one-sidedness of a nation-state and national interest dominant politics and recognize that in a global world the nation is part of a multilateral, multipolar, multicultural, and transnational system. A cosmopolitan globalization driven by issues of multipolar multilateralism, democratization and globalization from below, would embrace women's, workers', and minority rights, as well as strong ecological perspectives. Such cosmopolitan globalization thus provides a worthy way to confront challenges of the contemporary era ranging from inequalities between haves and have-nots to global warming and environmental crisis.

The Bush/Cheney administration intervention in Iraq showed the limitations of militarist unilateralism and that in a complex world it is impossible, despite awesome military power, for one country to rule

---

[12] On cosmopolitanism, see Cheah and Robbins (1998) and Featherstone (2002).

in a multipolar globe (Kellner, 2005). The failures of Bush/Cheney administration policy in Iraq suggest that unilateralist militarism is not the way to fight international terrorism, or to deal with issues such as "weapons of mass destruction," but is rather the road to an Orwellian nightmare and era of perpetual war in which democracy and freedom will be in dire peril and the future of the human species will be in question.

The Obama administration emerged in 2008 committed to multilateralism, but continued military intervention in the Middle East and a new type of liberal humanitarian intervention in Libya under the auspices of the UN and NATO. These policies and Obama's failure to close the Guantanamo military base in Cuba and to cut back on militarism raises questions concerning the nature of the Obama administration and the extent to which it is pursuing a cosmopolitan global agenda or simply promoting US national interests in a new form.[13] Since the future of the human race demands concepts of cosmopolitan globalization and the renunciation of Empire and militarism, it is the responsibility of global citizens to struggle against institutions that continue to promote outmoded and failed forms of economy, polity, and society and all forms of contemporary oppression.

References

Amoore, Louise (ed.). 2005. *The Global Resistance Reader*. New York: Routledge.

Appadurai, Arjun. 1996. *Modernity at Large: Cultural Dimensions of Globalization*. Minneapolis: University of Minnesota Press.

Aronowitz, Stanley A. and Henry A. Giroux. 1986. *Education under Siege: The Conservative, Liberal and Radical Debate over Schooling*. London: Routledge and Kegan Paul.

Barber, Benjamin R. 1996. *Jihad vs. McWorld*. New York: Ballatine Books.

Bacevich, Andrew J. 2005. *The New American Militarism. How Americans Are Seduced by War*. New York: Oxford University Press.

[13] In my book *Media Spectacle and Insurrections, 2011: From the Arab Uprisings to Occupy everywhere!* (London and New York: Continuum/Bloomsbury). These questions concerning the Obama administration and the ambiguities of liberal humanitarian war, as well as the new forms of struggle from the North African Arab Uprisings through Occupy Wall Street.

Best, Steven and Douglas Kellner. 1997. *The Postmodern Turn*. London and New York: Routledge and Guilford Press.

————. 2001. The *Postmodern Adventure*. London and New York: Routledge and Guilford Press.

Boggs, Carl. 2000. *The End of Politics*. New York: Guilford Press.

———— (ed.). 2003. *Masters of War. Militarism and Blowback in the Era of American Empire*. New York and London: Routledge.

————. 2005. *Imperial Delusions: American Militarism and Endless War*. Lanham: Rowman & Littlefield.

Bowles, Samuel and Herbert Gintis. 1986. *On Democracy*. New York: Basic Books.

Brecher, Jeremy and Tim Costello. 1994. *Global Village or Global Pillage: Economic Reconstruction from Bottom Up*. Boston: South End Press.

Brecher, Jeremy, Tim Costello, and Brendan Smith. 2000. *Globalization from Below*. Boston: South End Press.

Burbach, Roger. 2001. *Globalization and Postmodern Politics. From Zapatistas to High-Tech Robber Barons*. London: Pluto Press.

Castells, Manuel. 1996. *The Rise of the Network Society*. Oxford: Blackwell.

————. 1997. *The Power of Identity*. Oxford: Blackwell.

————. 1998. *End of Millennium*. Oxford: Blackwell.

Cheah, Pheng and Bruce Robbins (eds). 1998. *Cosmopolitics: Thinking and Feeling beyond the Nation*. Minneapolis: University of Minnesota Press.

Cohen, Joshua and Joel Rogers. 1983. *On Democracy*. New York: Penguin.

Cvetkovich, Ann and Douglas Kellner. 1997. *Articulating the Global and the Local. Globalization and Cultural Studies*. Boulder, Col.: Westview.

Dyer-Witheford, Nick. 1999. *Cyber-Marx. Cycles and Circuits of Struggle in High-Technology Capitalism*. Urbana and Chicago: University of Illinois Press.

Eisenstein, Zillah. 1998. *Global Obscenities: Patriarchy, Capitalism, and the Lure of Cyber Fantasy*. New York: New York University Press.

Featherstone, Mike (ed.). 1990. *Global Culture: Nationalism, Globalization and Modernity*. London: SAGE.

Featherstone, Mike (ed.). 2002, February–April. *Cosmopolitics and* Special Issue of *Theory, Culture & Society* on Cosmopolis, 19(1–2).

Falk, Richard. 1999. *Predatory Globalization*. London and Cambridge: Blackwell.

Friedman, Thomas. 1999. *The Lexus and the Olive Tree*. New York: Farrar Straus Giroux.

————. 2005. *The World Is Flat*. New York: Farrar, Straus and Giroux.

Fukuyama, Francis. 1992. *The End of History and the Last Man*. New York: The Free Press.

Hardt, Michael. 2002. "Porto Allegre: Today's Bandung?" *New Left Review*, 14 (March–April): 112–118.

Hardt, Michael and Antonio Negri. 2000. *Empire.* Cambridge, Mass: Harvard University Press.

———. 2004. *Multitude. War and Democracy in the Age of Empire.* New York: The Penguin Press.

———. 2009. *Commonwealth.* Cambridge, Mass.: The Belknap Press of Harvard University Press.

Harvey, David. 1989. *The Condition of Postmodernity.* Cambridge: Blackwell.

Hayden, Patrick and Chamsy el-Ojeili (eds). 2005. *Confronting Globalization: Humanity, Justice and the Renewal of Politics.* New York: Palgrave MacMillan.

Held, David. 1995. *Democracy and the Global Order.* Cambridge and Palo Alto: Polity Press and Stanford University Press.

Held, David, Anthony McGrew, David Goldblatt and Jonathan Perraton. 1999. *Global Transformations.* Cambridge and Palo Alto: Polity Press and Stanford University Press.

Huntington, Samuel. 1996. *The Clash of Civilizations and the Remaking of World Order.* New York: Touchstone Books.

Jameson, Fredric. 1991. *Postmodernism, or the Cultural Logic of Late Capitalism.* Durham, N.C.: Duke University Press.

Kellner, Douglas. 1984. *Herbert Marcuse and the Crisis of Marxism.* Berkeley and London: University of California Press (U.S.A) and Macmillan Press (England).

———. 1990. *Television and the Crisis of Democracy.* Boulder, Colorado: Westview Press.

———. 1998. "Globalization and the Postmodern Turn," in Roland Axtmann (ed.), *Globalization and Europe,* pp 23–42. London: Cassells..

———. 1999. "Theorizing McDonaldization: A Multiperspectivist Approach," in Barry Smart (ed.), *Resisting McDonaldization,* pp 186–206. London: SAGE Publications.

———. 2002. "Theorizing Globalization," *Sociological Theory,* 20(3): 285–305.

———. 2003a. *Media Spectacle.* London and New York: Routledge.

———. 2003b. *From 9/11 to Terror War: Dangers of the Bush Legacy.* Lanham, Md.: Rowman and Littlefield.

———. 2005. *Media Spectacle and the Crisis of Democracy.* Boulder, CO: Paradigm Press.

———. 2007. "Globalization, Terrorism, and Democracy: 9/11 and Its Aftermath," in Rossi (ed.), *Frontiers of Globalization,* pp 243–168.

———. 2012. *Media Spectacle and Insurrections, 2011: From the Arab Uprisings to Occupy everywhere!* London and New York: Continuum/Bloomsbury.

Laclau, Ernesto and Chantal Mouffe. 1985. *Hegemony and Socialist Strategy: Towards a Radical Democratic Politics.* New York and London: Verso.

Lash, Scott. 1990. *The Sociology of Postmodernism*. New York and London: Routledge.

Luke, Allan and Carmen Luke. 2000 "A Situated Perspective on Cultural Globalization," in Nicholas Burbules and Carlos Torres (eds.), *Globalization and Education*, pp 275–298. London and New York: Routledge.

Marx, Karl and Frederick Engels. 1978. *The Marx-Engels Reader*, 2nd ed. Ed. Robert C. Tucker. New York: Norton.

Mander, Jerry and Edward Goldsmith. 1996. *The Case Against the Global Economy*. San Francisco: Sierra Club Books.

Moody, Kim. 1988. *An Injury to One*. London: Verso.

———. 1997. "Towards an International Social-Movement Unionism," *New Left Review*, 225: 52–72.

McChesney, Robert. 1993. *Telecommunications, Mass Media, and Democracy: The Battle for the Control of U.S. Broadcasting, 1928–1935*. New York and Oxford: Oxford University Press.

McChesney, Robert. 1997. *Corporate Media and the Threat to Democracy*. New York: Seven Stories Press.

Ritzer, George. 1993. Rev ed 1996. *The McDonaldization of Society*. Thousand Oaks, CA: Pine Forge Press.

Robins, Kevin and Frank Webster. 1999. *Times of the Technoculture*. London and New York: Routledge.

Rossi, Ino. 2007. "From Cosmopolitanism to a Global Perspective: Paradigmatic Discontinuity (Beck, Ritzer, Postmodernism, and Albrow) Versus Continuity (Alexander and Collins) and Emergent Conceptualizations (Contributers to this Volume," in Ino Rossi (ed.), *Frontiers of Globalization*, pp 397–436.. New York: Springer.

Sklair, Leslie. 2001. *The Transnational Capitalist Class*. Cambridge: Blackwell Publishers.

Steger, Manfred. 2002. *Globalism. The New Market Ideology*. Lanham, MD: Rowman and Littlefield.

Stiglitz, Joseph E. 2002. *Globalization and Its Discontents*. New York: Norton.

Waterman, Peter. 1992. International Labour Communication by Computer: The Fifth International? Working Paper 129, Institute of Social Studies, The Hague.

Watson, James L. (ed.). 1998. *Golden Arches East: McDonald's in East Asia*. Palo Alto, California: Stanford Univ. Press.

Wallerstein, Immanuel. 2004. "Soft Multilateralism," *The Nation*,14–20, February 2.

2

After Developmentalism and Globalization, What?*

IMMANUEL WALLERSTEIN

In 1900, in preparation for the Exposition Universelle in Paris, the French Ministry of Colonies asked Camille Guy, the head of its geographical service, to produce a book entitled *Les colonies françaises:la mise en valeur de notre domaine coloniale*.[1] A literal translation of *mise en valeur* is "making into value." The dictionary, however, translates "*mise en valeur*" as "development." At the time, this expression was preferred, when talking about economic phenomena in the colonies, to the perfectly acceptable French word, "*développement*." If one then goes to *Les Usuels de Robert: Dictionnaire des Expressions et Locutions figurées* (1979) to learn more about the meaning of the expression "*mettre en valeur*," one finds the explanation that it is used as a metaphor meaning "to exploit, draw profit from."

Basically, this was the view of the pan-European world during the colonial era concerning economic development in the rest of the world. Development was a set of concrete actions effectuated by Europeans to exploit and draw profit from the resources of the non-European world. There were a number of assumptions in this view: Non-Europeans would not be able or perhaps even willing to "develop" their resources without the active intrusion of the pan-European world. But such development represented a material and moral good for the world. It was therefore the moral and political duty of the pan-Europeans to exploit the resources of these countries. There was consequently nothing wrong with the fact that, as a reward, the pan-Europeans who exploited the

---

*Keynote address at conference, "Development Challenges for the 21st Century," Cornell University, October 1, 2004.

[1] Volume III of *Les Colonies françaises*, Exposition Universelle de 1900, Publications de la Commission chargée de préparer la participation de la Ministère des Colonies, Paris: Augustin Challamel, 1900.

resources drew profit from them, since a secondary advantage would go to the persons whose resources were being exploited in this way.

This rationale of course completely omitted discussion of the cost in life and limb to the local people of such exploitation. The conventional calculus was that these costs were, as we would say in today's euphemisms, the necessary and inevitable "collateral damage" of Europe's "civilizing mission."

The tone of the discussion began to change after 1945, primarily as a result of the strength of anti-colonial sentiments and movements in Asia and Africa, and a new sense of collective assertiveness in Latin America. It is at this point that "development" came to be used as a code word for the belief that it was possible for the countries of the South to "develop" themselves, as opposed to "being developed" by the North. The new assumption was that, if the countries of the South would only adopt the proper policies, they would one day, some time in the future, become as technologically modern and as wealthy as the countries of the North.

At some point in the post-1945 period, Latin American authors began to call this new ideology *"desarollismo"* or "developmentalism." The ideology of developmentalism took a number of different forms. The Soviet Union called it instituting "socialism," which became defined as the last stage before "communism." The United States called it "economic development." Ideologues in the South often used the two terms interchangeably. Amidst this worldwide consensus, all the states of the North the United States, the Soviet Union (and its East European satellites), the West European colonial (now becoming ex-colonial) powers, and the Nordic countries plus Canada began to offer "aid" and advice concerning this development that everyone favored. The Economic Commission for Latin America (CEPAL) developed a new language of "core-periphery" relations, used primarily to justify a program of "import-substitution industrialization." And more radical Latin American (and other) intellectuals developed a language about "dependency," which, they said, needed to be fought against and overcome in order that dependent countries be in a position to develop.

The terminology may have differed but the one thing that was agreed upon by everyone was that development was indeed possible, if only.... When, therefore, the United Nations declared that the 1970s would be the "decade of development," the term and the objective seemed virtually a piety. Yet, as we know, the 1970s turned out to be a very bad decade for most of the countries of the South. It was the decade of the two successive oil price increases instituted by OPEC and of stagflation in the North. The consequent rise in the cost of imports for countries in the South combined with a sharp decline in the value of their exports because the stagnation in the world economy created acute balance of payments difficulties for just about every one of these countries (including those in the so-called socialist bloc), with the sole exception of those which were oil-exporting states.

The oil-exporting states acquired incredibly large surpluses, a large part of which they deposited in the banks in the United States and Germany, which thereupon needed to find a remunerative use for this extra capital. They found it in loans to states with acute balance of payments difficulties. These loans, actively promoted by the banks themselves, solved both problems: finding an outlet for the surplus money in the accounts of the banks of the North and solving the liquidity problems of the virtually insolvent states of the South. But, alas, the loans led to cumulative interest payments which, by 1980, had led to even greater balance of payments difficulties in these states. Loans unfortunately are supposed to be repaid. The world thus arrived at the suddenly discovered so-called debt crisis—Poland in 1980, Mexico in 1982, and then all over the place.

It was easy enough to find the villain in the piece. The finger was pointed at developmentalism, so universally praised just a decade before. Import-substitution industrialization was now perceived as corrupt protectionism. State-building was deconstructed as feeding a bloated bureaucracy. Financial aid was now analyzed as money poured down a sink, if not a gutter. And parastatal structures, far from being virtuous efforts at pulling oneself up by one's own bootstraps, were exposed as deadening barriers to fruitful entrepreneurial achievement. It was decided that loans to states in distress, to be beneficial, needed to be hedged by requirements that these states cut wasteful state expenditures on such deferrable items as schools and health. It was further proclaimed that state enterprises were almost by definition inefficient, and should be privatized as rapidly as possible, since private enterprises were again almost by definition responsive to the "market" and therefore maximally efficient. Or at least that was the consensus in Washington.

Academic buzz words and fads are fickle and usually last but a decade or two. Development was suddenly out. Globalization arrived in its wake. University professors, foundation executives, book publishers, and op-ed columnists all saw the light. To be sure, the optic, or better said the remedies, had changed. Now, the way to move forward was not to import-substitute but to export-orient productive activities. Down not only with nationalized industries but with capital transfer controls; up with transparent, unhindered flows of capital. In place of one-party regimes, let us all together study governance (a new word, splendidly erudite and quite inscrutable, if not meaningless). Above all, let us face Mecca five times a day and intone Allahu Akbar TINA—There is No Alternative.

The new dogmas took root in the 1980s amidst the decaying rot of developmentalist dreams. They flourished in the 1990s, bathed by the sparkle of the "new economy" in which the United States and Eastern Asia were supposed to be leading the world to its economic glory. But alas, the sheen began to tarnish. The currency crisis in East and Southeast Asia in 1997 (which spread to Russia and Brazil), the slide downward of the World Trade Organization from Seattle to Cancun, the fading of Davos and the spectacular rise of Porto Alegre, al-Qaeda, and September 11, followed by the Bush fiasco in Iraq and the current accounts crisis of the United States—all this and more leads one to suspect that globalization as rhetoric may be going quickly the way of developmentalism. And hence our question—After Developmentalism and Globalization—What?

Let us not be too acerbic about faded theorizing. The whole dis-cussion from 1945 to today has indeed been one long effort to take seriously the reality that the world-system is not only polarized but polarizing, and that this reality is both morally and politically intol-erable. For the countries at the bottom, there seemed nothing more urgent than figuring out how to improve their situation, and first of all economically. After all, all these people had to do was see a movie and they would know that there were other people and places in the world that were better off, far better off, than they were. As for the countries at the top, they realized, however dimly, that the "huddled masses yearning to breathe free" represented a permanent danger to world order and their own prosperity, and that therefore something, somehow, had to be done to dampen the tinderbox.

So, the intellectual analyses and the derived policy efforts repre-sented by the discussion about development and globalization were serious and respectable, if in retrospect quite misguided in many ways.

The first question we need to ask now is, is it at all possible for every part of the world to attain—one day in a plausibly not too remote future—the standard of living of say Denmark (and perhaps also similar political and cultural institutions)? The second question is, if it is not, is it possible for the present lopsided and highly inegalitarian world-system to persist, more or less as such? And the third question is, if it is not, what kinds of alternatives present themselves to all of us now?

> Is it at all possible for every part of the world to attain—one day in a plausibly not too remote future—the standard of living of say Denmark (and perhaps also similar political and cultural institutions)?

There is no question that Denmark and most OECD countries have a quite decent standard of living for a substantial proportion of their population. The standard measure of internal variation of income, the Gini curve, shows quite low numbers for most OECD countries, and by world standards reasonably good ones for all of them (Anthony Atkinson). To be sure, there are many poor people in these countries, but compared to almost any country of the South, far fewer. So, of course, people in these poorer countries aspire to be as rich as people in Denmark. In the last few years, the world economic press has been full of stories about the remarkable rates of growth of China—a country which not too long ago was considered to be one of the poorest—along with much speculation about whether or not and to what degree these rates of growth can continue in the future and thereby transform China into a relatively wealthy country in terms of GDP per capita.

Let us leave aside the fact that many, many other countries have shown remarkable growth spurts for as much as up to 20–30 years, which rates then nonetheless petered out. There are, for example, the recent cases of the Soviet Union and Yugoslavia. Let us also leave out of the equation the long list of countries whose GDP was better in the further past than in the present. Let us assume for a moment that China's economic growth continues unhindered for another twenty years, and that China's GDP per capita approaches, let us say, if not that of Denmark, at least that of Portugal or even Italy. Let us even speculate that up to 50 percent of its population benefits significantly from this growth spurt, which is then reflected in their real income.

Is it credible to hold everything else constant, and to assume that, at the very least, everyone else remains where they are today in terms of standard of living? Where is the surplus-value to come from that would permit 50 percent of China's population to consume at the level of 50 percent of Italy's population, while all the rest of the world consumes at a level at least as high as at present? Is this all supposed to come from the so-called greater productivity of world (or Chinese) production? It is clear that the skilled workers of Ohio and the Ruhr valley do not think so. They think they would pay for it, or that they are already paying for it, by significantly reduced standards of living. Are they really so wrong? Has this not been happening in the past decade?

The first piece of evidence is the entire past history of the capitalist world economy. In over five hundred years of its existence, the gap between the top and the bottom, the core and the periphery, has never gotten smaller, always larger. What is there in the present situation that should lead us to assume that this pattern would not continue? Of course, over those five hundred years, there is no question that some countries have improved their relative standing in the distribution of wealth in the world-system. Thus, it could be claimed that these countries had "developed" in some sense. But it is also true that other countries are lower in relative wealth rankings than earlier, some of them spectacularly so. And, although our statistical data is at most of even minimal quality only for the last 75–100 years, such comparative studies as we have do show a constant trimodal distribution of wealth in the world-system, with a few countries moving from one category to another.[2]

The second piece of evidence is that high levels of profit, and therefore of the possibility of accumulating surplus-value, correlate directly with the relative degree of monopolization of productive activity.[3] What we have been calling development for the last fifty years or so is basically the ability of some countries to erect productive enterprises of a type considered to be highly profitable. To the extent that they succeed in doing this, they thereby reduce the degree of monopolization of production in this particular arena and hence reduce the degree of profitability of such production. The historic pattern of successive

[2] The classic article is that by Giovanni Arrighi and Jessica Drangel, 1986. Arrighi is currently updating this argument in a forthcoming article.

[3] Although this is prima facie logical, it seldom enters into analyses of mainstream economists.

so-called leading industries—from textiles to steel and automobiles to electronics to computer technology—is a clear evidence of this. The US pharmaceutical industry is right now fighting a rear-guard battle against just such decline in potential profitability. Can Boeing and Airbus maintain their present profit levels in the face of competition by a putative Chinese aircraft construction industry twenty or thirty years from now?

So, basically, of two things one: either the rising, so-called newly developing countries will be crushed by some highly destructive process—warfare, plague, or civil war (and in this case, the existing economic centers of accumulation will remain on top, and the polarization will be still more acute), or the rising, newly developing countries will be able to reproduce some of the major productive processes of the present centers. And in this case, either the polarization will simply be inverted (which is unlikely), or there will be a flattening of the curve. But in this latter case, the ability to accumulate surplus-value in the world economy taken as a whole will diminish severely, and the raison d'être of a capitalist world economy will be undermined. In none of these scenarios does every country become a Denmark.

If there has come to be a general morosity about economic development and the positive benefits of globalization, it is, I would argue, because the sense that we are in a *cul-de-sac* has begun to creep in on more and more people—scholars, politicians, and above all ordinary workers. The optimism of the 1950s and 1960s, which was momentarily revived in the 1990s, is no longer with us.

I personally can see no way in which, within the framework of a capitalist world economy, we can approach a general equalization of the distribution of wealth in the world, and even less an equalization that would have everyone consume at the level of the modal Danish consumer. I say this, taking into account all possible technological advances as well as increases in that elusive concept, productivity.

If it is not possible for all countries to achieve a Danish standard of living within the framework of the world-system in which we live, is it possible for the present lopsided and highly inegalitarian world-system to persist, more or less as such?

I doubt it. But of course we must be careful here, since predictions of dramatic structural change have been made so frequently over the past two centuries, and have turned out to be inaccurate over a medium term because some crucial elements were left out of the analyses.

The major explanation of purported prospective fundamental structural change has been dissatisfaction of the exploited and oppressed. As conditions worsened, the people at the bottom, or some very large group, were destined—it was argued—to rebel. There would be what has usually been called a revolution. I shall not resume the arguments and counterarguments, which are no doubt quite familiar to almost anyone who has been seriously studying the history of the modern world-system.

The 20th century was, among other things, the moment of a long series of national uprisings and social movements, which proclaimed their revolutionary intents and which achieved state power in one form or another. The high point of these movements was the period 1945–1970, the period precisely of the flourishing of developmentalism, which was in some sense the credo of these movements. But we also know that the period 1970–2000 saw the downfall of most of these movements in power, or at least a drastic revision in their policies. This was the period of the flourishing of globalization, whose logic these movements—those still in power or those now seeking to play a role of parliamentary opposition—sullenly accepted. So, we have the era of triumphalism followed by the era of disillusionment.

Some of the cadres of these movements adjusted to what were thought to be the new realities and others jumped ship, either into passive withdrawal or into joining actively the erstwhile enemy. In the 1980s and until the mid-1990s, anti-systemic movements worldwide were in a bad way. By 1995, however, the momentary sheen of neo-liberalism had begun to wear off and there ensued a worldwide search for new anti-systemic strategies. The story from Chiapas to Seattle to Porto Alegre has been that of the emergence of a new kind of world anti-systemic movement, sometimes called these days *altermondialisme*. My name for it is the spirit of Porto Alegre and I think it is going to be an important element in the world political struggles of the next 25–50 years. I shall return to it in my discussion of real alternatives now.

However, I do not believe that a new version of revolutionary movement is the fundamental factor in what I see as the structural collapse of the capitalist world economy. Systems collapse not primarily because of rebellion from below but because of the weaknesses of the dominant classes and the impossibility of maintaining their level of gain and privilege. It is only when the existing system is weakened in terms of its own logic that the push from below can possibly be effective.

The basic strength of capitalism as a system has been twofold. On the one hand, it has demonstrated an ability to ensure, against all odds, the endless accumulation of capital. And on the other hand, it has put into place political structures that have made it possible to guarantee this endless accumulation of capital without being dethroned by the rash and dissatisfied "dangerous classes." The basic weakness of capitalism as a historical system today is that success is leading to failure (as Schumpeter taught us normally happens). As a consequence today, both the ability to guarantee the endless accumulation of capital and the political structures that have kept the dangerous classes in line are collapsing simultaneously.

The success of capitalism in ensuring the endless accumulation of capital has been in its ability to keep the three basic costs of production—costs of personnel, costs of inputs, and taxation—from escalating too fast. However, it has done this by mechanisms that have been exhausting themselves over historical time. The system has now begun to reach a point where these costs are dramatically too high to make production an adequate source of capital accumulation. The capitalist strata have turned to financial speculation as a substitute. Financial speculation, however, is intrinsically a transitory mechanism, since it is dependent on confidence, and confidence in the medium run is undermined by the very speculation itself. Allow me to illustrate each of these points.

The costs of personnel are a function of the ongoing, never-ending class struggle. What the workers have on their side is the concentration of production (for reasons of efficiency) and hence their ability over time to organize themselves in both the work place and the political arena to put pressures on the employers to increase their remuneration. To be sure, employers always fight back by playing one set of workers off against another. But there are limits to doing this within the framework of a single country or a single local area, since there are political means by which the workers can encrust their advantages (legally and/or culturally).

Whenever we are in a Kondratieff A-phase, employers, faced with militant workers' demands, usually prefer to allow remuneration to rise somewhat, since work stoppages do them more immediate damage than concessions. But as soon as we are in a Kondratieff B-phase, it becomes imperative for an employer who hopes to survive the bad times to reduce the remuneration package, since there is acute price competition. It is at this point that employers have historically resorted to relocation—the "runaway factory"—transferring their production to zones that have "historically" lower rates of remuneration. But exactly what history accounts for these historically lower rates? The answer is rather simple—the existence of a large pool of rural labor, for whom urban, waged employment, at whatever level of remuneration, represents a net increase in real income for the household. So, as remuneration goes up, more or less permanently, in one area of the world economy, it is compensated in terms of the world economy as a whole by the appearance of new cohorts of workers who will accept lower remuneration for the identical work, holding of course efficiency constant.

The problem with this solution to the regularly repeated problem of the owner/producers is that after 25–50 years the workers in this new zone of production are able to overcome their initial urban disorientation and political ignorance and proceed down the same path of class struggle as did others previously in other areas of the world. The zone in question thereupon ceases to be a zone of historically lower remuneration, or at least not to the same degree. Sooner or later, the employers are required, in their self-interest, to flee again, relocating to yet another zone. This constant geographical shift of the zones of production has worked quite well over the centuries, but does have an Achilles' heel. The world is running out of new zones into which to relocate. This is what we mean by the deruralization of the world, which is going on apace, and at a very accelerated rate since 1945. The proportion of world population that lives in cities went from 30–60 percent between 1950 and 2000 (Deane Neubauer, 2004). The capitalist world economy should run out of such zones entirely within twenty-five years at the most. There are already too few. And with modern means of communication, the time period for new zones to learn the lessons of how to organize has been drastically reduced. Hence, the ability of employers to keep remuneration in check has been drastically curtailed.

The cost of inputs is dependent on what percentage of the inputs the employer is required to pay. To the extent that he can get inputs free, his costs remain low. The major mechanism by which employers have over the centuries been able to avoid payment for inputs is by shifting the cost to others. This is called the externalization of costs. The three principal costs that have been externalized are detoxification, renewal of primary resources, and infrastructure.

Detoxification is easy to handle in the beginning. One dumps waste somewhere that is public or unoccupied. This costs next to nothing. The costs are usually not immediate, but delayed. The eventual difficulties become the problem of the "public"—either as individuals or collectively as governments. Clean-up, when it is undertaken, is seldom paid for by the original user. In premodern times, rulers moved to different castles as they ran out of sewage dumps. In the capitalist world economy, producers do more or less the same. The problem here is identical to the problem of runaway factories and remuneration levels. We are running out of new prospective dumps. In addition, the collective cost of toxification has caught up with us, or at least we are more aware of it because of scientific advances. Hence, the world seeks to detoxify waste. This is called concern with the ecology. And as concern mounts, the question of who pays comes to the forefront. There is increasing pressure to make the user of the resources who leaves toxic waste pay the costs of detoxification. This is called internalization of costs. To the extent that governments impose such internalization of costs, the overall costs of production rise, sometimes quite steeply.

The issue of the renewal of primary resources is basically analogous. If forests are cut down, they may renew themselves via natural processes, but often slowly. And the faster forests are cut down (because of increased world production), the harder it is for the natural renewal process to take place in meaningful time. So here too, as the ecological concerns have come to the fore, both governments and social actors have put pressure on users either to restrain use or to invest in renewal. And to the extent that governments impose internalization of these costs, the costs of production rise.

Finally, the same is true of infrastructure. Infrastructure, almost by definition, is expenditure on costly activities that cannot be attributed to a single producer—for example, constructing public roadways over which transportation of goods takes place. But the fact that these costs cannot be considered the costs of a single producer does not mean that they cannot be considered the costs of a multitude of producers. Furthermore, the cost of such infrastructure has escalated geometrically. Yes, they are public goods, but the public can be specified up to a point. And once again, to the extent that governments impose even partial internalization of such costs, the costs of production rise. The third basic cost of production is taxation. Any comparison of the total level of taxation in the world, or in any part of the world, with the world of a century ago reveals that everyone is paying higher taxes today, whatever the oscillation of the rates. What accounts for this? There are three major expenditures of all governments—the costs of collective security (armies, police, etc.); the costs of all kinds of public welfare; and the costs of administration (most importantly, the costs of collecting the taxes).Why have these costs of government risen so steeply?

The costs of security have risen simply as a result of technological advance. The toys security forces use are every day in every way more expensive. After all, security is a game in which all sides always try to have more than their opponents. It is like an endless auction in which the bids are always being raised. Perhaps if we had a generalized nuclear holocaust, and the surviving world went back to bows and arrows, these costs would go down. But in the wake of anything less, I see no way to expect such a reduction.

In addition, the costs of welfare have been going up steadily and nothing is slowing them down, despite all the hoopla about doing that. They are going up for three reasons. The first is that the politics of the capitalist world economy have pushed the dominant strata to make concessions to the dangerous classes, who have been demanding three things—education, health services, and guarantees of lifelong income. Furthermore, the level of the demands has been going up steadily and becoming more geographically extensive. In addition, people are living longer (partly the consequence of precisely these welfare measures), and hence the collective costs have increased because of the increase in the number of beneficiaries. The second reason is that advances in technology in education and health have increased the costs of providing the appropriate machinery (just as in the case of expenditures on security). And finally, the producers in each of these domains have taken advantage of this government-subsidized public demand to take a big cut of the pie.

Welfare, as the conservative complaint has said, has become an entitlement. And it is difficult to see how any government could survive a truly significant cutback in these expenditures. But of course, someone must pay for this. And producers in the end pay, either directly or via their employees who demand higher remuneration precisely to pay these costs.

We do not have good data on the steady increase of all these costs, but they are considerable. On the other hand, we cannot have a rise in the sales price of world goods to match the increase of production costs precisely because of the enormous expansion of world production, which has reduced the multiple monopolizations and increased world competition. So, the bottom line is that the costs of production have risen faster than the sales prices of production, and this means a profit squeeze that translates into difficulties in accumulating capital through production. This squeeze has been evident overall for some thirty years already which accounts for the speculative rage that has encompassed world capitalists since the 1970s and which shows no signs of letting up. But bubbles burst. Balloons cannot be infinitely expanded.

To be sure, capitalists collectively fight back. This is what neoliberal globalization is all about—a massive political attempt to roll back remuneration costs, to counter demands for internalization of costs, and of course to reduce levels of taxation. As has happened with every previous such counteroffensive against rising costs, it has succeeded partially, but only very partially. Even after all the cutbacks by the most reactionary regimes, the costs of production in the first decade of the 21st century are markedly higher than they were in 1945. I think of this as the ratchet effect—two steps forward and one step backward add up to a secular rising curve.

As the underlying economic structures of the capitalist world economy have been moving in the direction of reaching an asymptote which makes it increasingly difficult to accumulate capital, the political structures that have been holding the dangerous classes in check have also run into trouble.

The period of developmentalism, 1945–1970, was also the period of the triumph of the historic anti-systemic movements, which came into power in one form or another almost everywhere. Their biggest promise had been the developmentalist dream. When that failed, the support of their followers disintegrated. The movements, whether they called themselves communist or social-democrat or national liberation movements, fell from power almost everywhere. The period of globalization, 1970–2000, was the period of deep disillusionment with the historic anti-systemic movements. They fell from grace, and are unlikely to attract the deep loyalty of the mass of the populations again. They may be supported electorally as better than the other guys, but they no longer are deemed worthy of the faith they represented for a golden future.

The decline of these movements—the so-called Old Left—is not in fact a plus for the smooth functioning of the capitalist world economy. While these movements were anti-systemic in their goals, they were disciplined structures which controlled the spontaneous radical impulses of their followers. They mobilized for specific actions, but they also demobilized followers, especially when they were in government, insisting on the benefits in a distant future, as opposed to untrammeled disturbances in the present. The collapse of these movements represents the collapse on constraints on the dangerous classes, who thereby become dangerous again. The spreading anarchy of the 21st century is the clear reflection of this shift. The capitalist world economy is today a very unstable structure. It has never been more so. It is very vulnerable to sudden and swift destructive currents.

If it is not, what kinds of alternatives present themselves to all of us now?

It is not very comforting to anyone in countries of the South to say that the present world-system is in structural crisis and that we are in a transition from it to some other world-system over the next 25–50 years. They will want to know what happens in the meantime, and what if anything they can or should do to improve the lot of the populations of these countries right now. People tend to live in the present, as indeed they should. On the other hand, it is important to know the constraints of the present, in order that our actions are maximally useful, in the sense that they further the objectives we seek in some meaningful way. So, let me indicate what I think is the scenario over the next 25–50 years, and what that implies for the immediate present.

The scenario over the next 25–50 years is twofold. On the one hand, the collapse of our existing historical system is most likely for all the reasons I laid out just previously. On the other hand, what will replace the existing system is completely uncertain, inherently unpredictable, although all of us can have input into that uncertain outcome. It is inherently uncertain because whenever we are in a systemic bifurcation, there is no way of knowing in advance which fork in the road we shall collectively take. This is the message of the sciences of complexity (Ilya Prigogine, 1997).

On the other hand, precisely because this is a period of transition in which the existing system is far from equilibrium, with wild and chaotic oscillations in all domains, the pressures to return to equilibrium are extremely weak. This means that, in effect, we are in the domain of "free will" and therefore our actions, individual and collective, have a direct and large impact on the historical choices with which the world is faced. In a sense, to translate this into our concerns, we may say that the objective of "development" which countries and scholars have been pursuing for some fifty years now are far more realizable in the next 25–50 years than they ever were up to now. But of course there is no guarantee, for the outcome is uncertain.

In the larger geopolitical arena, there are presently three principal cleavages. There is first the triadic struggle between the United States, Western Europe, and Japan/East Asia to be the principal locus of capital accumulation in the capitalist world economy. There is secondly the long-standing struggle between North and South for distribution of the world surplus. And there is the new struggle that revolves around the structural crisis of the capitalist world economy and centers on which of the two possible forks the world will take in completing the transition to a new system.

The first two struggles are traditional within the framework of the modern world-system. The so-called triad are roughly equal contestants in the attempt to reorganize the world-system's production and financial systems. As with all such triadic struggles, there is pressure to reduce the triad to a dyad, which may occur in the next decade or so. I have long argued that the most likely pair is the United States and Japan/East Asia against Western Europe/Russia (Wallerstein, 1991). But I shall not repeat this argument here, since I consider this struggle secondary to the issue of overcoming the polarization of the existing system, that is, permitting what we have called "development" throughout the world-system.

The second struggle, that between North and South, has of course been a central focus of development issues for the last fifty years. Indeed, the great difference between the era of developmentalism and the era of globalization has been the relative strength of the two sides. While in the first era, the South seemed to be improving its position, if only slightly, the second period has been one of a triumphant push-back by the North. But this pushback has now come to a close, with the deadlock in the World Trade Organization and the split among the spokesmen of the North about the wisdom of the Washington Consensus. I think here of the increasingly open dissent of such figures as Joseph Stiglitz, Jeffrey Sachs, and George Soros, among many others, and the remarkable softening of the rigidities of the International Monetary Fund in the post-2000 period. I do not expect that in the coming decades there will be much off-center push in this contest.

It is the third cleavage which reflects the new situation, that of the structural crisis with its consequent chaos in the world-system and the bifurcation that is occurring. This is the split between the spirit of Davos and the spirit of Porto Alegre, which I mentioned previously. I should explain what I think are the central issues here. The struggle is not about whether or not we are in favor of capitalism as a world-system. The struggle is about what should replace it, given the implosion of the present world-system. The two replacement possibilities have no real names and have no detailed outlines. What is in question is essentially whether the replacement system will be hierarchical and polarizing (i.e., like the present system, or worse) or will be instead relatively democratic and egalitarian. These are basic moral choices, and being on one side of the other dictates our politics.

The contours of the actual political players are still uncertain. The side of the spirit of Davos is split between those whose vision of the future involves an unremitting harshness of strategy and institution-building and those who insist that such a vision would create an untenable system, which could not last. At the moment, it is a very divided camp. The side of the spirit of Porto Alegre has other problems. They constitute politically merely a loose alliance of variegated movements all over the world which, today at least, meet together within the framework of the World Social Forum (WSF). Collectively, they have no clear strategy as yet. But they do have a good deal of grassroots support, and they are clear about what they oppose.

The question is what those who would uphold the spirit of Porto Alegre should really do to advance this "other world" they assert is possible. And this is a double question. What is it that those few governments who share their vision, at least up to a point, should do, and what the multiple movements should do. Governments deal with the short-run issues. Movements can deal with both short-run and middle-run issues. Both kinds of issues affect the longer-run transition process. And short-run issues affect our daily lives immediately. An intelligent political strategy must move on all fronts at once.

The biggest short-run issue is the continuing drive of the neoliberal globalizers to achieve a one-sided expansion of open borders—open in the South, but not really open in the North. This is the heart of the persistent discussion within the framework of the World Trade Organization, and of all the bilateral discussions being conducted most notably by the United States but also secondarily by the European Union and its members—the creation of multiple "free trade agreements" like NAFTA, CAFTA, etc. Basically what the United States pushes for is guarantees for its monopolies (so-called intellectual property) and access for its financial institutions in return for limited tariff concessions on agricultural and low-value industrial goods produced in countries of the South.

The offensive within the WTO was stalled at Cancún by a coalition of medium powers of the South—Brazil, India, South Africa, etc.—who put forward a simple demand: free trade that works both ways. If the North wants us to open our borders to them, they said in effect, it must open its borders to us. But the North is basically unable to accept this kind of deal for two reasons. It would result in considerably increased unemployment and downsized income in countries of the North, which is politically impossible for governments subject to electoral contests to accept. And it is not clear to the triad which of them would profit most, or lose least, from such arrangements, and therefore they hesitate. After all, the triad is engaged with tariff/subsidy controversies with each other, and arrangements with the South would weaken their political positions in this economically even more important conflict from the point of view of the countries of the North.

One can draw two conclusions from this. This is a political quarrel doomed to a standstill. And it is politically very important for the countries of the South to maintain this stance, from their own point of view. This is the single most important action these governments can take to further the possibility of maintaining or raising the standard of living in their countries. To the sirens of the neoliberal dogmas, these countries are now responding skeptically, show me, and this skepticism is justified.

Of course, these governments have to remain in power. And the biggest threat to that is external interference in their politics. What the larger countries of the South are now doing, and will speed up doing in the next decade, is seeking to enter the nuclear club. What this will accomplish is to largely neutralize external military threat, and thereby minimize external political threat. And the third thing one can demand of these governments is social welfare distribution within their countries, which of course could include low-level development projects (such as digging wells, etc.) What one cannot expect of these countries is that some policy on their part is going to turn them into a Denmark in the next 10-, 20-, or 30 years. It's not going to happen, and is basically a diversion from an intelligent policy. The role of progressive governments is primarily to make sure that conditions in their countries and the world do not get still worse in the decades to come.

It is the movements that can do more than the governments, although the movements need to keep minimally progressive governments in power, and not engage in leftist infantilist critiques about the lack of achievements that are in fact impossible to expect. And here we must point out an important element that is often lost from observation. The first two geopolitical cleavages are geographic: conflicts among the Triad; North-South conflicts. But the conflict between the spirit of Davos and the spirit of Porto Alegre has no geography. It cuts across the entire world, as do the movements. It is a class struggle, a moral struggle; not a geographic struggle.

In the medium run, what the movements can best do is to push decommodification wherever they can, and to the extent that they can. No one can be quite sure how this would work. It will take a lot of experimentation to find viable formulas. And such experimentation is going on. It is going on, we must remember, within a basically hostile environment, in which there are systemic pressures to undermine any such attempts, and which can corrupt the participants with not too much difficulty. But decommodification not only stems the drive for neoliberal extensions but builds the basis for an alternate political culture.

Of course, the theorists of capitalism have long derided decommodification, arguing that it is illusory, that it goes against some presumed innate social psychology of humankind, that it is inefficient, and that it guarantees lack of economic growth and therefore of poverty. All of this is false. We have only to look at two major institutions of the modern world—universities and hospitals—to realize that, at least up to twenty years ago, no one questioned that they should be run as nonprofit institutions, without shareholders or profit-takers. And it would be hard to argue seriously that, for that reason, they have been inefficient, unreceptive to technological advances, incapable of attracting competent personnel to run them, or unable to perform the basic services for which they were created.

We don't know how these principles would work, if applied to large-scale production like steel production or small-scale, more artisanal production. But to dismiss this out of hand is simply blind. And in an era when productive enterprises are becoming far less profitable than previously, precisely because of the economic growth which the capitalist world economy has bred, is foolish. Pushing alternate forms of development along these lines has a potential for answering problems not only of the South but of the declining industrial regions of the North.

In any case, as I have insisted, the issue is not what will magically solve the immediate dilemmas of our world-system but the basis on which we shall create the successor world-system. And to address that seriously, we must first of all comprehend with some clarity the historical development of our present system, appreciate its structural dilemmas today, and open our mind to radical alternatives for the future. And we must do all this, not merely academically but practically, that is, living in the present, and concerned with the immediate needs of people as well as longer-run transformations. We must therefore fight both defensively and offensively. And if we do it well, we may, but only may, come out ahead in the lifetimes of some of the younger members of this audience.

References

Anthony Atkinson, Lee Rainwater, and Timothy Smeeding. "Income Distribution in European Countries," in A. B. Atkinson (ed.), *Incomes and the Welfare State: Essays on Britain and Europe*, Cambridge: Cambridge Univ. Press.

Giovanni Arrighi and Jessica Drangel. 1986. "The Stratification of the World-Economy: An Exploration of the Semiperipheral Zone," *Review*, X(i, Summer): 9–74

Deane Neubauer. "Mixed Blessings of the Megacities," *Yale Global Online*, http://yaleglobal.yale.edu/display.article?id=4573 (accessed on September 24, 2004).

Ilya Prigogine and Isabelle Stengers. 1997. *The End of Certainty: Time, Chaos, and the New Laws of Nature.* New York: Free Press.

Wallerstein, Immanuel. 1991. "Japan and the Future Trajectory of the World-System: Lessons from History?" in *Geopolitics and Geoculture*, pp 36–48. Cambridge: Cambridge Univ. Press.

3

21st Century Globalization

Sociological Perspectives

JAN NEDERVEEN PIETERSE

The 21st century momentum of globalization is markedly different from 20th century globalization and involves a new geography of trade, weaker hegemony, and growing multipolarity. This presents major questions. Is the rise of East Asia, China, and India just another episode in the rise and decline of nations, another reshuffling of capitalism, a relocation of accumulation centers without affecting the logics of accumulation? Does it advance, sustain, or halt neoliberalism? The rise of Asia is codependent with neoliberal globalization and yet unfolds outside the neoliberal mold. What is the relationship between zones of accumulation and modes of regulation? What are the ramifications for global inequality? The first part of this chapter discusses trends in trade, finance, international institutions, hegemony and inequality, and social struggle. The second part discusses what the new trends mean for the emerging 21st century international division of labor.

With 4 percent of the world population, the United States absorbs 25 percent of the world energy, supplies 40 percent of the world consumption, and spends 50 percent of the world military spending and 50 percent of the world health care spending (at $1.3 trillion a year). US borrowing of $700 billion per year or $2.6 billion per day absorbs 70–80 percent of net world savings. Meanwhile the US share of world manufacturing output has steadily declined and the share of manufacturing in US GDP at 12.7 percent is now smaller than that of the health care sector at 14 percent and financial services at 20 percent. This shrinking of the physical economy makes it unlikely that the massive American external debt can ever be repaid (Prestowitz, 2005).

According to IMF estimates, China and India are expected to overtake the GDP of the world's leading economies in the coming decades. China is expected to pass the GDP of Japan in 2016 and of the United States by 2025. In 2005, China surpassed the United States as Japan's biggest trading partner, surpassed Canada as the biggest trading partner of the United States, and surpassed the United States as the world's top choice of foreign direct investment. If current trends continue, China will become the biggest trading partner of practically every nation. By 2025, the combined GDP of the BRIC—Brazil, Russia, India, and China—would grow to one-half the combined GDP of the G-6 countries (the US, Japan, Germany, France, Italy, and Britain). By 2050, according to a Goldman Sachs report, the combined BRIC economies will surpass that group and "China, India, Brazil, and Russia will be the first-, third-, fifth-, and sixth-biggest economies by 2050, with the United States and Japan in second and fourth place, respectively." BRIC spending growth measured in dollars could surpass the G-6 countries' levels as early as 2009 (Whelan, 2004).

Both these data sets are uncontroversial, almost commonplace, yet combining them raises major questions. How do we get from here to there and what does this mean for the course and shape of globalization?

The United States, Europe, and Japan rode the previous wave of globalization, notably during 1980–2000, but in recent years their lead in manufacturing, trade, finance, and international politics is gradually slipping. The United States set the rules, in economics, through the Washington consensus, in trade, through the WTO, in finance, through the dollar standard and the IMF, and in security, through its hegemony and formidable military. Each of these dimensions is now out of whack. The old winners are still winning but the *terms* on which they are winning cede more and more to emerging forces. In production and services, education and demography, the advantages are no longer squarely with the old winners. In several respects in the maelstrom of globalization, the old winners have become conservative forces.

The 21st century momentum of globalization is markedly different from 20th century globalization. Slowly like a giant oil tanker, the axis of globalization is turning from North-South to East-South relations. This presents major questions. Is the rise of Asia and the newly industrialized economies (NIEs) just another episode in the rise and decline of nations, another reshuffling of capitalism, a relocation of accumulation centers without affecting the *logics* of accumulation? Does it advance, sustain, or halt neoliberalism? Is it just another shift in national economic fortunes, or is it an alternative political economy with different institutions, class relations, energy use, and transnational politics? What is the relationship between zones of accumulation and modes of regulation and what are the ramifications for global inequality?

Examining this poses methodological problems. Extrapolating trends is risky. The units of analysis are not what they used to be or seem to be. Statistics measure countries, but economies are crossborder. The story, of course, is not merely one of change but also continuity, and in some respects, seeming continuity. There is a certain stickiness and stodginess to social change. Power plays continue as long as they can. Policies continue old style until a policy paradigm change is inevitable, not unlike Thomas Kuhn's revolutions in science. There is a sleepwalking choreography to social existence, never quite in sync with actual trends; or rather, trends are only trends when they enter discourse. (In a similar way what we teach in universities is often years behind what we know or what we're thinking about because there is no convenient structure or heading yet under which to place and communicate it.) Changes manifest after certain time lags—an institutional lag, discursive lag, and policy lag; yet changes are underway even if the language to signal them isn't quite there yet. Some changes we can name, some we can surmise, and some escape detection and will catch up with us. So at times it feels much like business as usual. Thus we should identify structural trends and discursive changes as well as tipping points that would tilt the pattern and the paradigm.

About cutting-edge globalization there are two big stories to tell. One is the rise of Asia and the accompanying growth of East-South trade, energy, financial, and political relations. Part of this story is being covered in general media, often with brio (Marber, 1998; Agtmael, 2007). In the words of Paul Kennedy, "[W]e can no more stop the rise of Asia than we can stop the winter snows and the summer heat" (Kennedy, 2001: 78). The other story, which receives mention only in patchy ways, is that the emerging societies face major social crises in agriculture and urban poverty.

The first section of this chapter discusses the main trends in 21st century globalization by comparing trends during 1980–2000 and 2000 to present under the headings of trade, finance, international institutions, hegemony, and inequality and social struggle. In the second part I seek to understand what the new trends mean for the emerging 21st century international division of labor and the ramifications of the ongoing global economic crisis. The financial crisis that erupted in 2008 and led to ongoing global recession is part of the 21st century transition and confirms several trends discussed below: the crisis of neoliberalism and American capitalism, weakening American hegemony, finance as a central arena of international competition, and the rise of emerging societies, in particular China, exemplified in the shift from the G7–G20.

Trade

Growing East–South trade leads to a "new geography of trade" and new trade pacts.

Through the postwar period North-South trade relations were dominant. In recent years East-South trade has been growing, driven by the rise of Asian economies and the accompanying commodities boom (particularly since 2003) and high petrol prices (since 2004). According to the UN Conference on Trade and Development, a "new geography of trade" is taking shape: "The new axis stretches from the manufacturing might and emerging middle classes of China, and from the software powerhouse of India in the south, to the mineral riches of South Africa, a beachhead to the rest of the African continent, and across the Indian and Pacific oceans to South America which is oil-rich and mineral- and agriculture-laden" (Whelan, 2004).

During 1980–2000, American-led trade pacts such as NAFTA, APEC, and the WTO played a dominant role. In the 2000s these trade pacts are in impasse or passé. Dissatisfaction with NAFTA is commonplace, also in the United States. In Latin America, Mercosur, enlarged with Venezuela and with Cuba as associate member, undercuts the Free Trade Association of the Americas (FTAA). The association of Southeast Asian nations, ASEAN, in combination with Japan, South Korea, and China (ASEAN+3) sidelines APEC, which is increasingly on the backburner, and reduces Asian dependence on the American market. Michael Lind (2005) notes, "This group has the potential to be the world's largest trade bloc, dwarfing the European Union and North American Free Trade Association."

During 1980–2000, the overall trend was toward regional and global trade pacts. The G22 walkout in Cancún in November 2003 upped the ante in subsequent negotiations. Advanced countries that previously pushed trade liberalization now resist liberalizing trade and retreat to "economic patriotism." The United States has been zigzagging in relation to the WTO (with steel tariffs and agriculture and cotton subsidies). Given the WTO gridlock in the Doha development round and blocked regional trade talks (the Cancún walkout was followed by the failure of the FTAA talks in Miami), the United States increasingly opts for free trade agreements, which further erode the WTO (Nederveen Pieterse, 2004b).

In South-South trade, the trend is toward regional and interregional combinations such as Mercosur and ASEAN. China has established a free trade zone with ASEAN. In the future India may join ASEAN+3. Since 2003 there have been talks to establish a free trade zone of India, Brazil, and South Africa (IBSA).

So the old "core-periphery" relations no longer hold. The South no longer looks just north but also sideways. In development policies East and Southeast Asian models have long overtaken Western development examples. South-South cooperation, heralded as an alternative to dependence on the West ever since the Bandung meeting of the Nonaligned Movement in 1955, is now taking shape. "Already 43 percent of the South's global trade is accounted for by intra-South trade" (Gosh, 2006: 7).

The downside is that much of this growth is sparked by a commodities boom that will not last. Only countries that convert commodity surpluses into productive investments and "intellectual capital" will outlast the current commodities cycle.

Finance

The current imbalances in the world economy (American overconsumption and deficits and Asian surpluses) are unsustainable and are producing a gradual reorganization of global finance and trade.

During 1980–2000 finance capital played a key role in restructuring global capitalism. The financialization of economies (or the growing preponderance of financial instruments) and the hegemony of finance capital reflect the maturation of advanced economies, the role of finance as a key force in globalization, financialization as the final stage of American hegemony, and financial innovations such as hedge funds and derivatives. The return to hegemony of finance capital ranks as one of the defining features of neoliberal globalization (Duménil and Lévy, 2001).

The role of speculative capital led to the diagnoses such as casino capitalism and Las Vegas capitalism. International finance capital has been crisis prone and financial crises hit Mexico, Asia, Russia, Latin America, and Argentina. Attempts to reform the architecture of international finance have come to little more than one-sided pleas for transparency. The trend since 2000 is that NIEs hold vast foreign reserves to safeguard against financial turbulence; "the South holds more than $2 trillion as foreign exchange reserves" (Gosh, 2006: 7). As many historians note, the final stage of hegemony is financialization. Accordingly, emerging economies view competition in financial markets as the next strategic arena—beyond competition in manufacturing, resources, and services.

During 1980–2000 the IMF was the hard taskmaster of developing economies; now year after year the IMF warns that US deficits threaten global economic stability (Becker and Andrews, 2004: Guha, 2007).

Through the postwar period the US dollar led as the world reserve currency, but since 2001 there has been a gradual shift from the dollar to other currencies. After the decoupling of the dollar from gold in 1971, OPEC in 1975 agreed to sell oil for dollars and established a de facto oil-dollar standard. Now Venezuela, Iran, and Russia price their oil in other currencies. In 2001–2005 the dollar declined by 28 percent against euro and a further 12 percent in 2006. In 2002 the leading central banks held on average 73 percent world reserves in dollars, by 2005 this was 66 percent (Johnson, 2005) and the trend for 2006 is toward 60 percent. China and Japan with 70–80 percent of their foreign reserves in US dollars, reflecting their close ties to the American market, deviate markedly from the world average. Of China's $1.3 trillion in foreign reserves up to $1 trillion is in dollars. The current trend is for China to diversify its foreign reserves toward 65 percent in dollars (McGregor, 2006). For obvious reasons this diversification must be gradual.

In the wake of the 1997 Asian crisis, the IMF vetoed Japan's initiative for an Asian monetary fund. Since then Thailand's Chiang Mai Initiative established an Asian Bond Fund. Western financial markets have been dominant since the 17th century. In the 2000s financial sources outside the West play an increasingly important role, reflecting the rise of Asia, the global commodities boom, and high petrol prices. A new east-east financial network is emerging. China's initial public offerings are increasingly no longer routed via New York and London, but via Saudi Arabia (Timmons, 2006) and the Dubai Borse. Wall Street is losing its primacy as the center of world finance to London with Shanghai and Hong Kong as runners up (Tucker, 2007).

East Asian countries are active investors in Latin America and Africa. Thirty seven percent of FDI in developing countries now comes from other developing countries. China emerges as a new lender to developing countries, at lower rates and without the conditions of the Washington institutions (Parker and Beattie, 2006). China's foreign aid competes with Western donors and Venezuela plays this role in Latin America.

For all these changes, the net financial drain from the global South is still ongoing. Poorer nations sustain American overconsumption and the overvalued dollar. The world economy increasingly resembles a giant Ponzi scheme with massive debt that is sustained by dollar surpluses and vendor financing in China, Japan, and East Asia. The tipping points are that financialization backfires when it turns out that financial successes (leveraged buyouts, mergers and acquisitions and the rise in stock ratings) have been based on easy credit, and secondly, when finance follows the "new money."

Institutions

The 1990s architecture of globalization is fragile and the clout of emerging economies is growing.

The 1990s institutional architecture of globalization was built around the convergence of the IMF, World Bank, and WTO and is increasingly fragile. Since its handling of the Asian crisis in 1997–1998 and Argentina's crisis in 2001, the IMF has earned the nickname "the master of disaster." Argentina, Brazil, Venezuela, South Africa, Russia, and other countries have repaid their debt to the IMF early, so the IMF has less financial leverage, also in view of the new flows of petro money. IMF lending is down from $70 billion in 2003 to $20 billion in 2006. The IMF has adopted marginal reforms (it now accepts capital controls and has increased the vote quota of four emerging economies) but faces financial constraints.

The World Bank has lost standing as well. In the 1990s the Bank shifted gear from neoliberalism to social liberalism and structural adjustment "with a human face" and an emphasis on poverty reduction and social risk mitigation. But the poverty reduction targets of the Bank and the Millennium Development Goals are, as usual, not being met. Paul Wolfowitz's attempts as World Bank president to merge neoliberalism and neoconservatism have been counterproductive with an internally divisive anti-corruption campaign and focus on Iraq.

The infrastructure of power has changed as well. The "Wall Street-Treasury-IMF complex" of the 1990s has weakened. The 1990s architecture of globalization has become fragile for several reasons. The disciplinary regime of the Washington consensus has been slipping away. Structural adjustment has shown a consistently high failure rate with casualties in sub-Saharan Africa, most of Latin America, and the 1997 Asian crisis and how it was handled by the IMF. Research indicates a correlation between IMF and World Bank involvement and negative economic performance, arguably for political reasons: since IMF involvement signals economic troubles, it attracts further troubles (McKenna, 2005). Zigzag behavior by the hegemon—flaunting WTO rules, an utter lack of fiscal discipline and building massive deficits—has further weakened the international institutions. Following the spate of financial crises in the 90s, crisis mismanagement and growing American deficits, the macroeconomic dogmas of the Washington consensus have given way to a post-Washington no-consensus. Meanwhile increasing pressure from the global South is backed by greater economic weight and bargaining power.

Hegemony

Rather than hegemonic rivalry, what is taking place is global repositioning and realignments toward growing multipolarity.

In general terms, the main possibilities in relation to hegemony are continued American hegemony, hegemonic rivalry, hegemonic transition, and multipolarity. The previous episode of hegemonic decline at the turn of the 19th century took the form of wars of hegemonic rivalry culminating in the transition to the United States as the new hegemon. But the current transition looks to be structurally different from previous episodes. Economic and technological interdependence and cultural interplay are now far greater than at the *fin de siècle*. What is emerging is not simply a decline of (American) hegemony and rise of (Asian) hegemony but a more complex multipolar field.

During the 1990s American hegemony was solvent, showed high growth and seemed to be dynamic in the throttle of the new economy boom. The United States followed a mixed uni-multipolar approach with cooperative security (as in the Gulf War) and "humanitarian intervention" (as in Bosnia, Kosovo, and Kurdistan) as Leitmotivs. Unilateralism with a multilateral face during the 1990s gave way to unilateralism with a unilateral face under the GW Bush administration, a high-risk and high-cost approach that flaunts its weaknesses (Nederveen Pieterse, 2004a). By opting for unilateral "preventive war," the GW Bush administration abandoned international law. After declaring an "axis of evil," the United States has few tools left. The United States is now caught up in its new wars. In going to war with Iraq, the United States overplayed its hand. In its first out-of-area operation in Afghanistan, NATO meets fierce resistance. The United States has been forced to give up its access to a base in Uzbekistan.

During the cold war Muslims were cultivated as allies and partners on many fronts. Thus in the 1980s Ronald Reagan lauded the Mujahedeen in the Afghan war as "the moral equivalent of our founding fathers." As the cold war waned, these allies were sidelined. Samuel Huntington's "clash of civilizations" article in 1993 signaled a major turn by shifting the target from ideology to culture and from communism to the Islamic world. Thus erstwhile allies and partners were redefined as enemies and yesterday's freedom fighters were reclassified as today's terrorists.

New security axes and poles have emerged, notably the Shanghai Cooperation Organization (deemed a "counterweight to NATO") and the triangular cooperation of China, Russia, and Iran. Other emerging poles of influence are India, Brazil, Venezuela, and South Africa. The G77 makes its influence felt in international trade and diplomacy. For instance, it blocked intervention in Darfur on the grounds of state sovereignty, involving an Islamic government in a strategic part of the world, in part as a response to American expansion in the Middle

East and Africa. China has generally backed G77 positions in UN Security Council negotiations (Traub, 2006), a position that is now gradually changing.

On the military frontiers of hegemony, although the United States spends 48 percent of world military spending (in 2005) and maintains a formidable "empire of bases," the wars in Iraq and Afghanistan demonstrate the limits of American military power. As a traditional maritime and air power, the United States has traditionally been unable to win ground wars (Reifer, 2005). "Globalization from the barrel of a gun" is a costly proposition, also because of the growing hiatus between American military and economic power (Nederveen Pieterse, 2008).

The main tipping points of American hegemony are domestic and external. Domestic tipping points are the inflated housing market and high levels of debt. The main external tipping points are fading dollar loyalty, financial markets following new money, the growing American legitimacy crisis, and the strategic debacles in Iraq and the Middle East.

There are generally three different responses to American hegemony. The first is *continued support*—which is adopted for a variety of reasons such as the appeal of the American market, the role of the dollar, the shelter of the American military umbrella, and lingering hope in the possibility of American self-correction. The second option is *soft balancing*—which ranges from tacit noncooperation (such as most European countries staying out of the Iraq war and declining genetically modified food) to establishing alternative institutions without US participation (such as the Kyoto Protocol and the International Criminal Court). And the third response is *hard balancing*—which only few countries can afford either because they have been branded as enemies of the United States already, so they have little to lose (Cuba, Venezuela, Iran, and Sudan), or because their bargaining power allows them maneuvering room (as in the case of China and Russia and the SCO).

An intriguing trend is that the number of countries that *combine* these different responses to American hegemony in different policy domains is increasing. Thus, China displays all three responses in different spheres—economic cooperation (WTO, trade), noncooperation in diplomacy (UN Security Council), and finance (valuation of renminbi), and overt resistance in Central Asia (Wolfe, 2005) and in support for Iran.

American unilateralism and preventive war are gradually giving way to multipolarity if only because unilateralism is becoming too costly, militarily, politically, and economically. New clusters and alignments are gradually taking shape around trade, energy, and security. Sprawling and cross-zone global realignments point to growing multipolarity rather than hegemonic rivalry.

Inequality and Social Struggle

The flashpoints of global inequality are rural crises and urban poverty in emerging economies and chronic poverty in the least developed countries. International migration is a worldwide flashpoint of inequality.

Let us review these trends in a wider time frame. Postwar capitalism from 1950 to the 1970s combined growth and equity. Although overall North-South inequality widened, economic growth went together with growing equality among and within countries. Neoliberal "free market" economies during 1980–2000 produced a sharp trend break: now economic growth came with sharply increasing inequality within and among countries. The main exceptions to the trend were the East Asian tiger economies.

The trend in the 2000s is that overall inequality between advanced economies and emerging economies is narrowing while inequality in emerging societies is increasing. Overall global inequality is staggering with 1 percent of the world population owning 40 percent of the world's assets. The pattern of rising inequality in neoliberal economies (the US, the UK, and New Zealand) continues and has begun to extend to Australia, Japan, and South Korea (Lim and Jang, 2006). International migration has become a major flashpoint of global inequality and produces growing conflicts and dilemmas around migration and multiculturalism in many countries (Nederveen Pieterse, 2007b).

James Rosenau offers an optimistic assessment of global trends according to which rising human development indices, urbanization, and growing social and communication densities are producing a general "skills revolution" (1999). However, the flipside of technological change and knowledge economies is that with rising skill levels come widening skills differentials and urban-rural disparities. The second general cause of growing inequality is unfettered market forces promoted by multinational corporations, international institutions, and business media. Familiar short hands are shareholder capitalism (in contrast to stakeholder capitalism), Wal-Mart capitalism (low wages, low benefits, and temp workers), and Las Vegas capitalism (speculative capital). The third general cause of inequality is financialization because its employment base is much narrower than in manufacturing, and income differentials are much steeper. A fourth cause of inequality in developing countries is fast-growth policies that reflect middle class and urban bias and aggravate rich-poor and urban-rural gaps.

Practically all emerging economies face major rural and agricultural crises. In China this takes the form of pressure on land, deepening rural poverty, pollution, village-level corruption, and urban migration. In Brazil and the Philippines, land reform drags because the political coalition to confront landholding oligarchies is too weak. In South Africa, the apartheid legacy and the poor soil and weak agricultural base in the former Bantustans contribute to rural crisis.

These are classic problems of modernization. In the past, failure to bring the peasant hinterland into modernity gave rise to fascism. A major failing of communism in Russia was the collectivization of agriculture. Emerging economies need balanced development and "walking on two legs," yet urban bias (low agriculture prices, inadequate support for agriculture) and the intrusion of transnational market forces in agriculture (land appropriations, multinational agribusiness) are crisis prone.

Yet the *impact* of poor peoples' movements and social struggles in the 2000s has been greater than during 1980–2000, notably in China and Latin America. In China, where "a social protest erupts every five minutes," social crises are widely recognized and have led to the "harmonious society" policies adopted in 2005. In Latin America poor peoples' movements have contributed to the election of leftwing governments in Venezuela, Bolivia, Ecuador, and Nicaragua and to policy adjustments in Argentina and Chile.

Whereas the "Shanghai model" of fast-growth policies that are geared to attract foreign investment has been abandoned in China, it is being pursued with fervor in India. A case in point is the "Shanghaing of Mumbai" (Mahadevia, 2006) and the growing role of special economic zones.

What is the relationship between the India of Thomas Friedman (*The world is flat*) and P. Sainath (*Everybody loves a good drought*), between celebrating growth and deepening poverty, between Gurgaon's Millennium City of Malls and abject poverty kilometers away, and between dynamic "Cyberabad" and rising farmer suicides nearby in the same state of Andhra Pradesh? According to official figures, 100,248 farmers committed suicide between 1993 and 2003. Armed Maoist struggles have spread to 170 rural districts, affecting 16 states and 43 percent of the country's territory (Johnson, 2006) and are now the country's top security problem.

> For every swank mall that will spring up in a booming Indian city, a neglected village will explode in Naxalite rage; for every child who will take wings to study in a foreign university there will be 10 who fall off the map without even the raft of a basic alphabet to keep them afloat; for every new Italian eatery that will serve up fettuccine there will be a debt-ridden farmer hanging himself and his hopes by a rope. (Tejpal, 2006)

India's economic growth benefits a top stratum of 4 percent in the urban areas with little or negative spin off for 80 percent of the population in the countryside. The software sector rewards the well-educated middle class. The IT sector has an upper caste aura—brainy, requiring good education, English language—and extends upper caste privileges to the knowledge economy, with low cost services from the majority population in the informal sector (Krishna and Nederveen Pieterse, 2008). Public awareness in India is split between middle class hype and recognition of social problems, but there are no major policies in place to address the problems of rural majorities and the urban poor.

In addition to rural crisis, the emerging powers face profound *urban poverty*, as part of the "planet of slums" (Davis, 2005). The rural crisis feeds into the sprawling world of the favelas, bidonvilles, shanty towns, and shacks. Urban policies are at best ambivalent to the poor and often negligent. Thus Bangkok's glitzy monorail mass transit system connects different shopping areas, but not the outlying suburbs. As India's rural poor are driven out of agriculture, they flock to the cities, while land appropriations and clampdowns on informal settlements, hawking, and unlicensed stores squeeze the urban poor out of the cities, creating a scissor operation which leaves the poor with nowhere to go.

Trends in 21st Century Globalization

Now let us review these trends. Is the cusp of the millennium, 1980–2000 and 2000 to present, a significant enough period to monitor significant changes in globalization? Why in a short period of decades would there be significant trend breaks? My argument is essentially that two projects that defined the 1980–2000 period, American hegemony and neoliberalism—which are of course the culminating expressions of longer trends—are now over their peak. They are not gone from the stage but they gather no new adherents and face mounting problems (indebtedness, military overstretch, legitimacy crises, and rising inequality), and new forces are rising. The new forces stand in an ambiguous relationship to neoliberalism and American hegemony.

In sum, the overall picture shows distinct new trends in trade, institutions, finance and hegemony, and to some extent in social inequality. The trend break with the old patterns is undeniable, yet it is too early to speak of a new pattern.

Global Sociology

The perplexities of globalization are, so to speak, the demand side. Now consider the supply side: what does sociology contribute to this question? Among social sciences, sociology, more than others, plays a double role as a discipline and meeting place of social sciences. Arguably sociology is more open than other social sciences and better positioned to develop a social science synthesis. Addressing globalization requires an interdisciplinary rendezvous of sociology, global political economy, development studies, geography, history, anthropology, and cultural studies.

"Society" as the conventional unit of analysis, shaping the legacy of sociology, is gradually being surpassed in comparative, regional, and transnational studies. Historians (Mazlish, 2006) and sociologists (Beck, 2005) claim that we have entered a "global age," and a global sociology is taking shape. In global sociology the main theoretical synthesis remains world-system theory. Even so, the limitations of WST are familiar: WST is Eurocentric, preoccupied with the long

16th century as the genesis of the modern world-system and with capitalism in the singular. For instance, if the rise of Asia is a come-back that builds on and in some respects resumes the experience of prior oriental globalization, WST precludes this option and we must look for guidance outside the historical work of Andre Gunder Frank (1998) and others. Some variants of WST point to deeper historical lineages, yet the question of the analytics remains.

In effect, WST replicates on a global canvas the two main analytics and limitations of sociology: modernity and capitalism. *Modernity* remains wedded to a Eurocentric legacy. Its variants—new, reflexive, liquid modernity, and postmodernism—retain an occidental cast as well. Capitalism likewise is a powerful problematic, but *capitalism in the singular* remains implicitly embedded in 19th century stages theory with its unilinear cast.

To go beyond Eurocentric and historically fixed and biased con-ceptualizations, we must opt for the plural: modernities and capital-isms. The idea of multiple *modernities* has the potential to transcend Eurocentrism and accommodate the "new modernities" that are taking shape. It raises fundamental questions: which patterns of relations are structural invariables (yielding modernity) and which vary according to history, geography, and culture (yielding modernities)?

The modernities approach abandons linear history and the idea of advanced societies as models. This means that the most important variables are the domestic balance of forces and debates; it means not simply applying models but giving priority to domestic balance of forces and local debates and expecting local (national, regional) adaptations of transnational influences. This approach also has downsides. As an approach *modernities* is descriptive, interpretive, and open ended, rather than critical, normative, and programmatic. Critical theory may fall by the wayside and the critical edge may be blunted to make way for bland pluralism. An immanent critique becomes difficult for what are the criteria of judgment? Cultural relativism is the strength and weakness of this approach.

Implicitly the modernities approach may follow the "national" paradigm of sociology with accounts of different Thai, Indonesian, Chinese, Brazilian, etc. modernities, so "society" returns via a side door. Work on regional modernities (Latin American, Southeast Asian, East Asian, etc.) opens this window wider, yet leans toward a civilizational approach. A further concern is that what matters is not just modernities but also the *interaction of modernities*.

Capitalisms

Another major analytical tool is the variety of capitalism, or *capitalisms*, which is ordinary in global political economy, but rare and under researched in sociology. Conventional approaches mainly accommodate stages of capitalism (early, late, and advanced) and modes of regulation (Fordism, flexible production) and retain a unilinear bias. In contrast, *capitalisms* reckon with the actual variety of capitalist institutional practices. Just as the sociology of modernity gives rise to modernities (the variety of real existing modernities), the political economy of capitalism yields capitalisms. Let's consider the limitations of capitalism singular.

First, the orthodox approach frames the problematic as capitalism *or* socialism ("barbarism or civilization," in some accounts). This echoes 19th-century evolutionism and implicitly reiterates the Marxist "gospel of crisis" according to which capitalism has no other script than its inevitable undoing. Crisis has been pending since 1848. The gospel of crisis underestimates the ingenuity of capitalism: capitalism survives crises due to the biodiversity of capitalism; *capitalisms uphold capitalism* (Nederveen Pieterse, 2004a: 146). Rather than ignoring or bemoaning this, we should recognize and analyze it and examine what potential it holds as a diagnostic and for an emancipatory approach.

Second, capitalism singular tends to downplay variations in capitalism over time and by region. Capitalism's "golden years," 1950–1973, combined growth with equity; inequality between and within countries decreased. Neoliberal capitalism, 1980–2000, produces radically different effects: growth with growing inequality or polarizing growth.

Third, capitalism singular reinforces the cliché that "there is no alternative." It upholds the *idée fixe* that neoliberalism, rather than a rightwing utopia, is "real capitalism." As Dani Rodrik and many others note, we have globalization but not global capitalism (2000). Variations in national institutions matter and the contest between capitalisms, between Anglo-American capitalism and other variants, is at issue worldwide and reverberates in development policies, business decisions, finance, and geopolitics. Capitalism singular leads to a binary, polarizing approach that reproduces the old disputes between revolution and reform (revisiting Kautsky and Bernstein vs. Lenin, Luxemburg, and Trotsky). Now this takes the form of a false choice between neoliberalism and socialism. Anyone who works in development studies knows that these options are unreal. Neoliberalism is unworkable and socialism, in general, is not a realistic program.

According to Wallerstein (2003), the three main cleavages in 21st century globalization are rivalry within the triad (United States, EU, and Japan), the North-South divide in global inequality, and the divide between the World Economic Forum and the World Social Forum, or between Davos and Porto Alegre. In part, this can be understood as the interaction and contestation of different capitalisms. The latter rift is often interpreted as a choice between capitalism and socialism. I question this: the main divide now runs not between capitalism and socialism, but between capitalism and capitalism, or what kind of capitalism?

Fourth, capitalisms, then, pose the question: *which capitalism—* American, Rhineland, Scandinavian, Japanese, Chinese, etc.? This has the advantage of clearly posing the problem of future directions within societies rather than implicitly upholding American capitalism as the standard (in relation to which, only socialism is an alternative).

Fifth, capitalisms pose the question of *the interaction of capitalisms* as a core problem of globalization. The various capitalisms are intertwined through technology, finance, investments, trade, international institutions, and knowledge and ideology. Capitalisms plural draws attention to the *terms* of this interaction without posing one form of capitalism as the norm. Indeed it has become difficult to uphold American capitalism as the standard because it is dependent on cheap Asian imports, Asian labor, and Asian vendor financing.

Sixth, capitalisms and modernities also point to *globalizations*: each capitalism and each modernity pursues its preferred mode of globalization. Capitalisms and modernities concern different ways of analyzing and navigating different modes of regulation and social organization. Beyond the "rise of Asia" they pose the question what kind of Asia, what kind of capitalism, and what kind of modernity? Growth obsessed, consumerist, authoritarian, or polluting? Fast-track tycoon capitalism or development that combines and balances growth, equity, and sustainability? Social struggles, people's movements, trade unions, feminist and ecological movements, struggles for democracy, and new regionalism inflect modernities in different ways. A sociological approach means placing the analysis of the balance of forces center stage.

The spectrum of political and ideological positions that exists in each society cannot be captured in simple binary positions. However, this discussion takes place in a battlefield of paradigms, an arena in which few statistics, diagnoses, and policies are ideologically neutral. Economic success and failure don't come with radio silence but are immersed in ideological noise and filtered through representations. The World Bank claimed the "East Asian miracle" as evidence of the wisdom of its policies of liberalization and export-led growth, whereas according to Japan it showed the virtues of capable government intervention (Wade, 1996). According to Alan Greenspan, the Asian crisis of 1997 demonstrated that Anglo-American capitalism was the only viable economic model. Most others have drawn the opposite conclusion that American-led finance capital is crisis prone, and this has been one of the spurs of the turn of the millennium trend break in globalization patterns. The subprime mortgage crisis in the American housing market prompts a "liquidity crisis" (because banks reassess credit risks) which is really a confidence crisis that signals deeper weaknesses of Anglo-American financialized capitalism.

If the Washington institutions have lost clout, the knowledge grid of financial markets remains intact with ideological ratings such as the Economic Freedom Index and Competitiveness Index. Business media (such as the Wall Street Journal and the Economist) and the media big six (such as Time Warner and Rupert Murdoch's conglomerate) echo the ideological impression management of conservative think tanks and corporate interests. In the game of perceptions, western media reports often blame social unrest in emerging societies on state authoritarianism (and emphasize "human rights"), pro-market economists blame government inefficiency and corruption, whereas state and social forces focus on capitalist excesses (and local government incompetence). International institutions and free trade agreements, multinationals, financial markets, and World Bank economists weigh in on the debates. Meanwhile neoliberalism remains a prevailing adapt-or-die logic whose influence is transmitted via financial markets, international institutions, and free trade agreements. Does then the rise of China, India, and other emerging economies validate or invalidate neoliberalism?

According to American conventional wisdom and authors such as Thomas Friedman (2005), China's economic rise follows Deng's four modernizations and the subsequent liberalization, and India's economic rise dates from its 1991 liberalization. These views are ideology- rather than research-based because research indicates different itineraries. Rodrik's work on the "Hindu rate of growth" argues that the foundations of India's economic resurgence were laid during the 1970s and 1980s (2004). Recent studies of China break the mold of Mao stigmatization and find that improvements in industrial production, rural modernization, literacy, and health care during Mao's time laid the groundwork for the post-1978 transformation (Gittings, 2005: Guthrie, 2006).

Liberalization and export orientation—the Washington consensus and World Bank formulae—contributed to the rise of Asia. American offshoring and outsourcing have spurred rapid growth (Wal-Mart's imports alone represent 15 percent of the US trade deficit with China; Prestowitz, 2005: 68). But this would not have been possible or produced sustainable growth without Asia's developmental states. Their development policies enable Asian societies and producers to upgrade technologically and to foster domestic, regional, and alternative markets. China's spending on high-tech research and development now ranks third after the United States and Japan.

If we consider the *cultural politics* of neoliberalism, emerging economies surely match neoliberal trends. Middle class consumerism and its attendant features—marketing, commercial media, malls, and shopping culture—are a leading trend throughout emerging societies. It is now developing countries that underpin the "boom in advertising spending": "Advertising spending is soaring in the developing world, suggesting that US-style consumerism is alive and well from Brazil and Russia to Saudi Arabia and Indonesia" (Silverman, 2005).

If we consider *economic doctrine*, market fundamentalism is widely rejected. If we focus on neoliberal *economics*, the picture is less clear. If neoliberalism refers to *monetarism* and fiscal conservatism (which is doubtful), many developing countries are *more* neoliberal than the United States' fiscal profligacy. Monetarism and fiscal conservatism aim to counteract inflation and avoid a deficit and the risk of financial turbulence.

Emerging societies must strike a cautious balance. While through-out the global South it is a cliché that neoliberalism doesn't work, the international financial markets continue business as usual, so for developing countries diplomacy is in order. Deficit countries cannot afford to offend the hegemonic institutions and credit regimes. Most countries must walk the tightrope and remain on reasonably good terms with financial markets and credit rating agencies, lest their cost of borrowing and doing business goes up.

These are different reasons than during the 90s. Then the main considerations were debt and dependence on the Washington insti-tutions, which now applies to fewer countries, and a default belief in free market policies as the most dynamic and pro-growth, which has lost adherents since the crises of the 90s and economic and financial disarray in the United States. If American deficits are crisis prone and inequality in the United States is growing sharply, why follow this model? Now emerging economies follow neoliberal policies (in the sense of fiscal conservatism) to *escape* from neoliberalism (in the sense of the vagaries of the "free market").

If neoliberalism refers to *high-exploitation capitalism*, again the picture is mixed. It does not generally apply to the tiger economies, South Korea, Taiwan, or Singapore, at least in the sense that they have sizeable public sectors. It does apply to China where migrants from the impoverished countryside have been an essential component in the razor sharp "China price" and to India where the low-wage rural economy and the urban poor support the modern sector with cheap labor, services, and produce. Inequality has not been a just so circum-stance or minor quirk en route to growth but a fundamental factor in production and in establishing the international competitiveness of several emerging economies. In China this has begun to change since the adoption of the "harmonious society" policy in 2005. In India high-exploitation capitalism, buttressed by caste in the countryside, continues unabated without major changes in government policy.

Of the two major trends in 21st century globalization, the gradual East-South turn is widely recognized, but the deepening rural and urban poverty in emerging societies is not. Business media engage in emerging markets boosterism. Meanwhile for emerging societ-ies the key to sustainable development is to take the peasantry and the urban poor along. Discussions in emerging societies are about rehabilitating the developmental state (where it has been away), not an authoritarian developmental state but one that is democratic, inclusive, and innovative.

The East-South turn introduces a different vortex of capitalisms. China as workshop of the world competes with other developing countries; not just the US, Europe, and Japan see manufacturing jobs go to China, but so do Mexico, Kenya, and Bangladesh. Garment workers from Bangladesh to South Africa are under pressure from Chinese textile exports.

Alternatives that were sidelined during the epoch of neoliberal hegemony have taken on new influence and legitimacy since the turn of the millennium. The "Beijing consensus" is an emerging alternative in Asia and the Bolivarian alternative (ALBA) in Latin America. Countries that are financially independent and have relative maneuvering room, such as China because of its size and Venezuela because of its oil wealth, are in a strong position to articulate alternatives to neoliberalism.

In the world as a whole, the majority economic form is the mixed economy with the social market in the EU, bureaucratically coordinated market economies (Japan) and developmental states (with different leanings in Asia, Latin America, and Africa). On balance, mixed economies are doing better and several are more sustainable in terms of their growth paths and energy use. Social market and human development approaches have generally come back on the agenda. Global emancipation hinges on rebalancing the state, market, and society, and introducing social cohesion and sustainability into the growth equation. This means that each component changes: the state becomes a civic state, the market a social market, and growth turns green.

References

Agtmael, Antoine van. 2007. *The Emerging Markets Century*. New York: Free Press.

Beck, Ulrich. 2005. *Power in a Global Age*. Cambridge: Polity.

Becker, E. and E. L. Andrews. 2004. "IMF Says Rise in U.S. Debts is Threat to World Economy," *New York Times*, August 1.

Chi, Lau Kin and Huang Pin (eds). 2003. *China Reflected*, special issue *Asian Exchange*, 18, 2 and 19, 1.

Davis, Mike. 2005. *Planet of Slums*. London: Verso.

Duménil, G. and D. Lévy. 2001. "Costs and Benefits of Neoliberalism: A Class Analysis," *Review of International Political Economy*, 8(4): 578–607.

Frank, A. G. 1998. *ReOrient: Global Economy in the Asian Age*. Berkeley: University of California Press.

Friedman, Thomas L. 2005. *The World is Flat*. New York: Farrar Straus and Giroux.

Gittings, John. 2005. *The Changing Face of China: From Mao to Market*. Oxford: OUP.

Gosh, Parthya S. 2006. "Beyond the Rhetoric," *Frontline*, October 6.

Guha, Krishna. 2007. "IMF Warns of Risk to Global Growth," *Financial Times*, August 22.

Guthrie, Doug. 2006. *China and Globalization: The Social, Economic and Political Transformation of Chinese Society*. New York: Routledge.

Harris, Jerry. 2005. "Emerging Third World Powers: China, India and Brazil," *Race & Class*, 46(3): 7–27.

Johnson, Jo. 2006. "Insurgency in India—How the Maoist Threat Reaches beyond Nepal," *Financial Times*, 13, April 26.

Johnson, Steve. 2005. "Indian and Chinese Banks Pulling Out of Ailing U.S. Dollar," *Financial Times*, March 7.

Kennedy, Paul. 2001. "Maintaining American Power: From Injury to Recovery," in S. Talbott and N. Chanda (eds), *The Age of Terror: America and the World After September 11*, pp. 53–80. New York: Basic Books.

Krishna, Anirudh and J. Nederveen Pieterse. 2008. Hierarchical Integration: The Dollar Economy and the Rupee Economy in India. *Development and Change*, 39(2): 219–237.

Lim, Hyun-Chin and Jin-Ho Jang. 2006. "Neoliberalism in Post-Crisis South Korea," *Journal of Contemporary Asia*, 36(4): 442–463.

Lind, Michael. 2005. "How the U.S. Became the World's Dispensable Nation," *Financial Times*, January 26.

Magnus, G. 2006. "The New Reserves of Economic Power," *Financial Times*,11, August 22.

Mahadevia, D. 2006. *Shanghaing Mumbai: Visions, Displacements and Politics of a Globalizing City*. Ahmedabad: Centre for Development Alternatives.

Marber, Peter. 1998. *From Third World to World Class: The Future of Emerging Markets in the Global Economy*. Reading, MA: Perseus Books.

Mazlish, Bruce. 2006. "Global History," *Theory Culture & Society*, 23(2–3): 406–408.

McGregor, Richard. 2006. "Pressure Mounts on China Forex Management," *Financial Times*, 6, November 28.

McKenna, Barrie. 2005. "With Friends Like the IMF and the World Bank, Who Needs Loans," *Globe and Mail*, B11, August 16.

Nederveen Pieterse, J. 2004a. *Globalization or Empire?* New York: Routledge.

Nederveen Pieterse, J. 2004b. "Towards Global Democratization: To WTO or Not to WTO?," *Development and Change*, 35(5): 1057–1063.

Nederveen Pieterse, J. 2007. *Ethnicities and Global Multiculture: Pants for an Octopus*. Lanham, MD: Rowman & Littlefield.

Nederveen Pieterse, J. 2008. *Is There Hope for Uncle Sam? Beyond the American Bubble*. London: Zed.

Parker, G. and A. Beattie. 2006. "Chinese Lenders 'Undercutting' on Africa Loans," *Financial Times*, 3, November 29.

Prestowitz, Clyde. 2005. *Three Billion New Capitalists: The Great Shift of Wealth and Power to the East*. New York: Basic Books.

Reifer, T. E. 2005. "Globalization, Democratization, and Global Elite Formation in Hegemonic Cycles: A Geopolitical Economy," in J. Friedman and C. Chase-Dunn (eds), *Hegemonic Declines: Past and Present*, pp 183–203. Boulder, CO: Paradigm.

Rodrik, Dani. 2000. "How Far Will International Economic Integration Go?" *Journal of Economic Perspectives*, 14(1): 177–186.

Rodrik, Dani. 2004. "Globalization and Growth—Looking in the Wrong Places," *Journal of Policy Modeling*, 26: 513–517.

Rosenau, J. N. 1999. "The Future of Politics," *Futures*, 31(9–10): 1005–1016.

Sainath, P. 1996. *Everybody Loves a Good Drought*. New Delhi: Penguin.

Tejpal, Tarun J. 2006. "India's Future, Beyond Dogma," *Tehelka, The People's Paper*, 3, November 25.

Timmons, H. 2006. "Asia Finding Rich Partners in Middle East," *New York Times*, C1–C5, December 1.

Traub, J. 2006. "The World According to China," *New York Times Magazine*, 24–29, September 3.

Tucker, S. 2007. "Asia Seeks Its Centre," *Financial Times*, 7, July 6.

United Nations. 2007. *World Economic Situation and Prospects 2007*. New York: United Nations.

Wade, R. 1996. "Japan, the World Bank and the Art of Paradigm Maintenance: The East Asian Miracle in Political Perspective," *New Left Review*, 217: 3–36.

Wallerstein, Immanuel. 2003. *The Decline of American Power*. New York: Free Press.

Whelan, Caroline. 2004. "Developing Countries' Economic Clout Grows," *International Herald Tribune*, 15, July 10–11.

Wolfe, Adam. 2005. "The 'Great Game' Heats Up in Central Asia," *Power and Interest News Report*, August 3.

PART II

Explicating Postmodernism

4

The Emergence of Postmodern Theory in Sociology

ANDY SCERRI

Sociology As a Project of Modernization

Insofar as sociology is the discipline associated with inquiry into social relations and conditions—seeking to understand the "logic" of society based on interpretive generalizations drawn from empirical observations—it is explicitly a product and, therefore, a project of "modernization." That is, sociology arose as a way to understand society in tandem with the historical processes that arose in Western Europe and spread east and south into Asia and Africa and on to the Americas and Oceania from around the 17th century onward (Mukerji, 1983). Modernization as such implies a transformation of social conditions, *away* from the primacy of agricultural production located in the countryside and villages, often centered on a large place of worship such as a cathedral or temple or center of power such as a castle or fort, and *toward* the primacy of nonagricultural production concentrated in relatively large towns and cities, often centered on markets for goods and services or sites for distributing these, such as a factory or stock exchange. Modernization also implies a transformation of social relations, *away* from the primacy of interpersonal bonds of kinship or fealty and linked to historical interdependencies that draw upon a cosmological, that is, more or less religious, order that stretches back over time and establishes hierarchical relations between humans and between humans and the natural environment (Gauchet, 1997[1985]). Modernization ushers in a shift *toward* the prevalence of relatively abstract social relations (James, 1996) based around mediating "tokens" such as paper money or legal rules (Giddens, 1990).

Important to sociology has been the observation that modernization ushers in a cultural ideological principle of *individualism*. By contrast with the *holism* of traditional cultural ideology, in which individual desires, beliefs, and values are subsumed by hierarchical interpersonal relations dedicated to sustaining an eternal, cosmological order, the individualistic cultural ideology of modernization privileges abstractly mediated interactions amongst formally equal individuals, who are bound to exercise autonomy in relation to an objective world of material forces (Dumont, 1986[1983]), such that the social order becomes self-regulating or "secular." As such, and again by contrast with the relatively direct interpersonal relations governed by religious or aristocratic edict of nonmodern societies, social relations in conditions of modernization are governed by the functioning of secular institutions; capitalist markets, courts of law, representative parliaments, and bureaucratised administrations. These operate in accordance with abstract "scientific" principles of efficiency, calculability, predictability, and control through the replacing of human beings by human-organised technologies (Ritzer, 1992). Moreover, the "scientific" project within which sociology is situated is often regarded as one of *Enlightenment*: the pursuit of knowledge based in observation and interpretation of the universe construed as phenomena that are objectively knowable in themselves or in sum, as opposed to intuitive knowledge based in subjective experiential immersion within an all-encompassing cosmological order that predetermines the status of parts within the whole.

Implicit in this account is the need to recognize that sociology is by definition a *critical* exercise. Even in its most institutionalized forms, such as when informing a national census, the aim of collecting, categorising, and interpreting data is to appraise existing policy and practice in light of the possibility that these can be improved, that is, changed, and progress advanced (Boltanski, 2011[2009]). The collection and observation of data in the practice of sociology is thus a "scientific" exercise that is dedicated to observing and interpreting the workings of social institutions and their impacts upon the social collective and upon formally equal and autonomous individuals in order to improve the relations and conditions that shape their lives into the future. The early founders of sociology as a discipline, Karl Marx, Emile Durkheim, and Max Weber—a list to which some would add Auguste Comte, Herbert Spencer, Ferdinand Tönnies, Vilfredo Pareto, Thorstein Veblen, Karl Mannheim, and Georg Simmel—in this sense all developed key concepts to facilitate the collection of data, establishment of variables, conduct of observation, and interpretation of results aimed ultimately at contributing to controlling, into the future processes of modernization for the betterment of the individuals that constitute it.

To this extent, and as will become clear, the emergence of postmodern theory in sociology from the 1970s and 1980s onward poses a number of issues and challenges to the discipline. I examine two reasons for this situation. First, what I identify as the "strong" postmodern thesis tends to bring into question the possibility that "objective" knowledge is possible, thus radically undermining both sociology as a discipline and the project of modernization itself. Second, what I identify as the "weak" postmodern thesis tends to question the legitimacy granted to implicit assertions of the primacy of "objective" knowledge in sociology, challenging only those aspects of the discipline that privilege, for example, system over process or structure over agency. The main discussion of this chapter is thus structured around a historical narrative of change over time, through which the preferences of sociologists for knowledge that privileges system, structure, order, efficiency, calculability, and control became challenged by forms of knowledge that highlight the legitimacy of process, agency, chaos, complexity, and the "flow" of events. In the next section, I briefly describe the nature of the social conditions that supported a loss of faith in the role played by "modern" theory in sociology, before turning in the subsequent section to examine in more detail the emergence of conditions for the establishment of "postmodern" challenges to modern theory. In the chapter conclusion, I evaluate the contribution of postmodern theory to sociology and describe some of the ongoing debates that surround it.

The Social Sources of Postmodern Theory

By the mid-19th century, sociology had emerged as the primary tool for interpreting modernization as an ongoing social process. Under the influence of Marx and Durkheim, society was conceived in holistic terms, as a functional whole that was more than the sum of its parts. The actions of the individuals that constituted society through their actions, empowered by the growth of industrial capitalism as "free" bourgeois mercantilists or wage laborers, were understood as stretching the coherence of the whole, for example, in demands for citizenship

based in the civil "rule of law," political "representation," and, subsequently, social "welfare" rights (Marshall, 1965). That is, Marxian
concerns with the political-economic structure of industrial capitalism
and the antagonism between social classes that this fostered (Marx,
1973[1857-8]) and Durkheimian concerns with the role played by
the complex division of labor in producing anomie, the normlessness
that loosens constraints upon individual behavior to create feelings
of helplessness (Durkheim, 1966[1895]), were regarded as problems
rooted in the deepening individualization that modernization was continually unleashing (Giddens, 1971). Demands for practical equality in
relation to questions of religious belief, economic distribution, gender
and race, as well as pathologies such as crime, suicide, alcoholism, homosexuality, and madness, were seen as things that, left unmanaged,
could overburden the social system. In this sociological perspective,
modernization risked collapsing under the weight of the pressures
generated from within it, that is, placed upon it by the autonomous
"free" individuals who, relieved of the bonds of serfdom and religious
dogma, could pursue subjectively held drives and desires in organised
or disorganised ways.

Indeed, individualization, and the emergence of "subjectivity," that
is, self-awareness of one's autonomy in relation to the World, Others,
and, importantly, the future, is a key element of focus to emerge in
theories of sociology in the 20th century (Pippin, 2005). These concerns
with the impacts upon society of the ideology of individualism and with
individualization as a social process were especially central to the work
of the third founder of sociology as a discipline, Weber (1978[1922]).
It is with Weber's assimilation into a coherent sociological research
programme of philosopher Friedrich Nietzsche's concerns with the
impacts of individualism upon knowledge as a claim to truth (Vattimo,
1988[1985]) that sociology first fully accounts for the impacts upon
society of individualization and the converse impacts upon individuals
of the modernization process. For Weber, understanding the creation
and reproduction of a generalized "subjectivist culture" that privileged
one peculiarly modern ethic or spirit over another was central to the
sociological interpretation of modernization itself (2001[1904–1905]).
Weber recognizes that, in a social system that both creates and requires
"subjective" autonomy—rather than taking one's cue from tradition and
established roles, autonomous individuals must manage future uncertainties on their own, as problems requiring moral choices and effort in

the present (see also, Dumont, 1986[1983])—it is no longer possible to base claims to knowledge upon positive assertions of objective truth; rather, knowledge must be justified as one value-claim amongst many (1958[1946]). Moreover, Weber recognizes that for better or worse, the development of sociological knowledge is always *for* particular ends that individuals acting collectively as political agents choose to favor or not, such as building a strong nation through militarism, achieving social equality by harnessing the means of production, or liberal freedoms by fostering unbounded private property rights, for example. With Weber, knowledge in general and sociology in particular is set the task of explaining the *causes and effects of social phenomena* for the betterment of the individuals that constitute it.

Understood in these terms, I push a little further this argument; that Weber's incorporation of Nietzschean subjectivism sows the first seeds of the emergence of postmodern theory in sociology. In order to understand this situation from within a contemporary perspective, it is necessary to focus more attention upon Weber's famous thesis on the role of the *Protestant Ethic* in the constitution of modernization as a social process (2001[1904–1905]). For Weber, modernization prompted a distinctive *ethic*—that is, an orientation to the world and collection of ideas about what makes a good life that has particular moral and political implications—that was most visible in the places where secular institutions, capitalistic markets, and technological developments had been most prolific: Northwestern Europe. From this observation he deduced that a particular ethic or spirit was shared by individuals in these places, one that supported instrumentalist action dedicated to the rational pursuit of personal gain and sustained by the belief that effort in this world guaranteed a place in the afterworld. Weber drew a distinction between this ethic or spirit derived from Protestantism and what he saw as the ethic or spirit that derived from the other major strand of Christianity prevalent in Europe at the time, Roman Catholicism, which for him tended toward fatalism and as such, did not promote effort, thrift, and industriousness, rather, indolence, extravagance, and immediacy. For Weber, Protestantism motivated individuals to work hard and become successful and achieve personal wealth, rather than pursue immediate gratification of desires and enjoyment or Earthly pleasures. Importantly, it also tended to promote a form of atomism that undermined class-based morality and politics.

In other words, Weber drew attention to the role played by what had until the early 20th century been the most influential of the ethical responses to modernization by defining it in terms of what it was not. Indeed, by reflecting upon and incorporating Nietzsche's explicitly modernist ethic (Giddens, 1990), Weber recognizes that while modernization privileges the modern ethic, an essential feature of modernization is also an ethic of *modernism*. What Weber's work brings into view is the possibility of describing the interplay between two alternate ethical responses to modernization. In light of Weber's work, it is possible to delineate between *modern* and *modernist* ethical responses to modernization, and to outline a narrative of how changing social-historical conditions appear to privilege one in relation to the other at different times. It is by examining things in these terms that some of the social *causes* of the emergence of postmodern theory in sociology might be recognized, and its *effects* be understood.

On the one hand, what Weber defined as the Protestant ethic expresses a distinctly *modern* response to the experience of modernization; one that brings with it a particular kind of morality and politics. Such an ethic implies an experience of modernization as something that is existentially unsettling, impinges upon the coherence of subjectivity, and sustains a moral and political position that seeks to maintain and reinforce this coherence against such disruptions. On the other hand, the modernist ethic expresses an alternative experience that responds to "the maelstrom of modernization" by seeking self-realization "at the fringes of self-disintegration" (Berman, 1982). Henceforth, I take it that to be *modern* is to embrace a way of dealing with the experience of modernization that is based in asserting control and order amidst the disruptions that it brings to social and subjective life, while to be *modernist* points to a way of dealing with the experience of modernization that embraces an ethical orientation geared to achieving personal authenticity and self-realization. While modern ideology explicitly favors positive, objective (rational) knowledge that Humanity and with it the Self are separate from and above nonhuman phenomena, modernist ideology favors subjective (often avowedly "spiritual") knowledge that the Self is the final arbiter of one's position in relation to others and is immersed within the universe. In this view, individuals holding a modern ethic were more likely to participate in industrial production, mercantile trade, and politics as members of the capitalist class or "good" workers, while those holding to a modernist ethic were more likely to be marginalized or excluded from the political sphere, as artists or members of the societal fringes, such as bohemians or libertines.

From Industrial to Postindustrial Society: Postmodern Theory Eclipses Modern Theory

I now turn to develop further the view that the seeds of postmodern theory were effectively planted in the late 19th and early 20th centuries, if not earlier, and grew out of the normalising of the modernist ethic in the late 20th century as conditions shifted from the prevalence of industrial to postindustrial relations (Anderson, 1998; Eagleton, 1996; Giddens, 1990, 1991; Habermas, 1990[1985]; Ritzer, 2009). That is, I draw attention to how from the 1960s and 1970s onward a transformation within the Western societies took place, such that the primacy of the modern ethic was displaced by a modernist ethic that subsequently created a place for the emergence of postmodern theory within sociology.

Beginning in the early 1960s, sociologists as well as social and political theorists and cultural critics began to notice a major shift in how the processes of modernization were being played-out within the so-called "advanced" industrial societies. Whereas sociologists since Marx, Durkheim, and Weber had concentrated upon the impacts upon individuals of ever-further expanding *industrial* capitalism, vertically integrated *bureaucratic* administration and *technological* innovation, sociologists working in the 1960s began to draw attention to the impacts of emergent processes of de-industrialization and *financialization* in the economy, horizontal integration or *just-in-time* administration, and *techno-scientific, creative,* or *knowledge-intense* innovation (Harvey, 1990). Moreover, it was argued that this postindustrial phase of modernization was having the effect of "deepening individualization," which in turn was affecting social relations in new ways (Beck & Beck-Gersheim, 2002).

Central to the work of sociologists Luc Boltanski and Eve Chiapello (2005[1999]), and social and political theorists such as Axel Honneth (2004) and Nancy Fraser (2009) is a claim that many in the 1960s began to reject modern values, norms, and rules as sources of unjust cultural repression and political oppression. Amongst the relatively well educated, affluent, and articulate individuals that had emerged as central actors in the processes of postindustrialization, the modern orientation to the world was increasingly regarded as something inauthentic, lacking in autonomy and spontaneity, creativity, and self-awareness. These theorists contend that individuals' experiences of modernization—especially full-time employment, bureaucratically administered education and healthcare, compulsory military service, and the limitation of culture to "mass-consumerism"—had, with the advent of postindustrialization, begun to foster a wide-reaching and, by the 1970s and 1980s, deeply influential modernist critique of modern values, norms, and rules. From the early 1970s onward, the discipline, social conformity, and formal mannerisms that had been central to the industrial mode of production increasingly came to be regarded by a large section of the populace as key sources of injustice.

Several sociological factors combined to create this situation. Against the backdrop of de-industrialization, a general loosening of cultural concerns with conformity was compounded by the political decline of "old" class-based social movements. The increasing popularity of "countercultural" modes of expression, such as were found in the sexual revolution and more diffuse self-help, lifestyle and New Age fads (Frank, 1997; Heath and Potter, 2004) comingled with the so-called New Social Movements, led by anti-war, feminist, and environmental activists, who sought to universalize expectations that life should be meaningful and grounded in self-reflection rather than status-group expectations, as well as conducted in harmony with nature (Habermas, 1971[1968]: 121–122; 1987[1985]: 388). An explicitly modernist ethical agenda became increasingly normalised within postindustrial society just as the state's inability to manage series of large scale economic, political, and environmental crises—the Oil Crisis, stagflation, and regular terrorist hijackings, for example—as well as increasing media exposure of the human frailties of elites once held in high esteem, such as royalty, politicians, diplomats, and proponents of high culture (Anderson, 1998; Eagleton, 1996) had undermined the moral and political authority that was historically exerted by the modern ethic. What was normalised was a modernist ethic of dealing with the experiences of modernization by aiming to achieve authenticity and self-realization, and which stood in direct contrast with the modern ethic that defined the good life in terms of control over the disruptions that modernization brings to social and subjective life. Over the 1970s and into the 1980s, this modernism gradually filled the vacuum that was created by the declining legitimacy of the modern ethic.

The Strong Postmodern Thesis and Sociology As a Discipline

Into this situation, postmodern theory gave expression to the new modernist ethic. Social, political, and cultural theorists contributing to the emergence of postmodern theory in sociology from the 1960s, 1970s, and into the 1980s include Michel Foucault (1965, 1970[1966], 1972[1969], 1972[1977], 1978, 1984, 1986, 1986[1984], and 1991[1975]), Gilles Deleuze and Felix Guattari (1977[1972], 1987), Jacques Derrida (1978, 1981[1975]), Jean Baudrillard (1975, 1981[1972], 1983, 1990, 1993[1976], 1994[1981], and 1998[1970]), Richard Rorty (1979), Judith Butler (1990), Frederic Jameson (1984, 1991) and Jean-Francois Lyotard (1993). While the concerns of these authors vary greatly, from feminism to literary theory, architecture to television, they share in common an aim of legitimising norms and values that express desires for authenticity, self-realization, and subjective acceptance and "celebration" of the disruptive influences of modernization. That is, the postmodern theorists, theorists of postmodernity, or, simply, postmodernists championed the hitherto ignored or marginalised dimension of the ethical response to modernization as a social process. Postmodern theory or, more accurately, postmodernism in sociology, in this sense emerged as an attempt to think through and legitimise in epistemological terms the modernist ethical orientation.

On the one hand, closely associated with the radical politics of the late 1960s and early 1970s was what I am labelling the strong postmodern thesis. Theorists such as Foucault and Deluze and Guattari both partook in the protest movements of the era and undertook professional projects that aimed to challenge institutions that for them sustained the modern ethic, such as psychiatric hospitals or prisons. The tenor of the argument proposed by strong postmodernism might be summarised in the famous line, from Foucault's Preface to Deleuze and Guattari's *Anti-Oedipus: Capitalism and Schizophrenia*, one must constantly confront "the strategic adversary … the fascism in us all, in our heads and in our everyday behaviour, the fascism that causes us to love power, to desire the very thing that dominates and exploits us" (Foucault, 1972[1977]: xi-xiv). This clarion-call challenges the foundation of the Enlightenment project to which sociology contributes by linking organized knowledge itself with the morally and politically suspect idea of "fascism." Unfortunately, bringing into question the possibility that "objective" knowledge is even possible, the strong postmodern thesis radically undermines both sociology as a discipline and the project of modernization itself (Habermas, 1990[1985]). That is, a certain irony of course surrounds the incorporation of the strong postmodern thesis into sociology. Insofar as a generalized decline of support for "meta-narratives"—such as communism or nationalism—was normalized in the 1960s and 1970s (Lyotard, 1993), knowledge in general and sociology in paular require epistemological or narrative structure if it is to remain coherent. Examining the emergence of postmodern theory in sociology from within a broadly Weberian perspective that recognizes a tension between the modern and modernist ethical orientations, the strong postmodern thesis appears to give expression rather than support inquiry into the prevailing ethic or ideology of postindustrial society: that is, the modernist ethic that prioritizes self-realization and the search for subjective authenticity, which for Berman seeks to be "at home in the maelstrom" (1982: 345). In this view, when modernism is stretched beyond the boundaries of ethical claims to be defining the good life to encompass an epistemological position, it confronts precisely the sort of problem that it originally set out to critique (Habermas, 1986a, 1986b). For philosopher Charles Taylor, this is because any narrative requires a counter narrative; one side of the story, the postmodern side that is against metanarratives is in this sense utopian because it ignores or elides the presence of its own metanarrative and, so, by omission, allows it to remain implicit (2011).

Importantly, these attempts to realize the modernist critique of modern values in theoretical terms arose at the same time as modernism in all its forms was being incorporated into social reproduction more generally. That is, modernist ethical assertions that the good life was to be found in self-realization, personal autonomy, emotional expression, aesthetic authenticity, and the chaos of spontaneous creativity—as opposed to modern defence of the self against uncertainty, conformity

with status-group expectations, rational expression, and aesthetic or-
derliness—*coincided* with increased demand for just-in-time production
and management techniques, the de-regulation of financial markets,
displacement of fulltime waged employment in favor of casualization,
and dismantling of the bureaucratized welfare state institutions in favor
of fostering greater self-responsibility and an "opportunity society."
That is, the modernist ethic and the strong postmodern thesis that gives
expression to it in the academy contains an implicit political critique
that expresses new social movement and "counter-cultural" concerns
of the 1960s and 1970s. Modernism and postmodern theory offer a
critique of industrial, Fordist, and relatively state-organized, that is,
to some degree corporatist or at least Keynesian pluralist society; an
economy centered on "full-time" waged employment in large-scale,
often heavy industry; the mass-consumption of mass-produced goods
and services, including a unidirectional mass-media; a cultural realm
that privileges "fitting-in" with class and status group expectations;
an entrenched, large-scale "top-down", technocratic, and bureaucratic
government; and internal politics shaped by tensions between different
factions vying for the spoils of industrial production through some
form of welfare state "compromise," and external politics shaped by
the Cold War.

At issue for sociologists is the recognition that by the early 1990s
processes of postindustrialization had become entrenched at the cost
of industrial conditions and relations. In short, aspirations that had
a clear emancipatory thrust in industrial conditions—that is, modernism—assume a far more ambiguous meaning in postindustrial
conditions (Fraser, 2009: 108). In theoretical terms, "The price paid
by critique for being listened to, at least in part, is to see some of the
values it has mobilized to oppose the form taken by the accumulation
process being placed at the service of accumulation in accordance with
a process of cultural assimilation" (Boltanski & Chiapello, 2005[1999]:
29). This transformation of social relations had by the 1990s resulted
in a situation in which, for Axel Honneth, "the individualism of self-
realization has since [the 1970s] been transmuted—having become
an instrument of economic development, spreading standardization
and turning lives into fiction—into an emotionally fossilized set of
demands under whose consequences individuals today seem more
likely to suffer than to prosper" (2004: 474).

Conclusion: The Weak Postmodern Thesis in Sociology As a Discipline

Hence, on the other hand, what I label the weak postmodern thesis fruitfully draws into question the legitimacy granted to implicit assertions of the primacy of modern "objective" knowledge in sociology, challenging only those aspects of the discipline that privilege, for example, system over process or structure over agency, and instrumental or technical over practical, socio-cultural, or community rationality. In this view, work by sociologists such as Zygmunt Bauman (1988, 1997, 2001, 2001[1989], 2003, 2005, 2007, and 2008), Peter Miller and Nikolas Rose (1990, 1997, and 2008; Rose, 1999, 2001), or John Urry (2003, 2004, and 2010), for example, represent efforts to incorporate into sociology an awareness of the contribution, for better or worse, to social formation of contingency, groundlessness, arbitrariness, diversity, instability, and indeterminacy. By treating these aspects of social conditions and relations as having the same *analytic* status as the "traditional" scientific principles of order, efficiency, calculability, predictability, and control through the replacing of human beings by human-organised technologies (while of course applying different normative standards), the weak postmodern thesis sensitises sociology as a discipline to the impacts of the "other side" of modernization as a socio-historical process.

In the 2000s, sociology confronts a postindustrial, postFordist, disorganized, and networked global society, where regimes of horizontal governance have displaced "top-down" government; *laissez faire* neoliberalism has displaced Keynesianism in political-economic policymaking; full-time employment has given way to creative and independent work in all its forms (Supiot, 2006: 109); the unidirectional mass-media of print and television has given way to internet and peer-to-peer communications-advertising firms such as Google and Facebook. A cultural realm has emerged where it no longer makes sense to situate oneself according to the perceived collective viewpoint, that is, to conform with status or class expectations, but does make sense to do so in relation to a privatized search for authenticity through self-discovery (Gauchet, 2000: 34). Where "the problem of choice is now solved increasingly by the individual, whose capacity to act is coming to rest more and more on a reflexive relationship between experience and cultural options" and less on collective action or knowledge (Delanty, 2000: 161) and individual judgement of the value of collective representations in terms of optimal self-affirmation emerges as the guide for domestic state-craft and policy action (Gauchet, 1991: 7), the emergence and influence of the weak postmodern thesis in sociology has helped to shift the focus of observation away from one-sided concerns with order and progress and toward a more critical and reflexive account of social conditions and relations. While the influence of strong postmodern theory has been diffused and impacted more at a philosophical level, it might be argued that the emergence of weak postmodern theory in sociology has brought to the fore possibilities for framing observations of social conditions and relations in new terms, such as witnessed in approaches associated with social constructivism (Katzenstein, 1996; Wendt, 1999), Actor-Network Theory (Latour, 1993[1991], 2004), and critical pragmatism (Boltanski, 1999[1993], 2011[2009]; Boltanski and Chiapello, 2005[1999]; Boltanski and Thévenot, 2006[1991]).

References

Anderson, P. 1998. *The Origins of Postmodernity*. London: Verso Books.

Baudrillard, J. 1975. *The Mirror of Production*. Ed. M. Poster. St. Louis: Telos Press.

———. 1981[1972]. *For a Critique of the Political Economy of the Sign*. Ed. C. Levin. St. Louis: Telos Press.

———. 1983. *Simulations*. New York: Semiotext(e).

———. 1990. *Revenge of the Crystal*. Ed. P. Foss and J. Pefanis. Sydney: Pluto Press.

———. 1993[1976]. *Symbolic Exchange and Death*. Ed. I. Hamilton-Grant. London: SAGE Publications.

———. 1994[1981]. *Simulacra and Simulations*. Ed. S.F. Glaser. Ann Arbor: University of Michigan Press.

———. 1998[1970]. *The Consumer Society*. London: SAGE Publishers.

Bauman, Z. 1988. *Freedom*. Milton Keynes: Open University Press.

———. 1997. *Postmodernity and its Discontents*. New York: New York University Press.

———. 2001. *The Individualized Society*. Cambridge: Polity Press.

———. 2001[1989]. *Modernity and the Holocaust*. Ithaca: Cornell University Press.

Bauman, Z. 2003. *Liquid Love: On the Frailty of Human Bonds*. Cambridge: Polity Press.

———. 2005. *Liquid Life*. Cambridge: Polity.

———. 2007. *Consuming Life*. London: Polity Press.

———. 2008. *Does Ethics Have a Chance in a World of Consumers?* Cambridge: Harvard University Press.

Beck, U. and E.Beck-Gernsheim. 2002. *Individualization*. Ed. P. Camiller. London: SAGE Publications.

Berman, M. 1982. *All That Is Solid Melts into Air: The Experience of Modernity*. New York: Simon & Schuster.

Boltanski, L. 1999[1993]. *Distant Suffering: Morality, Media and Politics*. Ed. G.D. Burchell. Cambridge: Cambridge University Press.

Boltanski, L. and E.Chiapello. 2005[1999]. *The New Spirit of Capitalism*. Ed. G. Elliott. London: Verso Books.

Boltanski, L. and L.Thévenot. 2006[1991]. *On Justification: Economies of Worth*. Ed. C. Porter. Princeton: Princeton University Press

Boltanski, L. 2011[2009]. *On Critique: A Sociology of Emancipation*. Cambridge: Polity Press.

Butler, J. 1990. *Gender Trouble*. London: Routledge.

Durkheim, E. 1966[1895]. *The Rules of Sociological Method*. 8th ed. Trans S.A. Solovay and J.H. Mueller. New York: The Free Press/Macmillan Publishing.

Deleuze, G. and F.Guattari. 1977[1972]. *Anti-Oedipus: Capitalism and Schizophrenia*. Ed. R. Hurley, M. Seem, and H.R. Lane. London: Athlone Press.

Derrida, J. 1978. *Writing and Difference*. Ed. A. Bass. London: Routledge and Keegan Paul.

Derrida, J. 1981[1975]. "Economimesis," *Diacritics*. Ed. R. Klein.11: 3–25.

Dumont, L. 1986[1983]. *Essays on Individualism: Modern Ideology in Anthropological Perspective* (English ed.). Chicago: University of Chicago Press.

Deleuze, G. and F.Guattari. 1987. *A Thousand Plateaus: Capitalism and Schizophrenia*. Ed. B. Massumi. Minnaepolis: University of Minnesota Press.

Delanty, G. 2000. *Modernity and Postmodernity: Knowledge, Power, and the Self*. London: SAGE Publications.

Eagleton, T. 1996. *The Illusions of Postmodernism*. London: Blackwell Publishing.

Foucault, M. 1965. *Madness and Civilization*. New York: Vintage Books.

———. 1970 [1966]. *The Order of Things*. London: Tavistock Publishers.

———. 1972 [1969]. *The Archaeology of Knowledge*. Ed. A.M. Sheridan Smith. London: Tavistock Publications.

Foucault, M. 1972 [1977]. "Preface." Ed. R. Hurley, M. Seem, and H.R. Lane. In G. Deleuze and F. Guattari (eds), *Anti-Oedipus: Capitalism and Schizophrenia*, pp. xi–xiv. London: Athlone Press.

Foucault, M. 1978. *An Introduction* (Vol. 1). London: Peregrine Books.

———. 1984. *The Use of Pleasure* (Vol. 2). London: Random House.

———. 1986. "Kant on Enlightenment and Revolution," *Economy and Society*, 15(1): 88–96.

———. 1986 [1984]. *The Care of the Self* (Vol. 3). Ed. R. Hurley. London: Penguin Books.

———. 1991 [1975]. *Discipline and Punish: The Birth of the Prison*. Ed. A.M. Sheridan. London: Penguin Books.

Frank, T.1997. *The Conquest of Cool: Business Culture, Counterculture, and the Rise of Hip Consumerism*. Chicago: University of Chicago Press.

Fraser, N. 2009. "Feminism, Capitalism and the Cunning of History," *New Left Review*, II(56): 97–117.

Giddens, A. 1971. *Capitalism and Modern Social Theory: An Analysis of the Writings of Marx, Durkheim, and Max Weber*. Cambridge: Cambridge University Press.

———. 1990. *The Consequences of Modernity*. London: Polity Press.

———. 1991. *Modernity & Self Identity*. Cambridge: Polity Press.

Gauchet, M. 1991. "Democratic Pacification and Civic Desertion," *Thesis Eleven*, 29: 1–13.

———. 1997[1985]. *The Disenchantment of the World: A Political History of Religion*. Ed. O. Burge. Princeton: Princeton University Press.

———. 2000. "A New Age of Personality: An Essay on the Psychology of our Times," *Thesis Eleven*, 60: 23–41.

Habermas, J. 1971[1968]. *Toward a Rational Society: Student Protest, Science, and Politics*. Ed. J.J. Shapiro. London: Heinemann.

———. 1986a. "Foucault's Lecture On Kant," *Thesis Eleven*,1, 14: 4–9.

———. 1986b. "Taking Aim at the Heart of the Present," in D.C. Hoy (ed.), *Foucualt: A Critical Reader*, pp.103–108. Oxford: Blackwell.

———. 1987[1985]. *Lifeworld and System: A Critique of Functionalist Reason*. Ed. T. McCarthy. Boston Beacon Press.

Habermas, J. 1990[1985]. *The Philosophical Discourse of Modernity*. Ed. F. Lawrence. Cambridge: The MIT Press.

Harvey, D. 1990. *The Condition of Postmodernity: An Enquiry into the Origins of Cultural Change*. Oxford: Blackwell Books.

Heath, J. and A. Potter. 2004. *Rebel Sell:Why the Culture can't be Jammed*. New York: HarperBusiness.

Honneth, A. 2004. "Organized Self-Realization: Some Paradoxes of Individualization," *European Journal of Social Theory*, 7(4): 463–478.

Jameson, F. 1984. "Postmodernism, or the Cultural Logic of Late Capitalism," *New Left Review,* I (146): 53–92.

—————. 1991. *Postmodernism, or, the Cultural Logic of Late Capitalism.* Durham: Duke University Press.

James, P. 1996. *Nation Formation: Towards a Theory of Abstract Community.* London: SAGE Publications.

Katzenstein, P. 1996. *Cultural Norms and International Security.* Ithaca: Cornell University Press.

Latour, B. 1993[1991]. *We Have Never Been Modern.* Ed. C. Porter. Cambridge: Harvard University Press.

Lyotard, J.F. 1993. *The Condition of Postmodernity: A Report on Knowledge.* Ed. G. Bennington and D. Massumi. Vol. 10. Minneapolis: University of Minnesota Press.

Latour, B. 2004. *Politics of Nature: How to Bring the Sciences into Democracy* Cambridge: Harvard University Press.

Marshall, T.H. 1965. *Class, Citizenship, and Social Development.* New York: Free Press.

Marx, K. 1973[1857–1858]. *Grundrisse: Foundations of the Critique of Political Economy (Rough Draft).* Ed. M. Nicolaus. London: Pelican Books.

Mukerji, C. 1983. *From Graven Images: Patterns of Modern Materialism.* New York: Columbia University Press.

Miller, P. and N. Rose. 1990. "Governing Economic Life," *Economy and Society,* 19(1): 1–31.

—————. 1997. "Mobilizing the Consumer: Assembling the Subject of Consumption," *Theory, Culture & Society,* 14(1): 1–36.

Miller, P. and N. Rose. 2008. *Governing the Present: Administering Economic, Social and Personal Life.* Cambridge: Polity.

Pippin, R.B. 2005. *The Persistence of Subjectivity: On the Kantian Aftermath.* Cambridge: Cambridge University Press.

Rorty, R. 1979. *Philosophy and the Mirror of Nature.* Princeton: Princeton University Press.

Ritzer, G. 1992. *Sociological Theory.* 4th ed. Singapore: McGraw-Hill International.

Rose, N. 1999. *Powers of Freedom: Reframing Political Thought.* Cambridge: Cambridge University Press.

Rose, N. 2001. "The Politics of Life Itself," *Theory, Culture & Society,* 18(6): 1–30.

Ritzer, G. 2009. *Contemporary Sociological Theory and Its Classical Roots: The Basics.* 3rd ed. New York: McGraw-Hill.

Supiot, A. 2006. "Law and Labour: A World Market of Norms?" *New Left Review,* I(39): 109–121.

Taylor, C. 2011. "The Malaise of Modernity." Available online at http://www. cbc.ca/ideas/episodes/2011/04/11/the-malaise-of-modernity-part-1—5/ (downloaded on April 15, 2011).

Urry, J. 2003. *Global Complexity*. Cambridge: Polity.

———. 2004. "The 'System' of Automobility," *Theory, Culture & Society*, 21(4/5): 25–39.

———. 2010. *Mobilities*. Cambridge: Polity.

Vattimo, G. 1988[1985]. *The End of Modernity: Nihilism and Hermeneutics in Post-modern Culture*. Ed. J.R. Snyder. Cambridge: Polity Press.

Weber, M. 1958[1946]. *From Max Weber: Essays in Sociology*. Ed. H.H. Gerth and C.W. Mills. New York: Oxford University Press.

———. 1978[1922]. *Economy and Society*. Ed. E. Fischoff, H. Gerth, Mills C.Wright, F. Kolegar, A.M. Henderson, T. Parsons, E. Shils, and M. Rheinstein. Berkeley: University of California Press.

Wendt, A. 1999. *Social Theory of International Politics*. Cambridge: Cambridge University Press.

Weber, M. 2001[1904–1905]. *The Protestant Ethic and the Spirit of Capitalism*. Ed. T. Parsons. London: Routledge Classics.

5

Postmodernity as an Internal Critique of Modernity

PETER KIVISTO

For several decades, claims have been made about the advent of a new postmodern epoch. And from the very beginning counterclaims challenging this have issued forth. In the process, we have been forced to think again about what we mean by modern. Increasingly it appears that the salience of a number of questions regarding modernity has increased. What does it mean to be modern? When did the modern age begin? Are we modern? What should we make of the provocative argument advanced by Bruno Latour (1993), that "we have never been modern?" Or what precisely did Peter Wagner (2008: 1) have in mind when he asserted, "But modernity today is not what it used to be?" Further along these lines, how should we respond to those—a growing chorus in recent years—who assert that, although we did until recently, we no longer live in modern society, but instead have entered a distinctly new "postmodern" world (Lyotard, 1979; Harvey, 1989; Jameson, 1991). Finally, how do we unpack Charles Lemert's (2005) intensions in claiming that "postmodernism is not what you think?"

These and related questions preoccupy many contemporary sociologists and appropriately so given that sociology emerged as an effort to comprehend the form and content of modern society. The classic founders of the discipline are all theorists of modernity. Their insights into the nature of modern society have proven to be invaluable in making sense of the social world we inhabit. Collectively, the portrait they offer includes a number of features. First, modern society is made possible by industrialization and by advances in science and technology. Second, democratic ideals and aspirations are intimately connected to modernity. Third, modernity reconfigures the relationship of individuals to other people and to their society by promoting individualism.

One figure from the formative period of sociology stands out as singularly important in helping us to comprehend modern culture and the varied ways it is experienced by individuals: Georg Simmel. David Frisby (1984: 40) argued that "Simmel is the first sociologist of modernity. . . . [The reason for this assertion was that] no sociologist before him had sought to capture the modes of experiencing modern life." At the same time, while recognizing him as the sociologist par excellence of modernity, a case has also been made for viewing Simmel as a precursor to, or the first exponent of, a postmodern sociological vision (Weinstein and Weinstein, 1993; Bauman, 1992).

After providing some provisional definitions of the subject at hand, I will proceed to support this view of Simmel's particular significance, contending that he offers a perspective that can be used to understand postmodernity as constituting an internal critique of modernity. As such, his work also makes clear that ours is a modern world—Latour notwithstanding. In advancing the idea of postmodernism as a critique from within the modern, to make the case I will present an analysis of the radical postmodernism of Jean Baudrillard, followed by a brief examination of the more tempered position of Zygmunt Bauman. I will conclude the chapter by exploring the idea of the "late modern age" as it has been developed by Anthony Giddens.

Modernity and Postmodernity: Provisional Definitions

Both modernity and postmodernity are notoriously difficult terms to define. Modernity has often been viewed as being in opposition to and representing a break from tradition (Lyon, 1994:19-21). If tradition looked to the past, modernity presumably turned its eye to the future. Modern culture is frequently associated, as Swedish social theorist Göran Therborn (1995: 4) notes, "with words like progress, advance, development, emancipation, liberation, growth, accumulation, enlightenment, embetterment, [and] avant-garde." One might add to this the idea that modernism is often depicted as an expansive, and thus global, phenomenon. The association with these terms suggests that modern culture possesses an optimistic orientation about our ability to collectively resolve problems, to remedy human suffering, and to enrich social life. It presupposes our ability to acquire knowledge of both the natural and the social worlds and to use this knowledge to beneficially control and mold these worlds. As Wagner (2008: 1) sees it, until recently, "Modernity was associated with the open horizon of the future, with unending progress toward a better human condition brought about by a radically novel and unique institutional arrangement."

Postmodernism is a term of relatively recent vintage. As the term implies, it refers to a cultural sensibility that occurs in response to, and chronologically after, modernism (Lyotard, 1979; Smart, 1992). Insofar as it signals a move from one culture to another, it is a parallel term to postindustrialism. Postmodernism, however, differs from postindustrialism because whereas postindustrialism is seen as an outgrowth of industrial society, postmodernism indicates an exhaustion of modernism. Although some postmodernist theorists dispute this claim, I fully agree with Robert Antonio and Douglas Kellner (1994: 127), who wrote that "postmodernists provide a pessimistic vision of the current era."

Thus, the move from modernity to postmodernity is in many ways a shift from optimism to pessimism. This can be seen in the argument advanced by architectural critic Charles Jencks (as cited in Harvey, 1989:39) that postmodernity began at 3:32 p.m. on July 15, 1972—the moment when St. Louis's Pruitt-Igoe public housing project was dynamited into rubble. Built in the 1950s, this architectural award-winning project, designed by the Japanese-American modernist architect Minoru Yamasaki, was seen as far more than housing. It was construed to be a site where the problems of ghetto poverty could be solved and a place that would facilitate the sustenance of strong families, a vibrant community, active citizens, and economically productive employees. In short, the construction of Pruitt-Igoe was inspired by a modernist vision and hope.

In less than two decades, the project was primarily occupied by female-headed households mired in endemic poverty and dependent on welfare. It acquired a reputation as a dangerous, drug-infested, and crime-ridden place where residents moved out as soon as they could. Pruitt-Igoe came to be seen as part of the problem rather than part of the solution to inner-city poverty. Unable to envision any viable way to turn the project around, the local housing authority finally concluded that it had to be demolished. Thus, the fate of Pruitt-Igoe came to be seen as a sign of the failure of the modernist project and, as such, the beginning of the postmodern age.

The Ambiguous Legacy of Georg Simmel

Simmel's place in sociology's pantheon of founding figures is far less secure than that of Marx, Weber, and Durkheim. He is less widely known than this trio, is less frequently read, and has contemporary critics who refuse to see his work as being of equal value to the discipline as that of Marx, Weber, and Durkheim. He did not create a school of thought that could be inherited by subsequent generations of sociologists. Simmel, however, was held in very high regard by many of his contemporaries. Weber, in particular, was impressed by the fecundity of Simmel's thought, and he intervened in efforts to advance Simmel's career. Durkheim and Toennies, although critical of aspects of Simmel's work, took him seriously. Simmel was highly esteemed by many influential American sociologists of the era, particularly those associated with the Chicago school of sociology. Although not a Marxist, he significantly influenced leftist theorists such as Georg Lukács and Ernst Bloch (Leck, 2000).

The Culture of Modernity

Simmel was a key figure promoting cultural sociology. As a sociologist of modern culture, Simmel's thinking often appeared to be a reflection of what he took to be a central defining trait of modernity—namely, its fragmentary character. Known primarily as an essayist, in his writings he provided finely textured descriptions, or snapshots, of various social types, such as the stranger, the miser, and the adventurer, as well as various types of social interaction, including exchange, conflict, and sociability. Suzanne Vromen (1990: 319) points out that Simmel "stands alone [among the classic figures] as the one who explicitly questioned the future of women in modern society." Simmel's style was that of a detached observer. Unlike Marx or Durkheim, he did not appear to be interested in finding ways to change the world. Although he spoke about the tragedy of modern culture, his tone, although critical, was by and large devoid of the pessimism of his contemporary, Weber. Not surprisingly, he has been described as a sociological impressionist and a flâneur, given to acute descriptions of the passing scene but lacking an overarching view of the social totality (Frisby, 1981:68-101; Weinstein and Weinstein, 1993; Levine, 1995).

There is a growing appreciation among commentators on Simmel, however, of the fact that underlying these shards, the bits and pieces of contemporary social life that he scrutinized, was a well-articulated and coherent theoretical framework. To illustrate this fact, I single out for attention two important foci in Simmel's writings. The first is money because Simmel considered modern culture to be undergirded by an economic system based on money. The second is the city because Simmel considered the modern metropolis to be the site where contemporary culture revealed itself in its most pristine and stark form.

Although Simmel was not a systematic theorist, his magisterial and complex book, *The Philosophy of Money* ([1907] 1991), contains his most sustained and coherent assessment of the form and content of modern culture and would serve as a framework for subsequent writings. In an advertisement that he took out to promote his new book (a common practice at the time), Simmel defined his intention as providing a complement to historical materialism. Rather than being concerned, as Marx was, with the material conditions—the economic factors—that led to the emergence of a money economy, he was primarily interested in discerning the varied ways in which a society predicated on a money economy transforms culture and in turn the individual's relations with others (Poggi, 1993: 62–8). Simmel sought to delineate the social psychology characteristic of a money economy, describing the varied ways that it structures our "internal and external lives" (Kracauer, 1995: 250).

Money, Simmel ([1907] 1991:210) pointed out, possesses no value in itself but functions as a tool to facilitate the exchange of goods and services. Money is instrumental, abstract, and impersonal. To cite one example of what he had in mind, in one widely cited passage of the book, Simmel observes that the monetary exchange between prostitute and client reinforces the fundamental character of prostitution, which entails "a wholly transitory connection, leaving no trace behind itself" (quoted in Poggi, 1993: 140). To borrow a term from Eva Illouz (2007), such encounters can be aptly described as "cold intimacies."

Objectively, it is no more than a means to an end. Thus, money promotes a rational orientation toward the world, and here Simmel's discussion bears a distinct resemblance to both Marx and Weber.

Simmel goes on to note, however, that this rationality can become distorted for some individuals who treat money irrationally as an end in itself. The miser, for instance, is a social type who "finds bliss in the sheer possession of money, without proceeding to the acquisition and enjoyment of particular objects" (Simmel, 1971: 179). For the spendthrift, however, "the attraction of the instant overshadows the rational evaluation either of money or of commodities" (Simmel, 1971: 182). Money, by removing emotional involvements from economic transactions, makes it possible to expand considerably the range of one's trading partners. It expands individual freedom by severing the all-encompassing ties to a primary group and in so doing promotes an individualistic worldview. Money encourages the individual to be future oriented, and thus it serves to undermine a respect for and attachment to tradition. Although all this is liberating, Simmel also sees a negative side to money. Money places a barrier between people and tends to become an absolute value in and of itself. More pointedly, he ([1907] 1991: 344) wrote, "The whole heartlessness of money mirrors itself in the culture of society, which it determines." The world was thus conceived to function in a cold, instrumental manner, with an underlying assumption that it is possible to regulate the social world and to give it order without considering the values, beliefs, and emotional orientations of the people who constitute the society.

Turning to the topic of the city, I begin by noting that like Durkheim, Simmel was interested in the phenomenon of social differentiation. However, unlike Durkheim's focus on the division of labor, Simmel was more interested in the ways social differentiation permeated all facets of everyday social relations. He observed that in earlier societies, individuals derived their identities from the group, and insofar as this was the case, there was considerable homogeneity among the inhabitants of primitive societies. This changed in medieval Europe due to the existence of mediating institutions, such as professional guilds, that served as a buffer between the individual and the society at large. Nonetheless, although this made for greater heterogeneity in terms of the types of individuals in society, the individual's sense of identity was still largely determined by particular group identities.

The modern world changed this connection decisively. Simmel was fond of using geometric metaphors to describe social life, and in this connection, he spoke frequently about group affiliations as social circles.

Unlike the premodern world, modern society is inherently pluralistic, which means that people live at the intersection of numerous social circles. Each of these various circles occupies part of the time, energy, and commitment of the individual, with various kinds of affiliations being more or less compatible with other affiliations. In this milieu, the individual is accorded considerable autonomy and flexibility in negotiating the varied demands for allegiance by the social circles in which he or she voluntarily chooses to participate (Simmel, [1908] 1955). One of the significant changes that occurs as a result of the complex "web of group affiliations" that enmeshes the individual is that there are parts of the life of the individual that are hidden from the members of the differing groups in which the person is involved. The result is not simply that the distinction between the public and private realms becomes more pronounced but that the individual's inner world can contain secrets that are not revealed even to one's closest acquaintances and intimates.

Simmel was interested in the space where modern life was played out, and for this reason he was particularly interested in the city because modern society took form originally and evolved most deeply and completely in the metropolis. Although others among his contemporaries, such as Weber and the French scholar Fustel de Coulanges, had written perceptively on the city, Simmel was the first sociologist of modern city life. Because the money economy was crucial in shaping modern culture, and because it was in the metropolis that the money economy developed to its fullest, it was therefore in the city that one could expect to find modern culture most fully revealed. In "The Metropolis and Mental Life" (1903), Simmel provided an assessment of the impact of modern culture on the social psychology of urbanites. His thinking shares with Weber a concern for the fate of the individual in the face of the progressive rationalization of the world: "The deepest problems of modern life flow from the attempt of the individual to maintain the independence and individuality of his existence against the sovereign powers of society, against the weight of the historical heritage and the external culture and technique of life". (Simmel, 1971: 324).

Like Weber, he saw the demands for punctuality, calculability, and exactness as arising out of forces of the modern world. Simmel (1971: 328) speculated on the kind of chaos that would bring commercial life in Berlin to a standstill if, even for an hour, all the watches in the city went wrong in different directions. He said that in the city, one finds a greater emphasis on intellectuality because reason replaces tradition and habitual action as a primary factor in shaping the conduct of everyday life. Paralleling Weber, Simmel evidenced a concern for the threat that modern culture, with its emphasis on instrumental rationality, posed for individual autonomy. Simmel, however, harbored no romantic longings to return to the organic wholeness of traditional societies because he understood that, ironically, modern society made possible individualism and served to undermine it as well.

He was keenly interested in exploring ways that people acted to ensure that they would not be overwhelmed by modern life. For instance, Simmel explained the characteristic reserve of urbanites—their blasé attitude—as a response to the flooding of the psyche by such a wide array of ever-changing stimuli that to do otherwise the individual would simply become overwhelmed (Simmel, 1971: 325–29). What some took to be the coldness or apathy of city dwellers, he saw as a necessary safeguard against the threat to individuality.

Tragedy of Culture

Simmel ([1892] 1977) understood the tension between the individual and the social structure through the lens of a philosophical position shaped by the German philosopher Immanuel Kant that depicted human existence in terms of a dualistic tension that pitted life against form. Life was seen as an unbounded force of creativity, whereas forms become the containers that constrain and harness life. Thus, all of human existence is an unremitting struggle by life to overcome form, but as life liberates itself from one form it inevitably confronts—indeed, creates—a new form. The logic of cultural production entails acts of creation and destruction. It is the necessity of the destructive character of this process that leads Simmel to speak about the "tragedy of culture" (Nedelmann, 1991).

Simmel understood this in part in an ahistorical manner (Simmel, 1950; Weingartner, 1960). There was no possibility that this conflict could ever be resolved or overcome. Quite simply, it was part of the human condition. Marxists, such as his former student Georg Lukács, criticized him for his tendency to treat culture in a timeless manner. More in line with what Lukács would want, however, Simmel, in his special fascination with the particular types of conflict found in modern culture, also appreciated the historically conditioned character of this dialectical process.

Toward a Sociology of Leisure

Simmel was the first sociologist to turn his gaze toward the world of leisure and consumerism. This is evident, for instance, in an intriguing essay titled "Fashion" (1904), in which he inquired into the reasons that changes in fashion—be it sartorial, culinary, artistic, architectural, musical, or other—occur so frequently in modern culture. The main reason for this, he claimed, was that the modern world is a "more nervous age" because it offers, in contrast to the past, such a wide array of consumer choices that make it possible for individuals to differentiate themselves from others. In other words, people will be attracted to new and different fashions at an accelerated rate as they seek to forge what they take to be a distinctive personal identity.

Fashion, however, is not simply a matter of individual choices. Rather, these choices are structured by class divisions and by social mobility. Simmel identified an antithesis between the desire for individual differentiation—for the desire to stand apart and to be unique—and the tendency toward social equalization—the willingness of all people, regardless of class position, to embrace reigning fashions—as being both a part of the motivation behind fashion choices and a reason for the unstable and generally short-lived career of any particular fashion (Simmel, 1971: 296; Nedelmann, 1990). Simmel (1971: 313–14) believed, perhaps somewhat paradoxically, that fashion is one way that individuals seek to preserve their "inner freedom." Being willing to be dictated to and dependent on the external determinants of current fashions reflects a willingness to give up one's autonomy, but this, he thought, pertains only to "the externals of life." This willingness permits the individual to concentrate on preserving subjective freedom at its core (Weinstein and Weinstein, 1993: 101–29).

Should Simmel be viewed as someone who articulated the contours of a new social formation without actually calling it postmodern, or should he be seen as someone who captured the impact of the transition from a premodern to a modern social formation in an era of rapid social change? With regard to whether we should consider Simmel to be a modernist or a postmodernist, it is apparent that he does not appear to neatly fit the mold of either cultural orientation. This, as the long-time Simmel scholar Donald Levine (1985) has contended, is because the world we live in is one that is inherently ambiguous, and thus neither excessive optimism nor pessimism is warranted. Moreover, the lesson to be extrapolated from Simmel is that what we referred to as postmodern is, in fact, an aspect of the modern age: perhaps its dark side, perhaps one moment in a cycle of cultural fashion. Simmel, perhaps more than any other of the classic theorists seemed to have appreciated the ambiguity of his age, and his sociology is, in effect, a profound reflection of this recognition.

Postmodernism

The word postmodernism has been around for some time. For example, C. Wright Mills (1959: 166) proclaimed, that "the Modern Age is being succeeded by a postmodern period." Although the word has surfaced in various other places since Mills's proclamation, postmodernism did not burst onto the intellectual stage until sometime later. Nevertheless, in its brief and highly contested history, it has had a pronounced impact on certain fields, particularly in literature and in the broad interdisciplinary arena of cultural studies (Kivisto, 1994; Gottdiener, 1993).

Insofar as postmodern theorists focus particular attention on culture, they are located in a lineage of social thought dating back to the cultural sociology of the formative period, particularly in the work of Simmel but also in that of Durkheim. This lineage also includes various subsequent theoretical approaches, such as those contained in the German Frankfurt School and the French College of Sociology and those of mass society cultural critics. It is important to note that we are interested in what it means to speak about the postmodern as a theory of culture (Lash, 1990), and less so its epistemological claims or deconstructive method (Jameson, 1991; Derrida, 1981).

The Exhaustion of Grand Narratives

Grand narratives refer to large, panoramic accounts or explanations of current social circumstances and future trends: Marx on the logic of capitalist development, Weber on rationalization, Durkheim on the development of organic solidarity, and Parsons on the progressive inclusion of marginalized groups into the social and cultural mainstream are examples of grand narratives. However different these theories might be, they share the Enlightenment conviction that we have the ability to make sweeping generalizations about the social world we inhabit, and with the understanding obtained by these grand narratives, we have the power to change society for the better (Best and Kellner, 1991: 8).

Postmodernists cast suspicion on these convictions. The French theorist Jacques Derrida, for example, sees the construction of grand narratives as the product of what he refers to as "logocentrism," by which he means modes of thinking that refer truth claims to universally truthful propositions. In other words, our knowledge of the social world is grounded in a belief that we can make sense of our ever-changing and highly complex societies by referring to certain unchanging principles or foundations. The postmodernist stance articulated by Derrida (1976, 1978) calls for a repudiation of logocentrism, which entails taking what postmodernists refer to as an anti-foundational stance. In its most extreme versions, postmodernism constitutes a profound repudiation of the entire Western philosophical tradition and represents a form of extreme skepticism about our ability to carry on the sociological tradition as it has been conceived since the 19th century.

One might reasonably conclude that postmodernism is a contemporary form of nihilism. What is somewhat surprising is that many postmodernists define themselves as being situated on the political Left and, as such, as sympathetic to various progressive political movements: anti-imperialism, feminism, gay liberation, and so on. An example of how postmodernism proceeds, however, can provide a sense of its limited utility for leftist politics. In an essay titled "Can the Subaltern Speak" (1988), Gayatri Spivak contends that it is important to hear the voices of powerless, marginalized people rather than allowing more privileged and powerful voices to attempt to speak on their behalf. In this particular essay, she addresses the traditional Hindu practice of *sati* (or *suttee*), in which the widow climbs onto her dead husband's funeral pyre and immolates herself. During British colonial rule, the practice of sati was outlawed by colonial authorities. Spivak criticizes this act, claiming that it is a reflection of a desire to impose Western values on Indian society and as such is a form of cultural imperialism. The result was that the voices of these subaltern women were not heard. The colonial authorities failed to comprehend the women's belief that they were acting virtuously in performing this moral obligation. Spivak does not purport to defend sati. Rather, her intention is to criticize the British for presuming that their values should be seen as universal values, applicable to people everywhere. Such universalistic claims, she suggests, can only be the product of a worldview that is thoroughly logocentric.

In Spivak's thesis, one sees the linkage between antifoundationalism and cultural relativism. Critics contend that it becomes impossible to make a case for universal human rights or to respond to charges of Eurocentrism. Antifoundational postmodernism undercuts the moral grounds to challenge such phenomena as the torture of political dissidents by African military strongmen, infanticide in China, and female genital mutilation practiced in many Islamic countries (Kivisto, 1994: 726–27; Callinicos, 1989: 78–9). Ultimately, cultures are viewed as being discrete and incommensurate. There is no shared language that permits people to transcend local cultures and the parochialisms they embrace. Thus, the end of grand narratives signals the exhaustion of the modernist project, with its conviction that human knowledge could be used to remedy problems and facilitate more humane and sustainable societies.

The Real and the Hyperreal in Postmodern Culture

Whereas Marx and a tradition of sociological inquiry stemming from his thought have been preoccupied with the realm of production, postmodern theorists have turned their attention toward the realm of consumption. Indeed, one of the main claims of postmodernists about the transition from modern culture to postmodern culture is that people should be perceived as consumers rather than producers. Moreover, in advanced industrial societies, the sheer plenitude of goods and services available is seen as creating heretofore unimaginable consumer choices and with these choices a proliferation of new means of consumption (Ritzer, 1999). Jean-François Lyotard (1979: 76) wrote, "Eclecticism is the degree zero of contemporary general culture: One listens to reggae, watches a Western, eats McDonald's food for lunch and local cuisine for dinner, wears Paris perfume in Tokyo and "retro" clothes in Hong Kong; knowledge is a matter for TV games."

Contemporary culture in the advanced industrial societies is characterized as being saturated by the media, entertainment, and new information systems. What are the implications of this saturation? Jean Baudrillard (1981) has argued that this saturation has resulted in a world in which the difference between the real and the images, signs, and simulations of the real has dissolved. This leads to the creation of what Baudrillard refers to as *simulacra*—reproductions or simulations of the real that are difficult or impossible to distinguish from the real. The result is the emergence of what he refers to as *hyperreality*. The term is meant to imply something that is at once not real and more real than real (Baudrillard, 1983). Although one can point to fast-food restaurants, theme parks, and shopping malls as instances of simulacra, the purest example, according to Baudrillard (1988), is Disneyland because the Magic Kingdom is not a copy and does not purport to refer to a reality outside of Disneyland. Although nonpostmodern analysts of culture can concur with much of what Baudrillard has stated to this point, he proceeds to make sweeping generalizations that leave him open to criticism. This penchant for gross generalization is evident when Baudrillard (1983: 25) remarks, "Disneyland is presented as imaginary in order to make us believe that the rest is real, when in fact all of Los Angeles and the America surrounding it are no longer real, but of the order of the hyperreal and of simulation."

Recall that although Simmel saw leisure as an increasingly important arena of social life, he nonetheless maintained that leisure activities were set apart and distinct from the mundane world of work. In stark contrast, Baudrillard suggests that this distinction today is meaningless because he views the world almost entirely in terms of consumption. It is not easy to determine what Baudrillard's attitude is about postmodern culture. Jeffrey Alexander (1995: 27) considers him to be "the master of satire and ridicule, as the entire Western world becomes Disneyland at large." Stuart Hall thinks that Baudrillard celebrates postmodernity, whereas Douglas Kellner sees in his work a fatalistic bemoaning and accepting of the existing new social order, although it is a nightmare (Smart, 1992: 131). What is clear is that Baudrillard is less inclined to develop the conceptual tools that others might find useful in cultural analysis and more inclined, as Kellner (2000: 751) suggests, to serve as a "provocateur" challenging much of classical and contemporary social theory.

Easier to discern is Baudrillard's rather unflattering portrait of the role of individuals in postmodern culture. We appear to have been reduced to the roles of mall rats in quest of objects of desire and excitement, couch potatoes playing with the TV remote control, and voyeurs peering into the private lives of the rich and famous. We are thoroughly enmeshed in our social worlds but incapable of controlling them or of operating in a genuinely autonomous way. The implicit message of Baudrillard's work seems to be that we should passively accept—and even enjoy to the extent that we can—the spectacle and the carnival that is postmodern culture.

Because signs no longer refer to real referents, because the real has collapsed into the hyperreal, meaning has evaporated. In a rather notorious instance of applying this thinking to a concrete event, Baudrillard (1991) claimed that the Gulf War was nothing more than a television and computer graphics spectacle—the difference between this war and the war games in a video arcade presumably having essentially disappeared. Of course, there is an element of truth to this claim. Indeed, a similar claim was made by Slavoj Žižek (2002: 37) about the war in Afghanistan that took place in the aftermath of September 11, 2001, which he depicted as "a virtual war fought behind computer screens." Lost in Baudrillard's vision, however, as David Lyon (1994: 52) pointedly noted, is the fact that there really (i.e., not hyperreally) were "blood-stained sand and bereaved families." Lost, too, are beliefs about patriotic duty, geopolitical realities, the economics of oil, and similar very real considerations that lead nations into war. In his book on terrorism, which is described in the subtitle as a "Requiem for the Twin Towers," Baudrillard (2002) describes Al Qaeda's attack on the United States in terms of the "symbolism of slaughter" and "sacrificial death" as a mode of challenging American hegemony. Again, he treats a bloody event only as a spectacle and not as the consequence of a complex interplay of political, economic, and social forces that underlie the spectacle. Incidentally, and not noted by Baudrillard, the architect of the Twin Towers was Minoru Yamasaki, who had earlier designed the ill-fated Pruitt-Igoe.

My criticism of Baudrillard revolves around the obvious point that there is a reality that people experience, emotionally respond to, and attempt in some fashion to shape. There is a life outside of the television set and outside of cyberspace. The emotionless and meaningless worlds depicted in films such as David Lynch's *Blue Velvet* and Quentin Tarantino's films from *Pulp Fiction* to his more recent offerings, *Inglourious Basterds* and *Django Unchained*, are not synonymous with our lived experiences, nor do most people convolute the two (Denby, 2009; Bauman, 1992: 149–55; Best and Kellner, 1991: 137–44). Although it is certainly true that the world of consumerism has changed considerably in recent years, little evidence can be mustered to claim that we have left modern culture for postmodern culture. The continued potency of religious belief, for example, calls into question the pervasiveness of meaninglessness Baudrillard envisions. The existence of the new social movements concerned with such issues as the environment, peace, feminism, civil rights, and poverty also calls into question the extent to which people in advanced industrial societies have opted for political passivism and escapism.

By claiming that we have moved from production to consumption, this version of postmodernism shows evidence of a serious blind spot. It is obvious that goods continue to be produced, although in a global economy this might mean that they are being produced in poor countries, where workers are paid abysmal wages and are forced to work exploitatively long hours in unsafe and unsanitary factories. The clothes purchased at the shopping mall and online are the products of this darker side of our contemporary culture. Moreover, as Alex Callinicos (1989: 162) has pointedly noted, not only are most of the world's inhabitants excluded from the consumerism Lyotard and Baudrillard describe but also poor people in the advanced industrial societies have only a limited involvement in this kind of consumption.

In a generous assessment of Baudrillard that appeared shortly after his death in 2007, Robert Antonio (2007: 2) pointed out that Baudrillard's abandonment of leftist politics was a reflection of his assessment of the failure of the 1968 student/worker protests. This event led to his the abandonment of the Marxist dream of a radiant future. Unlike Žižek (2008), who some continue to describe as a Marxist,

Baudrillard was not inclined to argue "in defense of lost causes." Nor was he prepared to endorse the anti-utopian pragmatism of liberal democracy. Rather, in relentlessly promoting his often contradictory but deeply pessimistic diagnoses of our times, he became a media star, which included homage to him in one of the *Matrix* films and a US lecture tour that was part of the Institute of Contemporary Arts' "Big Thinkers" series. He played a major role in creating and sustaining the postmodern moment, but near the end of his life he claimed that the term that best defined him was nihilist.

Liquid Modernity

Baudrillard was the most explicit and insistent advocate for radical post-modernism (Lemert, 2005: 36–40). Other postmodernists have offered more tempered assessments of the postmodern condition, viewing it in many respects as a new phase of modernity rather than constituting a radical rupture between past and present. No one better exemplifies this position than the Polish-born sociologist, Zygmunt Bauman, who has published a series of books explicitly devoted to postmodern concerns (Bauman, 1993, 1995, and 1997). Of particular emphasis in these theoretical reflections is an appreciation of the significance of ambivalence in postmodernity. Peter Bielharz (2009: 97) sees a parallel between Bauman's thought and that of Simmel, contending that in both one finds a commitment "to the idea of *ambivalence* as a central orienting device and motif of modernity."

By the turn of the century, Bauman (2000) opted to replace the term postmodern with the idea of "liquid modernity." Perhaps to avoid the confusions and incessant debates about postmodernism and perhaps also to distance himself from postmodernism's more radical proponents, this original term can be seen as useful in carving out an intellectual space in which to articulate his own position. Agreeing with the claim that grand narratives had ceased to be compelling, Bauman (2007) sees the present as an "age of uncertainty." The preceding stage of modernity can be characterized as "solid." In contrast, the current stage is "liquid" insofar as patterned social conduct and the social structures essential to making such forms of everyday social relations durable no longer exist. Instead, we live during times in which these structures no longer keep their shape for very long, "because they decompose and melt faster than the time it takes to cast them…" The consequence is that structured forms today "cannot serve as frames of reference for human actions and long-term life strategies because of their short life expectations" (Bauman, 2007: 1).

In short, people in the contemporary world are consigned to living out their lives with a far greater focus on the present and immediate future rather than with the "open horizon of the future" that Wagner (2008: 1) associated with the early phase of modernity. What makes Bauman so dramatically different from someone like Baudrillard is that his assessment of our current condition does not lead him to nihilism. On the contrary, he thinks that today, more than ever before, ethical conduct must be grounded in a sense of personal responsibility. We may live in uncertain times, but we don't live in amoral times. It's for this reason that Bauman continues to define himself as a socialist. He would thus likely agree with Bielharz (2009: 140) that socialism today should be viewed, not so much as an alternative economic system to capitalism, but as its "alter ego."

The Late Modern Age

Some creative thinkers, such as Frederic Jameson, Ernesto Laclau, Chantal Mouffe, and Nancy Fraser, have sought to selectively fuse elements of postmodernist theory with various modernist theories, particularly those emanating from Marxism and feminism. By continuing to employ the term postmodernism, however, they persist in conveying the sense that a radical cultural break has recently occurred or is in the process of occurring. Put another way, they resist the idea that the world we live in "is not *all* about flux," and that "[w]e remain firmly stuck within modernity" (Bielharz, 2009: 27). This idea of a radical break has been criticized by a number of theorists, nowhere more cogently than in the work of Anthony Giddens. Rather than embracing the term "postmodernism," Giddens prefers to use alternative terms such as "high modernity" or the "late modern age," in order to stress the fact that despite the novelty of contemporary circumstances, nonetheless the present is embedded in and an outgrowth of the past. We occupy not something that goes beyond modernity, but rather a distinct phase of a powerful historical project. Embedded in his theory is a perspective that encourages what might be seen as a tempered optimism. Actors are not rendered powerless and thus have a role to play in directing, shaping, and managing the forces of modernity. Modernity, however, is a "juggernaut" that we are forced to ride: We are not in a position to abandon or transcend it at will (Giddens, 1990:151).

Giddens contends that we are, indeed, modern and have been so for quite some time, and will continue to be modern well into the foreseeable future. Rather than a postmodern world, he sees a radicalized modernity. In *The Consequences of Modernity* (1990), Giddens argues that modernity arose in the West under the twin impact of the modern expansionist nation-state and the system of capitalist industrialism. In its relatively brief history, modernity became a global phenomenon infiltrating non-Western cultures throughout the world. The modern world is composed of nation-states that are crucial in directing a society's allocation of resources. The centralization of power in the state gives it not only military might but also far-ranging administrative control over its citizenry. Nation-states make a major contribution in creating the modern information society because this institution paves the way for new and more pervasive modes of surveillance and control. Moreover, the nation-state is intimately linked to a capitalist industrial economy.

Modernity results in a process of what Giddens (1990: 19) calls "distanciation," which means that social relations are no longer tied to particular locales. Relationships with those who are not physically present become increasingly more characteristic of the modern world. Modernity also entails a related process known as "disembedding" (Giddens, 1990: 21–7). This involves "the 'lifting out' of social relations from local contexts of interaction and their restructuring across indefinite spans of time-space" (Giddens, 1990: 21). Like Simmel, Giddens sees one major type of disembedding in the expansion of a money economy. In some respects, like Durkheim, he sees a second type of disembedding in the increasing reliance on professional and technical experts. In both types, it is essential for people to operate with sufficient levels of trust, which Giddens (1991: 244) defines as "the vesting of confidence in persons or in abstract systems, made on the basis of a 'leap into faith' which brackets ignorance or lack of information." How to establish and maintain trust and to address threats to it represents a crucial and unresolved issue for late modern society.

Giddens (1990: 55–63) identifies four risks embedded in this politico-economic institutional framework. The first is the expanded ability of those with power to engage in surveillance in the interest of controlling information and monitoring and controlling people. Because the surveillance capabilities of the state and of capitalist enterprises have expanded dramatically in recent years, this ability creates the increased risk of the growth of totalitarian power. The second risk is associated with the rapid escalation in military power brought about by the "industrialization of war," a phenomenon that, beginning with World War I, signaled the end of "limited wars" and the dawn of the era of "total wars." The development of weapons of mass destruction, including nuclear weapons, has created heretofore unimaginable threats to human survival and has led to far more war-related deaths in the 20th century than in any other century.

The third risk relates to the potential collapse of economic growth systems. This risk is connected to the fourth, which involves the potential for ecological decay or disaster. Giddens's politics are on the political Left, and thus it is not surprising that he contends that capitalism must be regulated to remedy its "erratic qualities" or, as Marxists would say, its crisis tendencies. He also sees modern capitalism as yielding gross inequalities at the national and global levels. Added to these problems, Giddens argues that capitalism's need to constantly expand productive capacity comes up against ecological limits, and thus the pursuit of capitalist accumulation is a major cause of environmental degradation (Giddens, 1990: 163–70; Beck, 2009).

In summary, separately and in combination, these risk factors define the dark side of the late modern condition, and the seriousness of these threats might seem to justify a pessimism not unlike that expressed by many postmodernists. Giddens (1990: 154–63), however, does not succumb to pessimism because he sees these risks as potential and not as inevitable. Preventing dreadful scenarios from unfolding and ensuring that solutions to the four types of risk can be found is distinctly possible. In particular, Giddens sees considerable promise in various social movements that operate with an orientation that he refers to as "utopian realism." Although the success of these movements is not guaranteed, neither is their failure. What is essential for the viability of these movements is a worldview that considers plausible utopian realism. To that end, Giddens has become increasingly focused on explicating pragmatic political and policy choices, whether it be in examining the ways to enact reforms to Europe's social welfare model (Giddens, 2007) or finding solutions to the ecological threat posed by climate change (Giddens, 2009).

In the two books that followed *Consequences* (1990), *Modernity and Self-Identity* (1991) and *The Transformation of Intimacy* (1992), Giddens turned to more Simmelian concerns—that is, how people experience the modern condition. He attempts to indicate the growing connection between global developments and changes that are occurring in the shaping of self-identities and in establishing interpersonal relationships. For Giddens, the self becomes a project to be created rather than something decisively determined by tradition or habit. This project brings with it the possibility of considerable doubt and the threat of a sense of meaninglessness. It also, however, grants to individuals the possibility of engaging in life planning—in adopting a variety of lifestyle options. Whereas some critics of self-help manuals, 12-step programs, and so on, see in this lifestyle exploration a form of contemporary narcissism, Giddens has a more positive assessment. Indeed, he depicts this trend in terms of the emergence of "life politics," which is concerned with the freedom of individuals to make choices and to create answers to the existential question of how a person should live one's life. In other words, life politics involves the promotion of individual self-actualization (Giddens, 1991: 209–31).

Life politics has far-ranging implications for interpersonal relationships, especially intimate ones. The democratization of intimate relations and the quest for emotional self-fulfillment have transformed intimacy, creating the possibility in late modernity of "pure relationships," which are relations determined and defined solely on their own internal terms and not in terms of any external factors. Giddens (1992: 3) claims that "the transformation of intimacy might be a subversive influence upon modern institutions as a whole." What this transformation might entail outside of the realm of intimate relations remains unclear. It is certain, however, that the modern age is one characterized by reflexivity, which means that it is an age in which our acts and beliefs are constantly subjected to examination and reflection.

Conclusion

In the Fall of 2011, London's Victoria and Albert Museum opened an exhibit titled "Postmodernism: Style and Subversion, 1970-1990," which explored the impact of postmodernism on the arts near the end of the past century. In the curator's foreward to the book that accompanied the exhibit, postmodernism's "slippery nature" and the "toxicity" often associated with the word were duly noted. And mention was made of Louis Menand's comment that "postmodernism is the Swiss Army Knife of critical concepts. It's definitionally overloaded, and it can do almost any job you need done" (Adamson and Pavitt, 2011: 9–10). Although I have been critical of the radical postmodernism associated with figures such as Baudrillard for their postulation of a rupture with the modern that fails to offer an adequate portrait of the reality of both permanence and change, they have played a useful role in cultural criticism. As the exhibit clearly revealed, much of postmodernism—at least in the arts—is a matter of fashion, and as Simmel well understood, once a fashion takes root, it is on its path to destruction. Musician David Byrne said as much in the exhibit guide's postscript when he wrote that, "Before too long there was, according to some, a postmodernist look. Time to move on" (quoted in Adamson and Pavitt, 2011: 287). On the other hand, a healthy skepticism about the modernist project, connected to an appreciation of the limits of knowledge, our inability to control the world in quite the way expected by apostles of progress, growing awareness of risk, and the need to reckon with the unintended consequences of our actions is a product of postmodernism. If it does nothing else than to get we moderns to act with greater humility and care as we approach both society and nature, it will have provided an invaluable service.

References

Adamson, Glenn and Jane Pavitt. 2011. *Postmodernism: Style and Subversion, 1970–1990*. London: V&A Publishing.
Alexander, Jeffrey C. 1995. *Fin de Siècle Social Theory*. London: Verso.

Antonio, Robert J. 2007. "The Passing of Jean Baudrillard," *Fast Capitalism*,4(1). Available online at http://www.uta.edu/huma/agger/fastcapitalism/4_1/antonio.html (accessed on December 18, 2013).

Antonio, Robert J. and Douglas Kellner. 1994. "The Future of Social Theory and the Limits of Postmodern Critique," in D.R. Dickens and A. Fontana (eds), *Postmodernism and Social Inquiry*, pp 127–152. New York: Guilford.

Baudrillard, Jean. 1981. *For a Critique of the Political Economy of the Sign.* St. Louis, MO: Telos.

_____. 1983. *Simulations.* New York: Semiotexte.

_____. 1988. *America.* London: Verso.

_____. 1991. *La Guerre de Golfe n'a pas eu lieu.* Paris: Galilee.

_____. 2002. *The Spirit of Terrorism: And Requiem for the Twin Towers.* London: Verso.

_____. 2005. "War Porn," *International Journal of Baudrillard Studies*, 2(1). Available online at http://www.ubishops.ca/baudrillardstudies/vol2_1/taylor.htm (accessed on December 18, 2013).

Bauman, Zygmunt. 1992. *Intimations of Postmodernity.* London: Routledge.

_____. 1993. *Postmodern Ethics.* Cambridge, MA: Basil Blackwell.

_____. 1995. *Life in Fragments: Essays in Postmodern Morality.* Cambridge, MA: Basil Blackwell.

_____. 1997. *Postmodernity and Its Discontents.* New York: New York University Press.

_____. 2000. *Liquid Modernity.* Cambridge, UK: Polity.

_____. 2007. *Liquid Times.* Cambridge, UK: Polity.

Beck, Ulrich. 2009. *World at Risk.* Cambridge, UK: Polity.

Best, Steven and Douglas Kellner. 1991. *Postmodern Theory: Critical Interrogations.* New York: Guilford.

Bielharz, Peter. 2009. *Socialism and Modernity.* Minneapolis: University of Minnesota Press.

Callinicos, Alex. 1989. *Against Postmodernism.* Cambridge, UK: Polity.

Denby, David. 2009. "Americans in Paris," *The New Yorker*, 82–83, August 24.

Derrida, Jacques. 1976. *Of Grammatology.* Baltimore, MD: Johns Hopkins University Press.

_____. 1978. *Writing and Difference.* Chicago: University of Chicago Press.

_____. 1981. *Positions.* Chicago: University of Chicago Press.

Frisby, David. 1981. *Sociological Impressionism: A Reassessment of Georg Simmel's Social Theory.* London: Heinemann.

_____. 1984. *Georg Simmel.* London: Tavistock.

_____. 1992. *Simmel and Since: Essays on Georg Simmel's Social Theory.* London: Routledge.

Giddens, Anthony. 1990. *The Consequences of Modernity.* Stanford, CA: Stanford University Press.

Giddens, Anthony. 1991. *Modernity and Self-Identity*. Stanford, CA: Stanford University Press.

_____. 1992. *The Transformation of Intimacy*. Stanford, CA: Stanford University Press.

_____. 2007. *Europe in the Global Age*. Cambridge, UK: Polity.

_____. 2009. *The Politics of Climate Change*. Cambridge, UK: Polity.

Gottdiener, Mark. 1993. "Ideology, Foundationalism, and Sociological Theory," *Sociological Quarterly*, 34(4): 653–71.

Harvey, David. 1989. *The Condition of Postmodernity: An Enquiry into the Origins of Cultural Change*. Oxford, UK: Blackwell.

Illouz, Eva. 2007. *Cold Intimacies: The Making of Emotional Capitalism*. Cambridge, UK: Polity.

Jameson, Fredric. 1991. *Postmodernism, or, the Cultural Logic of Late Capitalism*. Durham, NC: Duke University Press.

Kellner, Douglas. 2000. "Jean Baudrillard," in G. Ritzer (ed.), *The Blackwell Companion to Major Social Theorists*, pp. 731–53. Malden, MA: Blackwell.

Kivisto, Peter. 1994. "Toward an Antifoundational yet Relevant Sociology: Can Gottdiener Have It Both Ways?" *Sociological Quarterly*, 35(4): 723–28.

Kracauer, Siegfried. 1995. *The Mass Ornament: Weimar Essays*. Cambridge, MA: Harvard University Press.

Lash, Scott. 1990. *Sociology of Postmodernism*. London: Routledge.

Latour, Bruno. 1993. *We Have Never Been Modern*. Cambridge, MA: Harvard University Press.

Leck, Ralph M. 2000. *Georg Simmel and Avant-Garde Sociology*. New York: Humanities Press.

Lemert, Charles. 1995. *Sociology after the Crisis*. Boulder, CO: Westview.

_____. 2005. *Postmodernism Is Not What You Think*. Boulder, CO: Paradigm.

_____. 2006. *Durkheim's Ghosts: Cultural Logics and Social Things*. New York: Cambridge University Press.

Levine, Donald. 1985. *The Flight from Ambiguity: Essays in Social and Cultural Theory*. Chicago: University of Chicago Press.

_____. 1995. *Visions of the Sociological Tradition*. Chicago: University of Chicago Press.

Lyon, David. 1994. *Postmodernity*. Minneapolis: University of Minnesota Press.

Lyotard, Jean-Francois. 1979. *The Postmodern Condition: A Report on Knowledge*. Minneapolis: University of Minnesota Press.

Mills, C. Wright. 1959. *The Sociological Imagination*. New York: Grove.

Nedelmann, Birgitta. 1990. "Georg Simmel as an Analyst of Autonomous Dynamics: The Merry-Go-Round of Fashion," in M. Kaern, B.S. Phillips, and R.S. Cohen (eds), *Georg Simmel and Contemporary Sociology*, pp. 243–57. Dordrecht, the Netherlands: Kluwer.

Nedelmann, Birgitta. 1991. "Individualization, Exaggeration, and Paralysation: Simmel's Three Problems of Culture," *Theory, Culture, and Society*, 8(3): 169–94.

Poggi, Gianfranco. 1993. *Georg Simmel's Philosophy of Money*. Berkeley: University of California Press.

Ritzer, George. 1999. *Enchanting a Disenchanted World: Revolutionizing the Means of Consumption*. Thousand Oaks, CA: Pine Forge Press.

Scaff, Lawrence. 2000. "Georg Simmel," in George Ritzer (ed.), *The Blackwell Companion to Major Social Theorists*, pp. 215–78. Malden, MA: Blackwell.

Simmel, Georg. 1950. *The Sociology of Georg Simmel*. Ed. K. H. Wolff. New York: Free Press.

———. [1908] 1955. *Conflict and the Web of Group Affiliations*. New York: Free Press.

———. 1959. *Georg Simmel, 1858–1918*. Ed. K. Wolff. Columbus: Ohio State University Press.

———. 1971. *On Individuality and Social Forms*. Ed. D.N. Levine. Chicago: University of Chicago Press.

———. [1892] 1977. *The Problems of the Philosophy of History: An Epistemological Essay*. Ed. G. Oakes. New York: Free Press.

———. 1984. *Georg Simmel: On Women, Sexuality, and Love*. Ed. G. Oakes. New Haven, CT: Yale University Press.

———. [1907] 1991. *The Philosophy of Money*. London: Routledge.

Smart, Barry. 1992. *Modern Conditions, Postmodern Controversies*. London: Routledge.

Spivak, Gayatri. 1988. "Can the Subaltern Speak," in C. Nelson and L. Grossberg (eds), *Marxism and the Interpretation of Culture*, pp. 271–313. Urbana: University of Illinois Press.

Therborn, Göran. 1995. *European Modernity and Beyond*. Thousand Oaks, CA: SAGE Publications.

Vromen, Suzanne. 1990. "Georg Simmel and the Cultural Dilemmas of Women," in Michael Kaern, Bernard Phillips, and Robert Cohen (eds), *Georg Simmel and Contemporary Sociology*, pp. 319–339. Dordrecht, The Netherlands: Kluwer.

Wagner, Peter. 2008. *Modernity as Experience and Interpretation: A New Sociology of Modernity*. Cambridge, UK: Polity.

Weingartner, Rudolph H. 1960. *Experience and Culture: The Philosophy of Georg Simmel*. Middletown, CT: Wesleyan University.

Weinstein, Deena and Michael A. Weinstein. 1993. *Post-Modern(ized) Simmel*. London: Routledge.

Žižek, Slavoj. 2002. *Welcome to the Desert of the Real*. London: Verso.

———. *In Defense of Lost Causes*. London: Verso.

6

Modernity and Postmodernity

NICO STEHR AND JASON L. MAST

Rooted in the modernist project of explaining such grand transformations as industrialization, the rise of urban centers, bureaucratic means of administration and domination, and the state formations of democracies and dictatorships, the social sciences in general and sociological theories in particular have sought to identify and name the hallmark features and processes that define an emerging historical epoch. The effort continues at the turn of the 21st century, when advanced societies once again appear to be experiencing profound changes in their constituent social and cultural elements. Scientific knowledge and technology played a central role in narratives of the rise of modernity, and they remain central characters in more recent theories of transformation as well.

Having penetrated all spheres of social (and natural) life during the 20th century, science and technology continue to exert considerable transformative power over social formations, leading contemporary theorists to diagnose the current epoch in a variety of ways. Do we live in postindustrial societies (Bell, 1973), knowledge societies (Böhme and Stehr, 1986; Stehr, 1994), network societies (Castells, 1996), or risk societies (Beck, 1992), we ask. As is the character of social theorizing, a clear answer eludes our grasp, yet probably lies somewhere in the middle of these formulations. What these social theories share, however, is a commitment to locating the roots of transformations in socio-economic processes. Yet alongside these debates the conceptual dichotomy of the modern and postmodern has arisen, an academic discourse with an altogether different epistemological approach to the question of how economy and culture shape one another.[1] Without

---

[1] In what is but a passing reference, Talcott Parsons (1977: 241) expresses, in his *The Evolution of Societies*, his certitude that the idea of postmodernity is premature since the trend of the "next century will be toward the completion of

describing the postmodern movement in all of its self-exemplifying and dazzling diversity, in the following pages we probe this difference in greater detail, and examine the very notion of an epochal break, the transition into a postmodern era, as well.

The postmodern theories and studies that originated in the 1970s, bloomed in the 1980s, and flourished through the 1990s, conceive of the postmodern epoch's emergence as residing in and responding to transformations within the *cultural* spheres of society.[2] In distinct contrast to theories of the postmodern, theories of modern industrial and postindustrial society have been more firmly rooted in the sociological, political, and economic discourses that assert if not the primacy then at least the immense importance of socio-economic activities for the life-worlds experienced in the contemporary, and perhaps more particularly, Western world. The theory of the knowledge society, for instance, continues to stress this theorem; while it does speak of a reversal in the relative importance of superstructure and substructure, it nonetheless refuses to deny the persistent relevance of the economic system, let alone exempt it from analysis.

Sentiments of Mortality

The following is not a grand overview of all relevant literature, but we aim to illuminate the efforts of some of the primary theorists of postindustrial and postmodern society in a new and interesting way.

---

the type of society that this book has called modern." Only fifteen years later, few social theorists would repeat the same position with similar conviction and lack of ambivalence.

[2] Albert Borgmann (1992), in his essay on *Crossing the Postmodern Divide*, is among the few observers who directly associates a postmodern culture with a postmodern economy. Borgmann argues that developments that lead to a *coherent* postmodern society, embracing all sectors of society, result from the general decline, that is, the rising disaffinity with the sentiments of realism (domination of nature), universalism (primacy of method), and individualism (sovereignty of the individual), characterizing the *modern* epoch. In the case of the economy, one is able to detect, as Borgmann (1992: 5) suggests, a more concrete and consequential postmodern paradigm, namely a "paradigm characterized by information processing, flexible specialization, and informed cooperation."

We start with one of the postmodern movement's signature artificers, Jean-Francois Lyotard. Citing the rapid innovations in scientific discourses, which have produced profound changes in media and communicative technologies, the miniaturization of machines, the proliferation of information-processing machines (aka computers), and advancements in transportation systems, to name but a few important developments, Lyotard ([1979] 1984: 3–4) argues that the "nature of knowledge cannot survive unchanged within this context of general transformation." (([1979] 1984: 4). What has been wrought by these technological developments and, more particularly, how has the sphere of modern knowledge been altered? Drawing on a neoWittgensteinian, "language games" perspective, Lyotard observed, "in contemporary society and culture—postindustrial society, postmodern culture—the question of the legitimation of knowledge is formulated in different terms. The grand narrative has lost its credibility, regardless of what mode of unification it uses, regardless of whether it is a speculative narrative or a narrative of emancipation" ([1979] 1984: 37). Two details stand out: Lyotard distinguishes society from culture, and associates postindustrialism with the former and postmodernism with the latter. Second, the "general transformation" has eroded the ability of broad, overarching understandings to make sense of the world, to render its disparate elements into a meaningful whole. In his own pithy turn of phrase, Lyotard defines postmodernism as characterized by an "incredulity toward metanarratives" ([1979] 1984: xxiv). Scientific knowledge, Lyotard argues, has lost its capacity to fold its endeavors and motivations into, or ground its legitimation on, narratives of emancipation and totalization, or understandings of freedom through accumulation on the one hand, and the promise of a unifying explanation or theory, on the other.

While it is tempting to read Lyotard as offering a metanarrative about the end of metanarratives,[3] one can also readily accept as compelling, on

---

[3] Such elective affinities lead Ernest Gellner (1992: 45), for example, to identify postmodernism, and its utmost obscurity and subjectivism ("the main stylistic marks of 'postmodernisms'"), as a contemporary specimen of the older and more established form of relativism; and, as an instance of relativism, it should be, as always, strongly repudiated. Carlo Mongardini (1992: 56) describes the paradox in question well, but does not display the same irritation with or resentment toward the "logical flaws" of what he calls the latest ideology of modernity: "The cleverness

the basis of impressive and intuitive evidence, that the contemporary world increasingly lacks cognitive stability[4] or an intellectual center, or that, despite the resurgence of some metanarratives in the wake of state socialism's retreat, its members tend to be more suspicious of totalizing philosophies of history than their ancestors. The world of ideas, science, and politics, it is asserted, is being "decentered."[5]

There is no doubt that in some quarters there still persist illusions of objectivity and assumptions about the existence of a calculus, even a *mathesis universalis* or a Newtonian anthropology, which will assemble knowledge's many disparate parts into a unifying whole. Despite these residues, expectations that this kind of consensus will rise from the ashes of the contemporary world's many inconsistencies and incongruities are waning. Instead, Lyotard's ([1979] 1984: xxiv–xxv) diagnosis suggests that postmodern societies are shaped by processes of local and regional determinism, and constituted by a heterogeneity of "language particles" that form "institutions in patches." In this context, contemporary knowledge does not operate solely under the command of a power elite or rest undisturbed and uncontested within the boundaries of ruling institutions. To the contrary, it is fragmented, multivalent, and created by and deployed from a diversity of locations and perspectives.

of the idea of postmodernity lies in setting up, as ideological fact, precisely what it claims it does not want to be, i.e., a uniform representation and a check on reality with regard to the segmentation of modernity, a form of historical consciousness with regard to *posthistorie*, a search for a single collective identity in face of the psychological and social inconsistency of the contemporary individual, a semblance of intellectual culture and spirituality in face of the fetishism of things and images."

[4] The postmodern perspective indeed is widely associated with a denial of the capacity of language, mind, or spirit to firmly establish standards in an objective, that is, consensual manner; in light of such displacement from more conventional norms of discourse, paradoxically perhaps, most affirmative discussions of postmodernity begin with efforts to firmly assert and ground a particular conception of postmodernity.

[5] Perhaps there is, in light of the cultural and intellectual fragmentation of the world reason to characterize postmodernism along with postindustrialism, late capitalism, and the end of history thesis as "a purely cultural phenomenon expressive of an evolution of western capitalist society" (Friedman, 1990: 311). This argument does have the merit of associating, perhaps reminiscent of a crude materialist perspective, the rise of postmodern thought with a particular economic formation of modern society.

As a result, these conditions facilitate the spread of disenchantment (ibid), a condition diagnosed and bemoaned by generations of social scientists. On the other, more uplifting hand, the eroding constitutive power of master ideologies and broad consensuses also sharpen our sensitivities to differences and precondition our tolerance for the incommensurable. On the more pragmatic level, postmodern dissension also adds new fuel to the motor of future invention.

This general characterization, asserting that increasingly social formations are composed of a multiplicity of "worlds," forms of life, Weltanschauungen, and different cultural or value spheres, is neither a novel discovery,[6] nor exclusively associated with late- or disorganized capitalism (Turner, 1989: 212–215). Perhaps the possible novelty of a postmodern perspective, therefore, must be constituted not by the mere insight into a multiplicity of communities but, as Zygmunt Bauman (1991: 246) perceptively put it, by the rise of "self-conscious contingency." After all, the realization of competing world-views may be dismissed as temporary, or understood as a strong incentive for even greater intellectual and political efforts to overcome diversity and the forces of fragmentation. For Bauman (1991: 272), we have reached the era of postmodernity once such (modern) efforts come to terms with their own impossibility. But other observers are more skeptical about the realities of a break in the traditions of the Enlightenment and prefer

---

[6] After all, Alexis de Tocqueville's description of a pluralistic *Democracy in America*, Friedrich Nietzsche's perspectivism, or Max Weber's values-spheres are not the only very early expressions of incompatible political and intellectual viewpoints as constitutive of modern society. Karl Mannheim ([1928]1990: 66), in his discussion of "Competition as a cultural phenomenon," locates one type of competition, namely atomistic competition, in the age of the enlightenment or as representative following the breakdown of the ecclesiastical monopoly in the interpretation of reality. Atomistic competition for Mannheim is characterized by the fact that many isolated social groups bid to inherit the official interpretation of the world. Once the "genuinely modern stage" of atomistic competition is reached, he observes, there exists "(a) no universally accepted set of axioms, (b) no universally recognized hierarchy of values, and (c) nothing but radically different ontologies and epistemologies." Similarly, and in a much more pejorative interpretation, Piritim Sorokin (1957: 700) offers his description of the last stages of decadent, sensate culture, which to a degree resonates with the contemporary conception of postmodernism.

to speak about contemporary conditions as reflexive modernity.[7] The intellectual disjunctures and transitions that have taken place in recent decades may be seen as a progressive and radicalizing self-clarification of both the limits and the basis of modern thought and thus represent a phase of modernity, as Anthony Giddens (1990: 51), for example, suggests. While the triumph of modern thought coincides with the European dominance of the world, its self-clarification corresponds to the gradual dissolution of Western hegemony by virtue of the global spread of its social structures. Similarly, the philosophical postmodernism as articulated by Lyotard may paradoxically be interpreted not as a "break with the modernization project but, potentially at least, its socio-political ally, a vigorous agent of the renewal and deepening of modernity's democratic potential (Keane, 1992: 84)." If we judge the current state of affairs by Bauman's definition of postmodernism, that we have reached the era when we acknowledge the impossibility of achieving Enlightenment goals, then we can see in the works of Gidden's and Keane that we have not quite arrived.

Does postmodernism represent a break between epochs or the further extension of a prior one; is its social contents merely old wine in new bottles or a distinctly unique elixir? The question of whether the label "postmodern" can be sociologically productive can be left open. What undoubtedly is worth special attention, however, is the apparent reversal of the classical sociological equation in much of the discussion of postmodern conditions: the bold or cautious claim, as the case may be, that the emergence of an "essentially contested culture"[8] is, in the

---

[7] The issue of finding an adequate periodization of historical periods or stages not surprisingly is, and will continue to be, an essentially contested issue not only in this case but in every other instance in which the attempt is made to differentiate between historical stages or to impose cognitive boundaries of any sort (cf. the discussion about industrial and postindustrial societies). This is not surprising because dichotomies and periodization tables constitute cognitive tools and perspectives in intellectual contests, which cannot be reduced except by force to a common denominator.

[8] The phrase coined is an analogy to William B. Gallie's and William E. Connolly's notion of "essentially contested concepts" in historical and political discourse (Gallie, 1964 and Connolly, 1983). According to Gallie's (1964: 158) interpretation, "essentially contested concepts" refer to cognitive disputes that are perfectly genuine but not resolvable by argument of any kind, but "nevertheless sustained by perfectly respectable arguments and evidence."

first place, the outcome of intellectual labor rather than the result of existential forces rooted in transformations of civilizational structures. Put another way, we are drawn to an unanswered question; what are the social processes, and the socio-economic ones in particular, that drove the "postindustrial society" in such as a way as to produce the rise of "postmodern culture" and further the delegitimation of grand narratives? What is it in the postindustrial order that threatens the organizing norms of "modern" intellectual practices (Bauman, 1987: 5), practices shaped by beliefs in universality, prediction, and control?[9] If one chooses to describe the process of intellectual "decentering" as postmodern, then we are not convinced that the socio-economic origins and base of postmodernity have been clearly discerned. While Lyotard refers to theories of postindustrial society and the extent to which knowledge has become the principle force of production, his allusions and references quickly recede into the background.

That the condition of an "essentially contested culture" is rendered an almost self-generated and largely self-propelled diversity becomes evident as one listens to the virtual absence of accounts concerning the socio-economic contributions to the "decline of narrative." This decline, we are told, is the "effect of the blossoming of techniques and technologies since the Second World War, which has shifted emphasis from the ends of action to its means" (Lyotard, [1979] 1984: 37). This description of modern conditions should have a familiar ring to the reader; for example, Georg Simmel ([1907] 1978: 482), in his *Philosophie des Geldes*, already indicates that then contemporary social conditions are characterized by "a preponderance of means over ends" and the disorienting effect this brings about. The reasons Simmel adduces for this reversal are similar to Lyotard's, namely the ascendancy of the "objective culture" ("sachliche Kultur") over the "subjective culture." And Simmel's ([1907] 1978: 484) description of the outcomes of this reversal for the nature of modern life sound as if Lyotard, or perhaps more accurately one of his postmodern disciples, could have written it: "The lack of something definite at the center of the soul impels us

---

[9] Perhaps prior to these epistemological features of modern knowledge claims is, as Bruno Latour (1991: 15) suggests, the "political constitution of truth," which establishes and sanctions two distinct and entirely separate spheres of knowledge, "one hidden for things; the other open for citizens," namely the division of social and natural phenomena.

to search for momentary satisfaction in ever-new stimulations, sensations, and external activities. Thus it is that we become entangled in the instability and helplessness that manifests itself as the tumult of the metropolis, as the mania for traveling, as the wild pursuit of competition and as the typically modern disloyalty with regard to taste, style, opinions, and personal relationships." Lyotard's theorem also resonates with Arnold Gehlen's views about the social consequences of the evolution of modern technology, as well as Marcuse's concerns about the penetration of rationality into most spheres of the life world inhabited by modern individuals.

Continuing his brief foray into socio-economic influences, Lyotard ([1979] 1984: 38) adds a second equally brief speculative remark intended to account for the delegitimation of grand intellectual designs, citing the "redeployment of advanced liberal capitalism after its retreat under the protection of Keynesianism during the period 1930-60." Unfortunately, he resists developing the plausibility of this observation and moves on without seriously investigating it. Instead, he searches for indications of origins of the decline of scientific reason within the boundaries of 20th century intellectual history. Any search for "causes" of the decline of the grand narrative in contemporary society, Lyotard suggests, will lead to disappointing results since efforts to precisely link structural and intellectual or cultural changes are bound to run up against the difficulty of detailing the precise nature of the connection between tendencies ([1979] 1984: 38). Thus, Lyotard reverts to a largely self-contained tradition of history of ideas as a way of elucidating the process of the delegitimation of grand narratives. In his foreword to *The Postmodern Condition*, Frederic Jameson (1984: xiii) suggests that a similar question arises in Lyotard's text, namely, "is this moment of advanced industrial society a structural variant of classical capitalism or a mutation and the dawning of a wholly new social structure in which... it is now science, knowledge, technological research, rather than industrial production and the extraction of surplus value, that is the 'ultimately determining instance'?" Jameson, alas, suggests that it is to Lyotard's credit that he does not pursue the question in "peremptory fashion," and, like Lyotard, turns the issue into a question of intellectual history, namely by asking if Marxist categories retain their explanatory power in the emerging age of multinational and media societies.

Characteristic of the discussion of the postmodern condition and some of its intellectual forerunners is therefore a narrow, even scientistic, conception of what issues from the scientific community and its discourse, namely cognitive-instrumental rationality. Since such structures are seen as linked to the autonomous sphere of truth, knowledge claims produced by science are viewed as ahistorical, transcending time and place. Lyotard ([1979] 1984: 7–9) obviously does not assert the hegemony of science. It shares the social world with "popular" ([1979] 1984: 28) or "narrative knowledge," which "does not give priority to the question of its own legitimation," and "certifies itself in the pragmatics of its own transmission without having recourse to argumentation and proof" ([1979] 1984: 27). These latter forms of knowledge are distinct from scientific knowledge; they cannot prevail over science and they fail to achieve the character of scientific knowledge. The opposition, or even incommensurability, between scientific and narrative knowledge, therefore animates Lyotard's discussion of the role of knowledge in modern society. It is "impossible to judge the existence or validity of narrative knowledge on the basis of scientific knowledge and vice versa: the relevant criteria are different," he argues ([1979] 1984: 26). In other words, Lyotard persists in assuming that a steep gradient obtains between scientific rationality and everyday knowledge. Though science is incapable of self-legitimation, it plays on its own field and according to its own rules, to stick with the language games metaphor.

Concluding his comparison of the pragmatics of scientific knowledge to narrative knowledge, Lyotard reflects, "[a]ll we can do is gaze in wonderment at the diversity of discursive species, just as we do at the diversity of plant or animal species" ([1979] 1984: 26). But the techniques, technologies, and knowledge in science have also variously been associated or held responsible for exactly the opposite cultural developments, namely a greater concentration and unity of ideas. Max Weber's notion of rationalization and the technocracy debate with its central thesis of the growing dominance of the technical imperative are only two prime examples. However, in each case, the pervasive and persuasive force of reason and systematic unity has been exaggerated.

We follow these observations with the suggestion that much of the discussion of postmodernity tends to be self-exemplifying and constituted by ambivalence. Not only the phenomena it proclaims to describe but the discussion of these phenomena lack specificity. One surely cannot deduce from this condition that modernity was orderly (Featherstone, 1989: 8). Is postmodernism the cultural logic of capitalism, late capitalism, or is it a manifestation of a split between the dynamics of society and culture in modern society?

Modernity as part of the central conceptual metaphor of the analysis requires critical reflection as well (see Habermas, 1981: 3–4). The notion of modernity is also frequently employed in a multifaceted and sometimes distinctly disparaging manner. If "modern" is merely seen as referring to that which is new or fashionable, varied usage is justified. The perpetual contest between preservation and change then becomes an anthropological constant. Modern is then not new, nor is the struggle to preserve it. But such usage of "modern" is also ahistorical. Yet, it is precisely its history-transcending efforts or even its deliberate present-mindedness that we would regard as characteristic of modern consciousness. "Modern" in this sense signifies a historical period by denying it and thereby recapitulates aspects of "traditional" (primitive) consciousness in as far as traditional society does not reflect on its own traditions. A modern consciousness has cut off its association with unique socio-historical circumstances, as captured in the Mannheimian notion of socially "unattached" intellectuals. It refers to and celebrates the virtues of ideas, which have transcended the multiplicity of their origins and have thereby fostered a new and distinctive identity—intellectual impartiality. In the scientific community, in Europe, North America, and elsewhere, efforts have been underway for centuries to create a style of modern thought increasingly freed from being bound to a specific time and a specific location. Success toward this goal had been experienced as emancipation and as liberation from sacred and secular bonds. Modern consciousness was and still is, on the whole, hardly unhappy with itself and represents an undeniable civilizational accomplishment, in science and elsewhere. However, it is increasingly evident that these aims and accomplishments are associated with multiple unanticipated consequences.

Among the unintended consequences of the search for a *mathesis universalis* and for the elimination of dissensus has been its virtual opposite, namely a condition of radical plurality (a condition which reminds us of features of the historical context which gave rise to the search for impartiality and unity in the first place). If the notion "postmodernity" (Welsch, 1987: 4) has any sociological import, perhaps it refers to such a condition of radical plurality associated, paradoxically, with a convergence of life orders within and across communities and social structures, in particular of economic structures, across societies. Time and place have indeed become increasingly irrelevant both in the sphere of production and in cultural figurations. Postmodernity reflects an increasing sense of disillusionment with the project of modernity in this sense. A postmodern consciousness is therefore best described as a consciousness disillusioned with modernity—a consciousness that is skeptical toward the possibility and virtues of impartiality, yet which retains the peculiar present-mindedness of modernity. What is historically new about such consciousness is its association not with profound socio-economic divisions but with new forms of social inequality based more directly on intellectual rather than material conditions.

Critiques of Postmodernity

As we observed in introducing this discussion on modernity and post-modernity, the proponents of postmodernity have tried to emphasize the desirability of decomposing traditional social science discourse with a view to uncoupling the analysis of contemporary society from the legacy of focusing on the modernization process and its impact on cultural life. More generally, the strong thesis of postmodernity asserts the autonomous strength of a divided culture in human existence. And consistent with this emphasis, the arguments of most critics of the notion of postmodernity are more firmly embedded in a comprehensive theory of modern society that a) affirms the intellectual ambitions of modernity, b) attempts to unmask postmodernism as ideology, as a source of anomie, or as representing a crisis of middle-class values, and c) insists that the social forces constitutive of modern society, especially its exploitative (capitalist) economic organization and bureaucratic power, have hardly been dismantled or severely disintegrated.

In this respect, the formal nature of the argument about the contested shift from one historical era to another, for all intents and purposes, closely resembles the debate about the genuineness of the change from industrial to postindustrial society. There are usually good warrants on either side of the divide. As a result, one is dealing with what are essentially contested perspectives that not only cannot be theoretically resolved but also typify the issues under debate in practical intellectual terms. Rather than adding and exemplifying the essentially contested debate further, we will instead inquire into the (usually) only vaguely articulated social conditions for the possibility of postmodernity as a cognitive social phenomenon. We return to Lyotard ([1979] 1984: 14), who, for example, offers a few hints, in a rather terse and bold manner, about some of the basic social transformations that could be held responsible for the emergence of postmodern intellectual conditions; that is, the old poles of attraction, as he calls them, "represented by nation-states, parties, professions, institutions, and historical traditions" are losing their appeal. Such an observation can easily be misconstrued to mean that these social constructs simply vanish from the scene and that postmodernity is something that fills the resulting created void. What is more likely is that the "attractions" in question are transformed; but why?

The societal frame for the possibility of disillusioned modernity certainly is not merely the outcome of cultural developments which can or must be traced to heroic figures in recent intellectual history; strong societal roots, in a nonreductionist sense of the term, ought to be found in changing features of the economic structure of contemporary society. For shorthand purposes, we mention only two of its features: (1) the decline in importance of the traditional forces of production of industrial society, namely property and labor in the classical meaning of the terms, and the rise of knowledge as a source of the growth of the economy, and (2) the reduced presence of the nation-state as an effective actor in the economic life of modern society. It will be most difficult, as long as the discussion of postmodernity and modernity remains largely self-exemplifying and merely dissects intellectual factors and the genealogy of its own emergence, to trace peculiar sociostructural conditions for the possibility and the character of the cultural life world in modern society. Any ruptures and breaks in the modern social order that allow for the emergence of pluralistic, multicultural, fragmented, and eclectic and cultural practices require reference to stronger, more lasting, and more consequential social criteria that then justify the reading of a new intellectual epoch.

Berger (1988: 232) also disputes and doubts the existence of a structural fissure in modern society because the transition to postmodernity occurs on the level of culture or consciousness, and because requisite value commitments today have to compete in a "market of opportunities" against the availability of other intellectual possibilities. In order to really sustain any argument about a rupture in modernity one has to be able to identify a break in the basic pattern of the social structure of modern society, or even more to the point, identify a displacement of the structural logic of social change. Social relations, it seems to Berger, are fatefully lodged in a certain structure, from which for the time being no escape appears to be possible. For Berger, the basic structure of modern, in contrast to traditional, social relations is the displacement of a "natural" stratification of domination by self-sufficient forms of social power that are based on clearly identifiable functions of specialized, that is, differentiated systems of social action. Thus, it makes no sense to speak of a structural break in contemporary society since there are no firm indications that the structure of modern social relations, linked to the logic of a differentiation of subsystems of social action, is in the process of being replaced. Any de-differentiation processes that may well occur are in fact only extensions of the basic social structure of modernity in the sense of alternative paths of modernization.

Daniel Bell (1976) perceived postmodernity as the most extreme and fashionable manifestation of the rejection of the motivational core of the pragmatic, puritan world-view of the bourgeoisie, and as the culmination of the collapse of a form of capitalism that was still able to penetrate and dominate cultural life. The distancing between the social structure and culture really means the establishment of a separate life space outside the immediate influence of the economy and traditional culture, and it provides the social basis for the emergence of postmodernism: "The traditional bourgeois organization of life—its rationalism and sobriety—now has few defenders in the culture, nor does it have any established system of cultural meanings or stylistic forms with any intellectual or cultural respectability" (Bell, 1976: 53). The separation of the world of society or social structure and culture obviously resonates with the age-old division and conflict of reason and meaning, fact and value, or intellectual and affective faculties. The distinct cultural spaces are enlarged and inhabited not only by the cultural elite but by innumerable actors. The emergence of popular mass culture with its new sensibilities emphasizing spontaneity, sensation, immediacy, and constant novelty are destructive, de-cohesive forces, Bell (1976: 54) asserts, eroding the "social structure itself by striking at the motivational and psychic-reward system which has sustained it." The two cultural codes of the economic system, the Protestant ethic and the Puritan temper, which also nurtured the traditional cultural value system, already broke up some time ago, in the first decades of the 20th century, but continue to leave a deep moral void in American society. Intellectual attacks on Puritanism were sustained and ultimately proved to be successful because of social and demographic changes in American society such as, for example, the end of small-town domination of American life, the emergence of a banal mass consumption society, and by technological inventions such as the automobile, motion picture, and radio, all of which compressed time, distance, and participation. In short, the traditional foundation of social cohesion linking individual to society is overthrown, and instead of a condition described as an end to ideology, society suffers a lack of social solidarity and is anything but immune to social conflicts and struggles.[10] At the same time, Bell's analysis resonates with the theorists of postmodernity because he too describes modern society as a plural society characterized by a multitude of values that cannot simply be reconciled. His critique of postmodernism, it should be mentioned, also echoes the critique of mass culture by intellectuals in the 1940s.

As the critics of postmodernism repeatedly have stressed, the crucial liability of the intellectual movement is its inability to ground social and political action. Postmodernism does not offer any moral principles that could guide social action and take full advantage of the potentials offered by the evolution of social structure into postindustrialism (Brick, 1986: 207–208). The modern social order, Bell (1976: 84) concludes, lacks "either a culture that is the symbolic expression of any vitality or a moral impulse that is the motivational or binding force.

---

[10] Thus, as Turner (1989: 206) concludes, while "Bell has been persistently criticized for presenting a consensus view of modern society free of ideological conflicts, in fact the reverse is an equally plausible interpretation of Bell's analysis, namely the persistence of conflicts over the state budget, the absence of a coherent cultural legitimation of politics, the emergence of the free-floating narcissistic self, the degradation of the person through the impact of consumerism and the emergence of a postmodern irrationalism which prevents any coherent analysis of society, while also precluding a coherence for the integration of the individual and society." Interpretations of Bell's views on the role of culture and social structure in modern society depend, to a considerable extent, we would suggest, on the critics' willingness to subscribe to a perspective which either embraces a conflation of culture and structure (whereby the powerful force of structural transformations represents a tendency toward some form of cultural monism in modern society) or is more likely to admit the possibility of cultural fragmentation despite a growing homogeneity of economic activities in modern society.

What, then, can hold society together?" In the final analysis, Bell's critique of postmodernism bemoans, as have Max Weber, Edmund Husserl, and Jürgen Habermas, the loss of meaning in an increasingly rationalized world.

The Limits of the Possible

In the final analysis, and paradoxically perhaps, the dispute about postmodernity as the end to an epoch, almost without fracture, passes and perhaps fades into classic, highly dichotomized, and highly charged debates about rationalism and relativism.

The debate on postmodernism once again demonstrates, in our view, that a sensible medium has to be located, much as was necessary in the debates between the extremes of the asymmetrical dichotomies of rationalism and relativism, universalism and particularism, epistemology and social science, local and global, and contextuality and transcendentalism, dichotomies that have haunted many social science controversies since the 19th century and continue to do so. In expressing skepticism toward the idea of postmodernity, one is not, for example, necessarily committed to the notion that the project of modernity continues to be implemented. A reasonable path beyond simple dichotomies should be grounded in socio-historical reality rather than in a logically construed vacuum alone. Such a path immediately diminishes the alleged moral and political threats that issue from relativism, contextuality, regionality, and particularism; at the same time, it tempers the possibility of eliminating diversity in favor of universality and a complete victory of rationalism. The limits, in each instance being socially constructed limits, not only prevent the realization of any of the extremes, but also decisively restrict any infinite permutation and modification of social and cognitive realities (Meja and Stehr, 1992).

References

Bauman, Zygmunt. 1987. *Legislators and Interpreters: On Modernity, Post-Modernity and Intellectuals*. Ithaca: Cornell University Press.

Bauman, Zygmunt. 1991. *Modernity and Ambivalence.* Ithaca, New York: Cornell University Press.

Beck, Ulrich. 1992. *Risk Society: Towards a New Modernity.* London: SAGE Publications.

Bell, Daniel. 1973. *The Coming of Post-Industrial Society: A Venture in Social Forecasting.* New York: Basic Books.

————. 1976. *The Cultural Contradictions of Capitalism.* New York: Basic Books.

Berger, Johannes. 1988. "Modernitätsbegriffe und Modernitätskritik in der Soziologie," *Soziale Welt,* 39(S): 224–236.

Böhme, Gernot and Nico Stehr. 1986. *The Knowledge Society.* Dordrecht and Boston: D. Reidel, 1986.

Borgmann, Albert. 1992. *Crossing the Postmodern Divide.* Chicago: University of Chicago Press.

Brick, Howard. 1986. *Daniel Bell and the Decline of Intellectual Radicalism. Social Theory and Political Reconciliation in the 1940s.* Madison: University of Wisconsin Press.

Castells, Manuel. 1996. *The Rise of the Network Society.* Cambridge, MA: Blackwell Publishers.

Connolly, William E. 1983. *The Terms of Political Discourse.* Princeton, New Jersey: Princeton University Press.

Friedman, Jonathan. 1990. "Globalization and Localization," in Jonathan Xavier Inda and Renato Rosaldo (eds), *The Anthropology of Globalization: A Reader,* pp. 233–246. Malden, MA: Blackwell Publishing.

Gallie, William B. 1964. *Philosophy and Historical Understanding.* London: Chatto and Windus.

Gellner, Ernest. 1992. *Postmodernism, Reason and Religion.* London: Routledge.

Giddens, Anthony. 1990. *The Consequences of Modernity.* Stanford: Stanford University Press.

Habermas, Jürgen. [1980] 1981. "Modernity versus Postmodernity," *New German Critique,* 22: 3–14.

Jameson, Frederic. 1984. "Foreword," in Jean-Francois Lyotard (ed.), in *The Postmodern Condition: A Report on Knowledge,* pp. vii–xxi. Manchester: Manchester University Press.

Keane, John. 1992. "The Modern Democratic Revolution: Reflections on Lyotard's *The Postmodern Condition,*" in Andrew Benjamin (ed.), *Judging Lyotard,* pp. 81–98. London: Routledge.

Latour, Bruno. 1991. "The Impact of Science Studies on Political Philosophy," *Science, Technology, Human Values,* 16: 3–19.

Lyotard, Jean-François. [1979] 1984. *The Postmodern Condition: A Report on Knowledge.* Manchester: Manchester University Press.

Mannheim, Karl. [1928] 1990. "Competition as a Cultural Phenomenon," in Volker Meja and Nico Stehr (eds), *Knowledge and Politics. The Sociology of Knowledge Dispute*, pp. 53–85. London and New York: Routledge and Kegan Paul.

Meja, Volker and Nico Stehr. 1992. "Social Scientific and Epistemological Discourse: The Problem of Relativism," in Diederick Raven, Lieteke van Vucht Tijssen, and Jan de Wolf (eds), *Cognitive Relativism and Social Science*, pp. 1–13. New Brunswick: Transaction Books.

Mongardini, Carlo. 1992. "The Ideology of Postmodernity," *Theory, Culture and Society*, 9: 55–65.

Parsons, Talcott. 1977. *The Evolutions of Societies*. Englewood Cliffs, NJ: Prentice-Hall.

Simmel, Georg. [1907] 1978. *The Philosophy of Money*. London: Routledge and Kegan Paul.

———. [1907] 1989. *Philosophie des Geldes*. Gesamtausgabe Volume 6. Frankfurt am Main: Suhrkamp.

Sorokin, Piritim. 1957. *Social and Cultural Dynamics*. New York: American Book Company.

Stehr, Nico. 1994. *Knowledge Societies*. London: SAGE Publications.

Turner, Bryan S. 1989. "From Postindustrial Society to Postmodern Politics: The Political Sociology of Daniel Bell," in John R. Gibbins (ed.), *Contemporary Political Culture: Politics in a Postmodern Age*, pp. 199–217. London: SAGE Publications.

Welsch, Wolfgang. 1987. *Unsere postmoderne Welt*. Weinheim: VCH Verlagsgesellschaft.

7

Sociology and Postmodern Risk

SAMIR DASGUPTA

I am not citing the discourse of postmodernism and critical thought in sociology. I am not interested to relate abstract discourse of postmodernism with the language game of poststructuralists. I am not going to write any critique on the issue of Marxism, Feminism, and postmodernism. I am in search of real and good sociology which is coming to an end. It is a fact that the postwar period of fantastic and robust technological giants that created a new shift in the arena of communication, interaction, information, and unreal (!) energy created a new language hegemony and discourse domination. Etzioni (1968) calls it normative values that guide technology and human beings. I think the postmodern discourse is a radical assault on good sociology. Lester Ward (1906) observes that the proportion of good and evil in life may be very sensibly affected by human action. He never heard anybody doubt that the evil may be thus increased, or diminished; and it would seem to follow that good must be similarly susceptible of addition or subtraction. And it is the knowledge which we borrow from Sociology that nobody professes to doubt that, so far forth as we possess a power of bettering things; it is our paramount duty to use it and to train all our intellect and energy to this supreme service of our kind.

Sociology is the study of human groups: their composition, organization, culture, and development. It combines scientific and humanistic perspectives and methods to explore a broad and relevant subject matter. The courses are diverse, but at the same time interrelated. Courses like social change, social stratification, family and kinship patterns, gender relations, urban and rural studies, crime, development, religion, social movements, health, ethnic relations, science and technology, and problems of development, environment, globalization, disaster studies applied sociology, and social problems and modernization are generally included in the mainstream sociology now.

Sociology is a valuable discipline for students who want to enter different professions and applied field and development-related arenas.

Whatever the career option, the study of sociology can help cultivate a critical responsiveness of society. Sociology has many faces and we feel the importance of using and applying our sociological knowledge for a brighter tomorrow. In short, sociologists study the many faces of society. Sociology around the world should encourage the study of many cultures and multinational studies along with the aspects of global sociological issues.

The dispute about the main purpose of sociology is whether it works to understand rhetoric discourse, or to cause human progress. In contemporary society there has emerged a radical movement among sociologists in various countries involving advocacy of complete commitment to action and practice on current social problems. Applications of sociology now appear to be spreading in a variety of directions, and here the possibilities of applied activities continue to spread.

Sociology: Importance of Social Reality

It is a good sign of the importance of sociology that it is both academic and applied. Some claim sociology as "a gauche newcomer" but accept its contribution. Nonsociologists sometimes "mock those who pursue it professionally" (Bruce, 1999). Most of the development policies to eradicate social problems mostly depend on sociological insights. Its theories and knowledge is based on the construction of the real society. Bruce (1999: 99) observes, "Sociology recognizes the socially constructed nature of reality; it identifies the hidden cause of action; it describes the unanticipated consequences of action." If the sociologists take up such issues, the attempt would be totally nonprofessional. The amateurism's view of sociological explanation is rhetoric and concerned with the world, but professional sociology serves the real purpose of the real world. If it is the discourse of the real world, then it has a humanistic perspective. Peter Berger (1963) views convincingly that sociology as a form of social consciousness includes skepticism about the official claims or common-sense interpretation of human behavior. Some argue that sociology has basic emphasis upon construction of sound and in-depth knowledge about society and social life. The wisdom of the ages thus signs the development of sociological theory and thinking. When this theoretical wisdom merges with empiricism, the route of sociology changes and divides. The debate of rhetoric versus reality, theory versus application, and knowledge sociology versus practicing sociology comes to the fore. Mills' (1961: 7–8) "Sociological Imagination" gives a new impetus to the theoreticians and practitioners. He argues,

> It is by means of the sociological imagination that men and women now hope to grasp what is going on in the world and to understand what is happening in themselves as minute points of the intersections of biography and history within society. In large part, contemporary means self-conscious view of himself as at least an outsider, if not a permanent stranger, rests upon an absorbed realization of social relativity and of the transformative power of history.

Mill's interpretation is very comprehensive, cogent, and philosophical; but, the disciplined and rational use of sociologist's perception or imagination (it is the reality!) is more important to know thyself. Society, as we know is not static one. It is always moving around the orbit of change, metamorphosis, transmission, and transformation. Crisis in one period might be the blessing in another period. Problems breed more problems. Social disorder might be perceived by a section of the sociologists as social order. Social disorganization is the prime part of social organization. And all these are difficult for the sociologist to experience, to understand, and to tackle with. Edward Shils (1961) points out that sociology has not succeeded in becoming a technological discipline. The sociological view that emerges in the course of the theoretical explanation is not sufficient enough to the technological explanation of sociology. Shils (1961) argues: "To be technological means to be manipulative. He observes, "Concrete empirical research of a descriptive sort can, of course, serve to make more exact and differentiated the knowledge…" (Wrong and Gracey, 1977: 623).

Sociological Imagination

Many theorists claim that rather than seeking some impossible objectivity, the sociologist required a "sociological imagination" that enables the understanding of "the large historical scene in terms of its meaning for the inner life and the external career of a variety of individuals. It enables him to take into account how individuals, in the welter of their daily experience, often become falsely conscious of their social position.... By such means the personal uneasiness of individuals is focused on explicit troubles and the indifference of publics is transformed into involvement with public issues" (C.Wright Mills, 1959: 5). Sociology must consistently remain committed to the impossible dream of seeking to find the ever contingent, but universally desired, social context of human freedom and equality, in the context of public debates over the pressing social issues of our time (Sydie, 2009).

But empirical *knowledge for sociology* is not the last word. "Because we live in an imperfect world, one that will always be imperfect and therefore always harbors injustice. *But we are far from helpless before this reality, we can make the world less unjust; we can make if more beautiful; we can increase our cognition of it*" (Wallerstein, 1977: 250). Sociologists' ideology put forward the idea of using sociology as a prime contributory discipline for a "more perfect world." From the enlightenment philosophers to the last theoretical sociologists, the importance of reasoning and truth mandates that the search for knowledge gets its proper due. Lyotard (1988: 312) notes that the new age would produce the "emancipation of humanity from poverty, ignorance, prejudice, and the absence of employment."

It is widely accepted that from Comte on, many sociologists "were confident in promising the truth about society" (Adams and Sydie, 2002: 266). In the words of Adams and Sydie (2002: 268), "Sociological theory is always an exciting but unfinished business as long as it encourages a fascination with and skepticism about the complexity and messiness of the social world, as well as about the efforts to clear up, order and control that messiness. It is an enterprise that, if it is true to its heritage, must be concerned with the promotion of ways and means to transform that world in order to offer dignity, health and security to all human beings." The theory-based applied tradition goes back to Jean-Jacques Rousseau in France who was very much in favor of applied motivation that can eradicate social illness and society's evils. So the chapter of use of sociology began with the conception of the discipline. The debate over theory and application is of course a very recent phenomenon, which I do feel compartmentalizes the unity, cohesiveness, and integrity of the approach of the discipline.

We may argue that sociology speaks the truth of the world society. "An important approach to sociological theory has been to examine the issues of order and integration in society, and to seek answers to questions such as what does it do?" Sometimes it is a positive program for "emancipatory practice" as in the words of Keynes, "Practical men, who believe themselves to be quite exempt from any intellectual influences, are usually the slaves of some defunct economist." Simplitistically speaking, sociological theory is concerned with space, time, and age.

The pure sociologists on the other hand encourage efforts to make use of knowledge in solving society's problems and developing social policies. They are very keen to come out from this shell of academic and intellectual snobbery. They may speak of how sociology can function in the community organization as being more important than how theory dominates over the academic world or how sociology may be used to investigate a variety of current social problems, domestic and international, and they present a panoramic view of sociology and its human uses in confronting the issues of the day (Gouldner and Miller, 1965). The blend of theory and practice with an open vision should indicate the task of what sociologists need to do for a better tomorrow. Social scientists might well make special pleas for sociology as broad-ranging, daring, adapting, and varying instruments for search, discovery, problem solving, model building, and social struggle" (Lee, 1976: 934). If the answer to the question of "Sociology for whom" is "Sociology for the service of humanity," then theory must be used as an application model or paradigm and it must give birth to newer theories which will be founded on knowledge, truth, reality, and social reconstruction. What good is it to strive after knowledge of reality if the knowledge we acquire cannot serve us in our lives (Durkheim, 1895[1938]: 85).

Sociologists' calling is to make a better world. Yet most sociologists today are afraid to openly profess sociology. But as the early sociologists knew, value relativism disappears once we ground the enterprise with human needs as our referent. They saw progress and human betterment as the goals of social science. They continue, "Our values are the human agenda. The purpose of our knowledge is to promote human well-being. The discourse of such a paradigm binds sociological knowledge with historicity—historicity with humanity and human values, virtues, truth and theoretical power, and the issues of social problems.

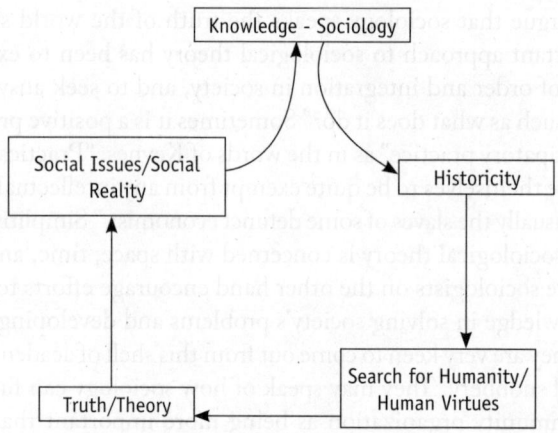

The major emphasis is mainly on the sociology of knowledge, human values and altruism, historicity of good sociology, truth behind theories, theory-practice dilemma, applied research methodology, importance of social analysis, issues relating to social reality like globalization and social policies, poverty, ethnicity and identity formation, issues relating immigration clinical research method and use sociology, population problems, and problems of sociology and anthropology in a developing world.

Good Sociology

Sociology, argues Bauman (1990) offers us a commentary—a refinement on the knowledge we possess and use in everyday life. It extends the social map beyond our personal experience so that we have a chance to understand areas of human activity, which we have had no chance to explore ourselves. There is the demand that sociology be practical. This idea is the basis of what scientific knowledge is supposedly about. Such knowledge permits us to predict how things will turn out. Sociology in this view is instrumentally useful.

The sociological writings provide numerous logical languages, strategies, and suggestions to be a "*do-gooder*" thinker, and urge us to develop knowledge sociology and practical sociology in order to service humanity and to abstain from the postmodern cliché of success.

Simmel was an active public intellectual being involved with feminist issues, workers rights, pedagogical reform, and poverty relief. Durkheim was equally engaged in the issues of the day, most especially in educational reform. Somewhat later the critical theorists of the so-called Frankfurt School maintained that the task for sociology was uncovering the "real" conditions underlying the "facts" and thus provide a blueprint for a future emancipated society (Horkheimer, 1947: 82). Critical theory claimed to overcome the "breach between theory and practice, ideas, and reality," and in this way remain "true to its Marxist heritage" as an emancipatory science (Adams and Sydie, 2001: 401).

As Saint-Simon (1814: 136) "the Golden Age of the human race is not behind us but before us; it lies in the perfection of the social order." But as Bauman (2000: 76) points out, order in the modern state is "not a 'given' but a task," and the modern state is concerned with "setting the rules, defining patterns and maintaining them, administration, management, surveillance and supervision; it is also about staving off or preventing all deviance from the pattern and all breaching of the rules, that is, everything haphazard, erratic, unanticipated and accidental." Sociological research has, in the past, contributed to the protection of the modern state from deviant, troubling challenges to social order (Sydie, 2009).

Another important concern of sociology is the issue of social and moral values. No one could deny the relevance of human values to the concept of development of sociology. It is by and for the people because the people are the start and end product of development. And sociology always deals with the value paradigm. If someone views techno-economic foundation as the only prime mover in sociological development process, he would not do justice. The development of any country identifies the development of collective personalities and self-identities. But postmodern circle created such an orbit where the faces of humanity merged with the rationality of irrationality. This is the root source of crisis of real and good sociology today.

The philosophy of social science facilitated by the triangular interaction or "transaction" between man, Communication and Institution or between *Person, value and Culture* (Radhakamal Mukerjee, 1960: 1). Of the triad, the crucial phase is values that, Mukerjee views, are not only "motivations, underlying the behaviour of Man in Society, but also heuristic principles that explains both individual behaviour in relation to the physical and the social world as well as an objective social relationship, behavior, institution and social system."

The basic notion of sociology is the emancipation of humanity from value crisis, anxiety, and dejection. Let us recall the note of Sorokin (1963: 3–11), which he quoted from Jesus' hymns:

The Sermon on the Mount and Beatitude forecast happiness for those without wealth or comfort on earth: "Blessed are the poor, the sorrowful, the week, the hungry, the merciful, the faithful, the peacemaker, and the pure of heart, for they all shall be comforted and rewarded. Overcome anger, conquest, love your enemies, do not lie or Judge others." Sorokin analyzes the social crisis and develops a blue print for social construction. He perceives human pain and suffering and its relationship to social structure. Altruism, a sense of sociology of humanity, according to Sorokin, is an integral part and system of philosophy of sociology.

The true altruism and social values mean, "do unto others what you would want others do unto you." The classical sociologists like Comte, Durkheim, and Ozinga feel the need for altruism as a prerequisite for a better tomorrow. "Doing good" is the inner motive of altruists. Sorokin's "amitology" signifies "the applied science or art of developing friendship, mutual aid and love in individual and intergroup relations". His interpretation of altruistic love is unique. The "Good neighbors," he means, "a quest for sympathy, understanding, and inconsequent – the desire to find a co-sympathizer in either despair or loneliness—is just as strong in human beings as the need for food or clothing."

Beginning of Postmodernism

Habermas, Jurgen (1969) argues that the project of modernity created in the 18th century by the philosophers of the Enlightenment consisted in their efforts to develop objective science, universal morality and law, and autonomous art according to their inner logic. At the same time, this project intended to release the cognitive potentials of each of these domains from their esoteric forms. The Enlightenment philosophers wanted to utilize this accumulation of specialized culture for the enrichment of everyday life—that is to say, for the rational organization of everyday social life. He also states that the postmodernists explore the beginnings, ambivalences, histories, subjects, fallacies, and contradictions of postmodernism. Sometimes postmodernity appears as a fashion of contemplation, which is apprehensive of orthodox impressions of truth, reason, identity and objectivity, of the thought of common progress or freeing, or single scaffolds, grand narratives, or ultimate grounds of elucidation. Against these enlightenment norms, it sees the world as contingent, ungrounded, varied, unbalanced, imprecise, a set of patchy cultures, or interpretations that breed a degree of cynicism about the objectivity of truth, history and norms, the givenness of natures, and the consistency of identities.

Values may only be devalued when one fails to comply with the modernization. Mind it, today always represents modernization with the values of that day, but yesterday, to some people, may be signified as values with *goodness*, and tomorrow will identify today as tradition. It means values are very much associated with the space and time. Globalization is not a new phenomenon that changes our culture and values. It has started with the emergence of colonialism. And sine then our culture and values began to change. F. Fanon (1967) writes, "One of the gravest consequences of the colonialization of Africa, Asia and Latin America has been the systematic destruction of the cultures and historic value systems of each people.... Ferocious exploitation, misery, famine, discrimination, inferiority complexes and the loss of personality and self respect are so many aspects of colonialism which induced a deep inhibition of cultures and knowledge."

Postmodern Shock

Ours world had witnessed two great wars which invited modernity on the one hand and slaps against human rights on the other. Now it may claim that modernization means a dehumanized enchanting world. Starting with the Jews to the hunting of Afghans and Iraqi people justifies that truth. The great bombing in Hiroshima and Nagasaki, the Japanese attack on Pearl Harbor, the Gulf war, the attack of Americans on Iraq and Afghanistan with bureaucratic and technologically enriched weapons and war machinery are the symbols of modernity. So it is undeniable that modernism began at the cost of human lives. During a single quarter century, for the first time in the world's history, imperialism unleashed two world wars. World War I claimed 20 million lives, more than all of the European wars for the three preceding centuries. During the 17th century, 3.3 million persons; during the 18th century, 5.4 million persons; and from 1901–1914, 5.7 million people died in wars on European territory (Dadayan, 1988). During World War II, which was waged on the territory of forty countries, 55 million people were killed and 35 million were severely injured of which 25 million remained physically handicapped for life. In the field of social science it may be argued that modernization has entered with a political power equation. Rise and fall of the superpowers, the trend of political domination, and economic superiority are the prime but hidden causes and effects of modernization. So it can be assumed that political modernization with the help of technological innovations and diffusions shape and remake world economy. But what is the contribution of modernity to the fund of human development? Is it a "species-threatening" phenomenon? Is the other name for modernization *inequalization?* The postmodern debate recently dominates over the intellectual arena. It mainly penetrates the cultural and aesthetic field and the focal theme of the debate is whether or not the tradition has closed its chapter. The postmodern specialty, rejecting the traditional social, cultural, moral, and aesthetic versions has now stepped into the world of new discourse and new rationality. In each and every era, this process unfolds similarly. But analysis of postmodernism mostly pinpoints the surface rather than the depth of concerns. But it is the reality that people in any age always like the previous one and they always call the previous age golden. Likely the people in the modern age following the instinctive paradigm of goodness of human quality favor traditional age and the postmodern men would like the previous one, i.e., modernity. Sociological theories therefore suffer from language vertigo. In society, polemics emerged over whether tradition in culture, economics, and polity was dead or what sort of modernization was succeeding. In case of metamorphosis from modernism to postmodernism, the same twist of rationality and communicative language happens. We are now on the crossroad of debate whether modernization has closed its chapter or emerged with new philosophy, new discourse, and new rationality. Sociologists are mostly confused with the concept of such metamorphosis. First of all we should know whether the metamorphosis happens only in the case of language, of thinking, or in the case of the reality of social living and moral values. Whether the realities of values are changing or not should be the prime concern of applied sociology. Practically, the time has come to examine the hidden nature of such value vertigo, which should be the focusing issue of today's seminar. If we back to our original roots, we could notice that sociology was very much concerned with the idea of progress, values, humanity, freedom, and peace.

Many people around the world fear that globalization brings the decay of social values. India is a multicultural, spiritually diverse country, now very much engaged in the global economy, culture, and technology, and a country where globalization is much more than a concept; it is the reality of our everyday lives. We are living in the era of profound social, economic, and cultural change. Rapid changes are taking place not only in the institutional settings but also in the mental frame of human beings. Achievement, aspiration, and motivation are shifting very promptly. Time has taken its place over space. Technology and knowledge dominate over humanity. All are suffering from a peculiar and unpredictable hyper-real vertigo. The philosophers call it postmodern shock.

Starting by the end of the 1960's and rapidly accelerating into the 21st century, technological, economical, political, and other forces have crafted a world in which this interdependence has reached an unprecedented level. In his 1999 Reith lectures, Anthony Giddens labelled this globalizing world a "runaway world." "We live," so he says, "in a world of transformations, affecting almost every aspect of what we do." It is my privilege to take note of a few cases in this Runway World. When the values change with the emergence of a new society and new culture the value-myth appears as a crisis. Globalization brings such a value crisis in our society. And this is the actual value crisis that emerges from postmodern vertigo. The social and political evolutions during this era of globalization, as I have said before, are giving rise to a moral disarray and cynicism, as can be heard in phrases and laments like "the end of modernity," "against ethics," "the closing down of humanism," "simulacra fashioned human existence," "moral aestheticism and relativism," and so on.

Another factor fuelling this moral perplexity of our age is the radicalization of the tension between, on the one hand, a much needed long-term vision for human aspirations and, on the other hand, the always threatening urgency and short-term applicability of policies. The moral perplexity of the era of globalization has rendered us, in the words of Jerome Bindé, a *"temporal myopia."*

What would be the future of ideal social and moral values? Will it be faded away by the imposition of postmodern cult? Will the traditional and modern culture be in conflict? Will the postmodern value-spell engulf our identity of humanity? Will it be human more than human? Will morality be a sin? I am afraid; we are going to be plunging into such a new dark age of hate, mistrust, intolerance, violence, greed and luster, family disaster, interaction-fragmentation, poverty, and global-local disorder. Modernists focus on variables such as capitalism, industrialism, surveillance capacity, and rise of military power (Giddens, 1990). All of these are faceless and represent only a shadow of human interaction. The postmodernists perceive the cultural logic as a metamorphosis of form into anti-form, purpose into play, design into chance, hierarchy into anarchy, presence into absence, genre into text, and root into rhizome or surface (Ihab Hassan, 1982). In the postmodern age, there is no linguistic normality, only "pastiche." In this context, it is important to note Baudrillard's (1970, 1980) comments. In his "Vanishing Point," he defines postmodernism as "the death of meaning, the death of reality, the death of the social and political and the death of sexuality" (cited in Dasgupta [2004]).

These are hyper-rational (Ritzer, 1996) or hyper-real expressions; that is, the "irrationality of rationality." The inclusion of mind, culture, civilization, reality, and the whole, on the one hand, and repression of body, nature, tradition, appearance, and the part, on the other, signifies the state of uncertainty that Ulrich Beck (1995) referred to as "risk society." Modern and postmodern cultures, each in their own way, thus reject the possibility of species consciousness. True altruism is excluded from the discourse of both because both attend to the surface of the road to the future, not to the underlying foundation of humanity on which the road is constructed. Thus, the obsession with our "body" and the denial of our "mind" render as deviant the very act of being human.

Using Sociology for good purposes reflects the renewed status in the practice of sociology at the present changed moment, for making a better world. It is difficult because postmodernism appears as a misnomer to the social scientists now, which only deals with abstract sociological components. It is doubtless to comment that mirroring other faces and using our mindset for a better world is the only key to real sociology which links with the truth and then merges with the reality which ultimately paves the path of social reconstruction and lights the spirit of altruism and humanity. Sociology should have "a floor and a ceiling ... and its ceiling remaining open to the sky." But the postmodern sociology melts into the air. Abstractism dominates over social reality, technological off world language appears to us as social and interactional replicant, root of love and passion which binds our traditional human identity becomes hallucinatory and mystical. Language vertigo swallows our sociological do goodness.

When people speak about postmodernism, the problem is that they are referring to something very fuzzy and slick. It is a new philosophy of virtual life—a new organizing code in thought, action, and reflection, connected to many changing factors in modern society. "The term postmodern was first applied, around 1971, to a new architectural style which combined old, classical forms with modern common sense and technical engineering. Since then, the postmodernists have used the term to elucidate their movement as a reaction to the varied crises of modernity—the betrayals of the modernist movement in different spheres of social process like industrialization, urbanization, centralization, and 'izations Postmodernism takes a step forward or beyond modernism and becomes something like trans-concept. In terms of social imagination it is a pseudo-project or half-finished project or postmodernism of nothing. Here lies the main concern of postmodern critique. Still sociology now enters into the arena of virtual society or in the mind of virtual people and describes an unreal and untrue lifestyle and defines human being as an animal perhaps live in the off world. As Mike Featherstone suggests, "postmodernism has to be understood against the background of a long-term process involving the growth of a consumer culture and expansion in the number of specialists and intermediaries engaged in the production and circulation of symbolic goals. It draws on tendencies in consumer culture which favour the aestheticisation of life, the assumption that the aesthetic life is ethically superior and that there is no human nature or true self; with the goal of life an endless pursuit of new experiences, values and vocabularies" (Featherstone, 1991: 126).

Oleg Kharkhordin views that social scientists are reluctant to grasp the fashionable labels and quickly changing cliches of the media-saturated world. They wait until the label is circulated for a considerable period of time so that they can recognize a serious social phenomenon to be studied, not a hype. Thus, postmodernism—uncared for through the 60s and 70s—has come to the front position in the 80s. The term "postmodernism," which appeared in the 60s as a characteristic of art and culture, has been integrated into mainstream social science through the work of some commentators on Habermas, who subsumed his French opponents in a debate on the fate of the Enlightenment (Derrida, Foucault, Lyotard) under the group name of "Postmoderns" (see also Bernstein, 1986).

The group was named after the title of the seminal work of Lyotard, who claimed that the breakdown of metanarratives of progress, which gave a coherent set of coordinates to ground different spheres of human activity, led to the disintegration of this coherent whole into a pluralism of language games, which can no longer be included in one general account. Derrida's work on the deconstruction of binary oppositions pervading Western philosophy and Foucault's genealogies of different human practices (which seem to have eschewed these oppositions) proposed new standards for philosophy and history (Lyotard, 1982. See also Norris, 1987; Dreyfus, 1982). Since then "postmodern thought" has sent ripples through all terrains of social inquiry.

Cultural studies and political science were fast to jump onto the postmodern bandwagon. Jameson's classic essay provided an interpretation of postmodernism as the dominant cultural logic of the third stage of capitalism together with an account of the characteristics of postmodernism: the depthlessness of the art product, the prevalence of the figural over the discursive, the waning of affect, and the abolition of the critical distance of an artist/theorist. This powerful intervention set the framework for a debate in cultural studies, which still rages (Jameson, 1988. See also Kaplan, 1988).

Sociology was the last to catch up. The two pieces of the jigsaw puzzle called "postmodernism" and "sociology" could not be made fit for a long time; but once a link was established, an avalanche of literature was produced at the turn of the 1990s. As usual, the last convert to a new faith was most eager to prove that it is the most fervent adherent: "postmodernity" and "postmodernization" were invented to accommodate postmodernism into sociological discourse (with their counterparts in the past as "modernity" and "modernization"). "Modernity" was most suitable for sociologists because it looked comfortably like "industrial society," although viewing this familiar society from a new vantage point of "postmodernity" gave the possibility of finding some previously unnoticed details.

Turner (1990) states in a rough generalization that "a sociology of postmodernism tends to locate postmodern culture in a context of disorganized capitalism, of consumer society and cultural mass production." This seems right, but to discriminate finer details it is more useful to employ the notion of three aspects of sociology of postmodernism as proposed by Featherstone (1988a: 205–7). Firstly, the analysis of changing activities of artists and intellectuals in postmodern culture.

The second direction of sociology of postmodernism comprises the analysis of changing relations between artists and intellectuals and the rest of society. How has the transmission and circulation of cultural goods changed? Featherstone proposes to study it in the terms of group interrelationships. The rise of the so-called "New cultural intermediaries" is central here. But the most prominent sphere of analysis, which is supposed to provide solid foundation for sociology of postmodernism is the "changes in everyday life of some groups, who may be using regimes of signification in different ways and developing new means of orientation and identity structures" (Dreyfus and Rabinow, 1982).

Thus, postmodernism is viewed as a godsend to salvage the bourgeoisie because it pacifies both its critics:

- It replaces realism and by means of that, de-centers working class identity, and
- it removes modernism as an ideology of the critical elite.

Postmodernists undermine the traditional Cartesian dualism that is ubiquitous to mainstream sociology. In sociology, which relies on a separation between subjective opinions and objective facts, the subject/object opposition provides grounds for establishing "true objective knowledge." But if subject/object opposition is suspended and a Cartesian mind/body dichotomy crumbles then Murphy can employ Merleau-Ponty's notions of knowledge, which have a fleshy texture, and of language as a connective tissue of reality. This means that language is not treated as the means to represent "real" events, but is given the status of an event itself. Language and reality are inseparable; and "... social life derives its meaning from speech acts. Rather than a conduit, language is a creative force" (Murphy, 1988: 603).

Postmodernism is "the ghost in the machine" of sociology which pervades its oppositions: it cannot be appropriated totally without destabilizing the regime, but it cannot be exorcised either—it inhabits sociological concepts thereby precluding a comfortable existence for arrogant sociologists.

When you will dissect and cross dissect the rhetoric body of globalization, something occurs in your mind. Is it just a buzzword or real? If it is real then what are the realities? In the era of globalization some virtual images stand before us as the perils that deface the concept of humanity. And perhaps so an expected trauma is waiting for our doomsday when the cloud of uncertainty, economic insecurity, and identity crisis will dominate over the sky of the world. Human species may be the replicants and will act like more human than human. The abstract identity of human existence will turn into simulacra-fashioned ecstasy. The impact of genetic engineering, a virtual innovation of postmodern science and technology introduces such a simulacrum that has overcome the boundary of time, space, and humanity. The dominance of information and communication technologies uproots the fetters of community feeling, family bondage and emotional interaction, and community closeness. It seems to dominate over real-life individuals. Alvin and Heidi Toffler's (2001) view after thirty years of Toffler's future prediction of society is more contextual. It is evident from the records that there are more than 3 million digital switches for every human being alive on the planet. There are nearly half a billion PCs over the world—one for every 13 human beings, if not more. The Internet and cell phone are spreading at high speed. In future these technologies will be more ultra modern. Is the hi-tech revolution virtual or real? Whatever it might be, it is certainly alarming for the comfortable growth of humanity, ethics, and human values, which they possess and nurture, with the process of socialization and upbringing. Another important and alarming consequence of globalization is biological revolution—a product of interdisciplinary knowledge like chemistry, medicines, genetics, and cloning that are related to the "bio-digital convergence." "Biochips, which are on the horizon, will give birth to bio-computers, bio-politics, bio-ethics, bio-wars, bio-investing, and bio-everything before long. Economies will be revolutionized and human history changed forever." It is the postmodernity—an expression of globalization that will reshape and remake our future world. The concept of postmodernism in sociology is a new entry. When people speak about postmodernism, the problem is that they are referring to something very vague and slippery. In the academic world, it is best understood as a new philosophy of virtual life—a new organizing code in thought, action, and reflection, connected to many changing factors in modern society. Lyon (2002: IX) states, "Postmodernism is a multi-layered concept that alerts us to a variety of major social and cultural changes taking place at the end of 20th century within many advanced societies." Rapid technological advance, involving communication networking and the cultural, political, and economic shifts all are implicated. A few days back an old rickshaw puller said, "Sir, have you seen Sparrow or Vulture very recently?" I was very careless of his saying and uttered in a very low and ignoring tone, "No." But something was happening in my mind and after a brief silence I asked, "You are right. The Sparrows, Vultures, and a good number of traditional birds are not quite visible either in our courtyard or on the branches of trees or on the roof of our houses; but why?" The illiterate old rickshaw puller replied very excitedly, "I am an illiterate man. But I do feel it is mainly because of the overuse of cell phones, its magnetic dimension and towers of accesses." Yes, the traditional poor fellow was hundred percent correct. The information technology removes the spatial distance, links time over space, and helps a lot to spread the vision of global capitalism; but, side by side, it has damaged not only the health and brains of the individuals, but also invited a world of future without insects, birds, and reptiles which always keep harmony with environmental equilibrium. This is perhaps the possibility of technological risk, which should remain outside the orbit of globalization, or it is itself the creation of globalization. This is the error of present-day globalization, which may give life to the volcano of globalization in future.

Smart (1993) argues that globalization is far less controversial than postmodernism. But I believe that globalization is the shadow of postmodernism that creates postcapitalism(?) Time-space compression and creation of hyper-real social, cultural, economic, and communication technologies invite a world of absence, of play of chance, of dispersal, of text and inter-text, anti-form and surface, and lastly of anarchy. (Ihab Hassan, 1982). Anyone observing us from outer space might experience a feeling of disgust and pity at the same time, concluding that the human race on a global scale has fallen victim to social and cultural insanity and economic inequality. This is very much true when we explain postmodernism and globalization. For example, communication technology performs a vital role in storing knowledge. The students nowadays do not demand or require classroom lessons or extensive written study materials or books and journals. Learning is no longer intertwined with the training minds with "*Gurus.*" Knowledge now can easily be borrowed and stored from the Websites. One who is economically weak can have little knowledge from free versions like the abstract or the outline of the knowledge content. But he who is economically capable or has Internet access can store the amount of knowledge he requires. He has to purchase it. Here two points are very important: knowledge selling and secondly, knowledge quantity. In future the storehouse of knowledge, I am afraid, will be computer with Websites facility. A few days back, I was in a Doctor's chamber for medical check-up. The nameplate was very interesting. It was written in the nameplate: "My endeavour is to Sign out pain and Sign in happiness in your life." I thought that the nature of language now begins to suffer from globalization disease and consequently postmodern vertigo. The language of "cure" and "recovery," which should be the right word, has been deconstructed and has gained technological code like *Sign out* and *Sign in* which is unknown to the illiterate, the economically depressed and disadvantaged masses. This sort of postmodernist or virtual *technological-language vertigo* in the third world countries will create a dilemma between local and global language and knowledge nomenclature, which may create an off world to the local people.

The concept of knowledge as the emancipation of soul or asylum of ideas and the taste of the last generation will be converted into knowledge-commodity. Not only that for the transmission and storage of information will no longer depend on human beings but on computers. Information will be produced and sold. Nations and State will fight for information and zip it around the world at the speed of electricity, and people will try to steal it. The role of the Nation will grow weaker. Taking the place of states, huge multinational corporations will take over the world. (Lyotard, 1984). If it were the ideal type postmodernism then the future society would be in great identity trouble. What was then Postmodernism? Ihab Habib (2001) explains it as: "What was postmodernism, and what is it still? I believe it is a revenant, the return of the irrepressible; every time we are rid of it, its ghost rises back. Like a ghost, it eludes definition. Certainly, I know less about postmodernism today than I did thirty years ago, when I began to write about it. This may be because postmodernism has changed, I have changed, and the world has changed." But it is undeniable that postmodernism cult began with the process of globalization and accordingly of capitalistic mechanism. Jameson (1991) argues that the ideological task of the concept remains that of coordinating new forms of practice and social and mental habits with the new forms of economic production and organization thrown up by the modification of capitalism. It is, in a word, the new face of capitalism and deface of local and communitarian epoch. Barbaric capitalism has created a surface-oriented deconstructed social and cultural language called postmodernism. It is best understood as the reflex of yet another mutation of capitalism. Jameson (1984) sees postmodernism as an intensification and latest phase of a capitalist world system where we witness the unrestricted growth of mul-tinational corporations as the offshoot of neoglobalization. Here the chance of fragmented language, art and culture, high degree of alienation and frustration, shadow of virtual imagination, and hal-lucination, consumerism, and technological repetitions is immense which may create a society of the absurd—may create a virtual image that will express majority's misery. Baudrillard (1968) argues that just as a young boy who is nurtured by wolves behaves like a wolf. Likely human beings in the era of postmodernism growing up in a world of objects become more object-like. He states, "Though postmodern society is based on the consumption of commodities—on buying and using things—this consumption can never make us happy." It was written in the Vedic Scripture: Truth is one—but the Sages call it by different names. Likely, we can say that capitalism is one, but the Masters call it by different names: Economic liberalization, reform and recovery, globalization, postmodernism neoglobalization, fair globalization, or civil society and good governance. Wallerstein argues, "*We move into the uncertain immediate future, and in moment of systemic anarchy such as the present, almost anything can happen.*"

Will the postmodern simulacra engulf our identity of humanity? Will it be human more than human? I don't know. We can only say we are in transition and the nightmare of alien future frightens us.

Social, political, and cultural theorists have been contributing to the emergence of postmodern theory in sociology from the 1960s, 1970s, and into the 1980s with the writings of philosophers. But it got its place in sociology with the development of simulacra-fashioned technology. Secondly, the emergence of globalization and development which many postmodernists claim that national boundary appears as a hindrance to human communication and propose internationalism and uniting separate countries. So sociology in the context of postmodern approach demands a new turn, a renewal. But it causes identity crisis of the content and context of the discipline. Here lies the debate and critique of postmodernism. I am afraid the relevance and identity of modern sociology may become the victim of clash between Sociological imagination and postmodern sociology. Postmodernists (they are mostly philosophers not sociologists in the sense of reality) therefore, perhaps ignoring or denying social reality and human existence, fabricated original and traditional versions of sociological insights and, under the shadow of technological innovation, created postmodern hyper-realism. Sociology deals with the mapping of individuals in society and society in individuals. It is the reality that such a "sociological imagination" gives birth to the concept and context of sociological practices and theory building that locates both the parts and the whole of the discipline. Moreover, from the very beginning of the discipline, efforts to make sense of the social world have been tied to a desire to find the tools necessary for creating a brighter tomorrow for better living. Social interaction, love, passion, hatred, and group solidarity cannot be interpreted as a hyper-real magical language of spell. Sociology is not merely a subject of language game—it is very much concerned with the presence of human beings. So society in men and men in society are the dual aspects of the same process. But sociology of postmodernism, a philosophical and abstract slogan of Western countries, makes sociology a deconstructive tradition, language, and anti-justificatory and anti-representational. It is always real, not hyper-real; it is the root of human voice, not the rhizome of human destiny; it is the continuity of human discourse, not the deconstruction of social and human language; it is the purpose of human welfare, not the language game; it is the centering, not the dispersal; it is the genre, not the inter-text; and, last but not least, it is very concerned with presence, not absence. So sociology has sought to find its place as a discipline linking theory and praxis, and it is the constructed discourse it has forged over time that should be the prime mover in keeping sociology relatively autonomous from any and all factions in society.

References

Adams, Bert, N. and R.A. Sydie. 2002. *Contemporary Sociological Theory*. London: SAGE Publications.

Adams, Bert, N. and Sydie, R.A. 2002. *Contemporary Sociological Theory*. California, London, New Delhi: Pine Forge Press.

Alvin and Heidi Toffler.1993. *War and Anti War*. London: Little Brown & Company.

Baudrillard. Jean. 1998. The *Consumer Society: Myths and Structures*. USA: SAGE. Originally published in 1970 by Paris, Éditions Denoël.

Bauman, Z. 1987. *Legislators and Interpreters*. Cambridge: Polity Press.

———. 1988a. "Sociology and Postmodernity," *The Sociological Review*, 6: 4.

———. 1988b. "Is There a Postmodern Sociology?" *Theory, Culture and Society*: 2–3.

———. 1989. "Modernity and the Holocaust," *Ithaca*. New York: Cornell University Press.

———. 1990. "Philosophical Affinities of Postmodern Sociology," *The Sociological Review*, 38: 3.

———. 1992. *Intimations of Postmodernity*. Cambridge: MIT Press.

———. 2000. *Liquid Modernity*. Oxford, UK: Polity Press.

Beck, Ulrich. 1992. *Risk Society*. London: SAGE Publications.

Benedict, James, trans. 1996.*The System of Objects*. London and New York: Verso.

Berger, Peter L. 1963. *Invitation to Sociology*. England: Penguin Books.

Berger, Peter L. and Brigitte Berger. 1972. *Sociology—A Biographical Approach*. New York: Basic Books.

Bernstein, R.J. (ed.). 1985. *Habermas and Modernity*. Cambridge: Polity Press.

Best, Steven and Douglas Kellner. 1991. *Postmodern Theory*. London: The Macmillan Press Limited.

Brown, R.H. 1983. "Theories of Rhetoric and the Rhetorics of Theory," *Social Research*, 50(1, Spring).

Bruce, Steve. 1999. *Sociology—A Very Short Introduction*. Oxford: Oxford University Press.

Comte, Auguste. 1855. *The Positive Philosophy*. Ed. H. Martinue. New York: Blanchard.

Cooley, Charles Horton. "Now and Then," in *Sociological Theory and Social Research: Being Selected Papers of Charles Horton Cooley*, pp 283–285. Also published in *Journal of Applied Sociology*, 8(1924): 259–262.

Dadayan, V. 1988. *The orbits of the Global Economy*. Moscow: Progress Publication.

Dallmayr, F.R. 1981. *Twilight of Subjectivity. Contributions to a Post-Individualist Theory of Politics*. Amherst: University of Massachusetts Press.

Dasgupta, S. 2004. *The Changing Face of Globalization*. New Delhi: SAGE.

D'Amico, R. 1986. Going Relativist. *Telos*, 67.

De Certeau, M. 1982. "Micro-techniques and Panoptic Discourse: A Quid Pro Quo," in *Foucault and Critical Theory: The Uses of Discourse Analysis*, 5:3–4.

Derrida, J. 1978. *Edmund Husserl's Origin of Geometry: An Introduction*. New York: Stony Brook.

———. 1981. *Positions*. London: Athlone Press.

Dews, P. (ed.). 1986. *Autonomy and Solidarity: Interviews with J. Habermas*. London: Verso.

———. 1987. *Logics of Disintegration: Poststructuralist Thought and the Claims of Critical Theory*. London: Verso.

———. (1987) *Post-Structuralist Thought and the Claims of Critical Theory*. London: Verso.

Dreyfus, H. and P. Rabinow. 1982. *Michel Foucault: Beyond Structuralism and Hermeneutics*. Berkeley: University of California Press.

Durkheim, Emile. 1933. *The Division of Labour in society*. New York: Glencoe III. The Free Press.

———.1950. *The Rules of Sociological Method*. NY : The Free Press.

Edward, Shils.1961. *Readings in Introductory Sociology*, cited in Wrong and Gracey. New York: Free Macmillan Press.

———. 1895[1938]. *The Rules of Sociological Method*. Ed. George E.G. Catlin. New York: The Free Press.

Etzioni, Amitai.1968.*The Active Society: A Theory of Societal and Political Processes*. New York: Free Press.

Fanon, F. 1967. *The Wretched of the Earth*. Trans. Constance Farrington. Harmondsworth: Penguin.

Featherstone, M. 1988a. "In Pursuit of the Postmodern: an Introduction," *Theory, Culture and Society*, 5 (June): 2–3.

———.1991. *Consumer Culture and Postmodernism*. London: SAGE Publications.

———. 1988b. "Towards a Sociology of Postmodern Culture," in H. Haferkamp (ed.). *Social Structures and Culture*. Berlin: de Gruyter.

Giddens, A. 1987. *Social Theory and Modern Sociology*. Cambridge: Polity Press.

———. 1990. *The Consequences of Modernity*. Cambridge: Polity Press.

———. 1992. *Sociology*. Cambridge: Polity Press.

Gouldner, Alvin, W. 1965. "Explorations in Applied Social Science," in Alvin W.

Gouldner, Alvin, W. and S. M. Miller (eds). 1965. *Applied Sociology: Opportunities and Problems*. New York: The Free Press. Available online at http://lucy.ukc.ac.uk/csacpub/russian/oleg.html (accessed on December 18, 2013).

Habermas, Jurgen.1969. "Modernity—an Incomplete Project," in Hal Foster (ed.) *The Anti-Aesthetic: Essays on Postmodern Culture*. Seattle: Bay Press.

———. 1980. "Modernity: An Incomplete Project," in P. Brooker (ed.), *Modernism/Postmodernism*, pp. 127. Harlow: Longman, 1996.

Haferkamp (ed.). 1989. *Social Structures and Culture*. Berlin and New York : de Gruyter.

Hassan, Ihab. 1982. *The Dismemberment of Orpheus: Toward a Postmodern Literature*. New York: Oxford University Press.

———. 2001. "From Postmodernism to Postmodernity: The local/global Context," *Philosophy and Literature*, 25(1): 1–13.

Horkheimer, Max.1947. *Eclipse of Reason*, London: Continuum Press.

Jameson, F. 1984. "Postmodernism, or the Cultural Logic of Late Capitalism," *New Left Review*, 146.

———.1991. *Postmodernism: The Cultural Logic of Late Capitalism*. Durham, NC: Duke University Press.

Johnston, Barry, V. 1998 (eds). *Pitirim Sorokin—on the Practice of Sociology*. Chicago: The University of Chicago Press.

Kaplan, E.A. (ed.). 1988 *Postmodernism and Its Discontents: Theories, Practices*. London: Verso.

Lee, Alfred McLhung. 1976. "Sociology for Whom?" *American Sociological Review* (USA) 41(6, December).

Lyon, David. 2002. *Post Modernity* (South Asian edition). New Delhi: Viva Books Private Limited.

Lyotard, J.F. 1984. *Habermas and Modernity*. Cambridge: Polity Press.

———. 1988. *The Differend. Phrases in Dispute*. Minneapolis: University of Minnesota Press.

Miller, S.M. 1965. "Prospects: The Applied Sociology of the Center-city," in Alvin W. Gouldner and S.M. Miller (eds.), *Applied Sociology: Opportunities and Problems*. New York: The Free Press.

Mills, C. Wright. 1959. *The Sociological Imagination*. London: Oxford University Press.

Mukherjee, Ramkrishna. 1973. "Indian Sociology; Historical Development and Present Problems," *Sociological Bulletin* (New Delhi) 21(1).

Murphy, J.W. 1988. "Making Sense of Postmodern Sociology," *The British Journal of Sociology*, 9: 4.

Norris, C. 1987. *Derrida*. New York: Pantheon.

Pieterse, Jan Nederveen. 2001. *Development Theory*. New Delhi, India: Vistaar Publications.

Powell, Jim. 1998. *Postmodernism for Beginners*. Hyderabad, India: Orient Longman.

Ritzer, George. 1996. *Modern Sociological Theory*. New York: McGraw Hill.

Smart, Barry. 1993. *Post Modernity*. London: Routledge.

Sorokin, Pitirim, 1941. *The Crisis of Our Age*. New York: E.P. Sutton.

———. 1929. "Some Contrasts between European and American Sociology," in Barry V. Johnshon (ed.), *Pitirim Sorokin: On The Practice of Sociology*. Chicago: The University of Chicago Press.

———. 1937. *Social and Cultural Dynamics* (3 vols). New York: American Book Company.

———.1963. *Long Journey: The Autobiography of Pitirim A. Sorokin*. London: Rowman & Littlefield.

Spencer, Herbert. 1857. "Progress," *Westminister Review*, LVII (N.S. Vol. XI) April.

Sydie, R.S. 2009. *Theoretical Applications in Discourse on Applied Sociology-Theoretical Perspective*. Ed. Samir Dasgupta and Robyn Driskell. London: Anthem Publishers.

Turner, B.S. 1990. "Periodisation and Politics in the Postmodern," in B.S. Turner (ed.), *Theories of Modernity and Postmodernity*. London: SAGE.

Wallerstein, Immanuel. 1977. "Wall Erstein's World Capitalist System: A Theoretical and Historical Critique," *American Journal of Sociology*, 82(5): 250.

———. 1998. *The Heritage of Sociology, The Promise of Social Science*. Available online at http://www2.binghamton.edu/fbc/archive/iwpradfp.htm (accessed on December 18, 2013).

Ward, Lester. 1906. *Applied Sociology*. Boston M.A.: Ginn.

Weber, Max. 1947. *Theory of Economic and Social Organization*. New York: Oxford University Press.

———. 1973 [1917]. "The Meaning of Ethical Neutrality in Sociology and Economics," in Edward Shils (ed.), *Max Weber on Universities*, pp. 47–54. Chicago: University of Chicago Press.

Weinstein, Jay. 2001. Available online at: file://A:\01 weinstein_revised.html

———. 2002. "The Place of Theory in Applied Sociology: A Reflection," in *Theory & Science*, U.S.A.

Wright C. Mill. 1959. *The Sociological Imagination*. New York: Oxford University Press.

Wrong, Dennis Hume and Harry L. Gracey. 1977. *Readings in Introductory Sociology*. N.Y: Free Macmillan Press.

8

Postmodernism and Sociology

Can Solidarity Be a Substitute for Objectivity?*

MURRAY MILNER, JR.

The Rise of Skepticism

Sociologists' understanding of what they are about has varied and vacillated considerably during the last half of the 20th century. Some have seen relatively little difference between sociology and the natural sciences—other than the specific subject matter they study (Black, 1976, 1993; Gibbs, 1972; Homans, 1967; Lundberg, 1975). According to this view we should apply the "scientific method" to social behavior, and seek to identify "laws," which are to be incorporated in broader theories. This would supposedly enable us to predict and explain social behavior the way that the natural sciences do for other empirical phenomena.

Interpretation, Hermeneutics, and Structuralism

There have long been members of the profession—not to speak of nonsociologists—who stressed that there were fundamental differences between the social sciences and the natural sciences (Furfey, 1953; MacIver, 1973; Winch, 1970).[1] The possibility of law-like positivistic knowledge of social behavior was called into question or significantly

---

* This is a revision of a paper first presented as a public lecture for the Postmodernity Project at the University of Virginia in 1999.

[1] In most respects Furfey was a positivist who closely identifies social sciences with the natural sciences, with the qualification that the experimental method is much more problematic. Where he differed from many of his contemporaries was

qualified. The goal of interpreting social and cultural patterns, that is, showing the logic of the relationship of social patterns, what these mean to people, and how such meaning shapes their interactions, was proposed as an alternative (Dilthey, 1976; Weber, 1949, 1968: 4–22; Blumer, 1969; Wuthnow, 1987). Some anthropologists such as Geertz (1983) have asserted that in important respects there is only "local knowledge"—knowledge rooted in the historical experience of a particular community— just as there are only specific languages. Hence, the task of the social analyst is analogous to the translator who makes the meaning of a foreign text available to those of his own community. The goal is interpretation not explanation and this requires "thick descriptions" not abstract theories.

Sometimes this process involves treating social patterns as if they were analogous to written texts; the analytical project is to offer a credible interpretation similar to those offered by literary critics (Ricoeur, 1981, Chap. 8; Brown, 1987). Initially such efforts were modeled after the hermeneutical methods that were developed for interpretation of texts (Schleiermacher, 1986; Heidegger, 1962: 31 2, I.5; Gadamer, 1992).[2] This involved the use of the "hermeneutic circle": that is, the meaning of any given word or phrase was derived largely from the context of the whole document, while the meaning of the text as a whole was derived from the related meanings of its various elements. The initial intent of hermeneutics was to determine the meaning of a text in its own historical context and hence it was, in part, concerned with what the author had intended to communicate.

Closely related, but distinct in its origins from hermeneutical perspectives, was structuralism. What it shared with hermeneutics was an insistence that meaning emerged primarily from the relationship between the elements of a symbolic system. In contrast to hermeneutics, however, structuralism downplayed the intended and explic-

---

that he insisted that sociology could not and should not be value-free in the same sense that was relevant to the natural sciences.

McIver defended the common sense notion of causation, but argued that the causal processes in the natural and the social sciences differed because social processes were mediated by psychological process, which meant that causation had to be thought of in different ways.

[2] Of course these writings on hermeneutics are concerned with much broader issues than methods in the social sciences. Gadamer is especially clear that the techniques for interpreting text are not his primary concern.

itly communicated meaning and focused on latent and unintended deep structures. The approach was first systematically articulated in Saussure's structural linguistics (1966), which focused, not on individual people speaking, but on the structure of a language as a whole. Structuralism, more broadly conceived, emphasized that all meaning systems tended to have structures comparable to those found in languages. Levi-Strauss made this approach famous by first applying it to kinship systems (1969) and later to the analysis of myths of premodern societies (1975). Barthes (1968) and others (e.g., Guiraud, 1975) developed semiology by extending this perspective to the analysis of sign systems in general, including fashions, food and dining, manners, street signs, and advertisements as well as literature. Althusser (1969 [1965]) combined structuralism with Marxism as a mode of analyzing capitalism; not only do structural factors shape the future, but the individual's consciousness is simply a reflection of the dominant ideology. All of these approaches tended to emphasize the determinative effect of latent structures and to downplay or ignore the role of individual actors. The acting subject was increasingly "de-centered."

Poststructuralism

To oversimplify things considerably: hermeneutics was primarily interested in intended meaning embodied in texts; structuralism was primarily interested in unintended meaning embodied in any system of signs. Both, however, tended to assume that there were a limited number of legitimate interpretations of a text or meaning system. If the first focused on the author (and his/her immediate context) and the second focused on the text itself, it is not surprising that before long a perspective would emerge that focused on the reader or interpreter.

According to this third perspective, any attempt to seek the true meaning of a text, whether that intended by the author or that latent in the text, is seen as an elusive goal. More generally, the very process of mutual understanding is seen as much more problematic than is usually assumed. Texts no longer have one or even a few meanings, but they have a virtually unlimited number of possible meanings and interpretations. This is not just a matter of different people seeing different things—though that, of course, happens. In addition the very process of creating meaning involves the privileging of some notions over against others. Moreover, since all meaning comes from metaphor, even the elements that are privileged contain ambiguities that must be papered over. Therefore, the construction of symbolic order involves the creation of latent disorder, that is, the disorder of repressed meanings that stand in contradiction to what is privileged. The apparent common sense meaning in any given historic context is partial and contingent. Just as apparent order was created by social construction, the superficiality of this order can be shown through "deconstruction."

Any text reveals ambiguities and inconsistency rooted in the privileging of one term over against its alternatives. That is to say, the very creation of a text implicitly creates one or more "subtexts." The more general result is to make some human possibilities seem obvious and foreclose others. What is required, according to Derrida (1976, 1978), is a "close-reading" which puts the key terms "under erasure." These key terms are treated as unavoidable, but problematic. Such close readings demonstrate the metaphorical nature of all meaning, the figurative nature of all knowledge, and that all texts have "subtexts." Identifying the key terms that must be put under erasure is accomplished in part by the same method used by structuralism, that is, the meaning of any term derives from its difference from other terms. But in contrast to structuralism, which still sees the link between the signified and the signifier as central, post structuralism demotes or rejects the significance of this link (Baudrillard, 1988: Chap. 3). Since all meaning is metaphorical, this means that it is created by an endless linking of such metaphors. Hence, meaning is created not only by the difference between terms, but also by deferring any attempt to finalize meaning.

This is the significance of Derrida's play on the French words *différence*, to differ, and *différance*, to defer or put off. These terms are pronounced the same, but have separate meanings. Derrida's point is that the creation of meaning unavoidably involves both, that is, creating differences, but differences whose final meaning is always deferred. (There are some similarities here with the notion of indexicality used by ethnomethodologists.) Final meaning is deferred, in part, because the next reader may rely on new and different metaphors to interpret the same text. There is yet another twist in the story of creating meaning: the processes of close reading and deconstruction are themselves historic social constructions; and so deconstruction is never complete or final, but, like all human efforts, temporary and contingent.

These ideas, along with a number of related developments in literary theory came to be known as poststructuralism. It tended to reject not only the authority of the author or the structure of the texts, but it called into question the relevance of authority itself—at least in determining meaning. It rejected the notion that any given reading or interpretation was authoritative. Hence, the process of interpretation ceased to be a technical or subsidiary intellectual activity; rather, it was an act of creation. The distinction between authors and interpreters became increasingly irrelevant. Moreover, since all knowledge and communication was mediated by language, human experience was conceptualized, at least figuratively—and all meaning is ultimately figurative and metaphorical—as a vast set of texts. Hence, all texts were seen to be about other texts. Abstract generalizations are either misleading or irrelevant. The most we can hope to do is compare and contrast particular texts. The goal is neither truth, nor even interpretation per se, for that would imply that there was some fixed meaning that had to be accurately discovered and communicated. Rather, playfulness, suggestiveness, stimulation, and originality are the goals.

Closely related to this notion of the problematic and contextual nature of meaning is skepticism about human identity. Not only does the author's intended meaning have no privileged status, but the identity of the author is enigmatic. In addition to consciousness being problematic, as Freud taught us, there is no taken-for-granted acting subject with a self-evident identity. The ego is demoted in the Freudian trinity and the id, usually re-conceptualized as "desire," becomes a central focus of psychoanalysis (Lacan, 1977). The identity of individual actors is seen as multiple and time bound; so, like all meanings, the subject is de-centered and deconstructed. Moreover, not only social order, but language, meaning, and human identity all necessarily involve the repression of alternative possibilities. Hence, free association of ideas and symbols becomes not only a technique of psychoanalysis used for therapeutic purposes, but also a more general mode of expression. This is true not only in art and literature, but in the healthy life itself, which is characterized not so much by logical consistency, but by symbolic playfulness (Barratt, 1993).

Foucault (1973b) develops a poststructuralist perspective for the "human sciences." According to Foucault, the supposed continuities of history are the result of making the rational subject of bourgeois individualism the fundamental assumption of analysis. Such an integrated subject requires that the present be logically connected to the past and the future. If this were not the case, who we are today would have no connection with who we were yesterday or will be tomorrow (Foucault,

1972). The assumption of such connections usually leads to positing some notion of "underlying" structures—an assumption characteristic of structuralism in general and Marxism in particular. It is in at least these two ways that Foucault wishes to be "poststructuralist." Abandoning the notions of the integrated subject and structured history allows us to see that it is fragmentation and discontinuities, rather than continuities, which should be the focus of analysis. Just as texts require a close reading to discern subtexts, history requires not causal analysis, but, following Nietzsche (1956), a genealogy of the past that pays attention to language. This is a kind of close reading of history that focuses on the neglected, the deviant, even the bizarre, for example, madness, sickness, crime, and sexuality, which are, of course, some of the preoccupations of Foucault (e.g., 1973a, 1979). These are the aspects of human life, which traditional history has ignored or even covered up in the process of constructing what is supposedly knowledge. Hence, what is required, according to Foucault, is an "archeology of knowledge"—the title of one of his key methodological books (1972). When such a method is used the Enlightenment story of superstition being replaced by rationality must be reconsidered. Instead of rational knowledge transforming force and prejudice into legitimate authority, blatant forms of power are replaced by more subtle forms of control rooted in knowledge. Hence the sick, the insane, and criminals are not simply shunned, restrained, or punished; they are treated and disciplined. But this requires new institutions of social control: the asylum, the modern reformatory prison, and the clinic. Instead of power being transformed by knowledge, the construction of knowledge becomes the primary means of power; or conversely, power produces its own knowledge. In the modern world the two become indistinguishable, that is, they become "power/knowledge" (Foucault, 1980).

Postmodernism

While there is no clear line between poststructuralism and postmodernism, an important strand of the latter is a critique of modernism in architecture, the arts and literature, rather than an argument about social theory per se. If modernism in art and architecture tended to emphasize the functional, the abstract, and the elegant, postmodernism is more eclectic and playful, mixing and counterpoising different styles. Modernism's abstractness and universalism—for example, the "international style" of steel and glass in architecture—is seen as an orthodoxy which must be made fun of by, among other means, eclecticism. For example, a massive pseudo neoclassical facade is placed on the front of a steel and glass skyscraper. Before long, these themes from the arts and art history (e.g., Jencks, 1986) are articulated by philosophers and theorists.

Just as artists attack the abstractness of modernism, Lyotard (1984), and others attack modernity's "grand narratives" and general theories of history, and more specifically Marxism and structuralism. There is an emphasis on the importance of the new technologies of communication and information as now the main force of production. Moreover, consumption, with its mind-numbing advertising, rather than production is increasingly seen as the core, societal shaping activity (Baudrillard, 1988). The enormous multiplication of information and databases involves a change in the very nature of knowledge. There is a use of Wittgenstein's (1968) notion of the lack of commensurability of different language games as a critique of universal or transcendent philosophical categories and epistemological realism. This provides a philosophical basis for pluralism.

The critique has been broadened and some reject the key project of the Enlightenment: the use of reason to develop systematic, universally valid knowledge. A postmodern age has been proclaimed in which the historical relativity and contingency of even our most rational and objective processes are emphasized. Not only the interpretation of literary texts and the findings of science, but any claim to transcendent categories, universalism, objectivity, or nonpartisanship must be demystified. The concept of irony is used to express this critical attitude toward all understandings, especially ultimate values—or more accurately (following the "linguistic turn"), what Rorty would call "final vocabularies" (Rorty, 1989: 73–95). All human knowledge and values are to be placed under what Ricoeur called the "hermeneutic of suspicion" (1981: 6–7, 34).

Structural and Political Sources of Skepticism

There are, of course, important nonacademic and extraintellectual sources of poststructuralism and postmodernism. These same factors are also important sources of the skepticism about objectivity and universalism. The end of formal political colonialism combined with a more integrated global economy, the feminist movement, and the increasing resistance of various minorities to discrimination and domination all have contributed to a questioning of the traditional categories of Western culture—which for the most part were created and sustained by Western white males (Said, 1979, 1994; Dirks, Eley, and Ortner, 1994). More specifically, some interpreters of poststructuralism and postmodernism see this questioning as arising directly from the rebellions of the late 1960s and especially the Paris uprising of 1968 (e.g., Lemert, 1992:29; Sarup, 1993). Hence politics has been at the core of these perspectives. A central concern of these politics has been to give voice to groups that had been marginalized in various ways. Often this took the form of a greater appreciation—and sometimes glorification—of cultural pluralism. Conversely, it led to criticism, and often rejection of notions of cultural and social assimilation. Ironically, this ideological appreciation of pluralism occurred at roughly the same time when the difficulties of maintaining social solidarity and peace in pluralistic societies was being made all too evident in places like Yugoslavia, Rwanda, East Timor, Sri Lanka, Lebanon, Palestine-Israel, the U.S.S.R., and even Czechoslovakia. On the intellectual level the concern to demote colonial and Euro-centric views of the world has been associated with criticisms of the traditional academic canon and calls for various kinds of multiculturalism.

At the end of the 20th century such skepticism was not restricted to those who had been excluded. It was also rooted in a reaction against the main structure of modernity that supposedly was intended to assist those who were marginal: the democratic welfare state. Those of relative privilege are resistant not only to being taxed to provide for the less fortunate, but also to the massive bureaucracies that are the core structure of the modern state. Not surprisingly, one reaction has been to revive and reinforce the centrality of the market and the ideologies associated with it. Market capitalism has become even more dominant as a mode of production throughout the world. The North American Free Trade Agreement (NAFTA), The World Trade Organization (WTO), the economic and political transformation of former Communist countries, and the adoption of market mechanisms in the last sizeable Communist society, China, are only the most obvious examples of the hegemony of the market and a de facto commitment to allowing the process of the market to play the central role in allocating human resources.

So ironically the praise of pluralism and decentralized power comes both from groups that have been marginalized, and from those who see their privileges threatened by more extensive demands for universalism—though the specific content each gives to pluralism is quite different. There is a double irony. The social constituencies that were once highly resistant to universalism—when it meant equal rights for women and minorities—now become the defenders of this notion as a way of criticizing "affirmative action," i.e., compensatory programs for social categories that have suffered past discrimination. Conversely, disadvantaged groups who initially demanded universalism, often now perceive it as a mechanism for perpetuating historic patterns of inequality.

The skepticism is not limited, however, to the state's efforts to help the disadvantaged and increase egalitarianism. There is, at least in the United States, increasing cynicism about the core structures of the democratic state: the ability of the legislative branch to reach acceptable compromises and avoid stalemate, the ability of the executive to effectively implement programs and policies, and the ability of the judiciary to justly resolve disputes and punish criminals. The leaders of the first two branches of government, politicians, are looked at with suspicion, if not outright contempt. They are assumed to be pursuing their own interests or the special interests of those who give them campaign funds, rather than some notion of the general interest. The leaders of the third branch, members of the legal profession, are also held in low esteem.[3]

But the public's cynicism is not restricted to government activities. Polls show that there is also less public confidence in business. This has almost certainly been accentuated by "downsizing," the replacement of regular employees with temporary workers who receive no retirement or health care benefits, and the supplanting of well-paying manufacturing jobs with low-paying service jobs, and various financial crises. Corporate accounting scandals in which billions of dollars were wasted or appropriated by corporate officers further eroded confidence

---

[3] In the United States, skepticism toward the judicial system was accentuated by the O.J. Simpson case. The difference in blacks' and whites' attitudes about the case illustrates the dramatically different ways those of different social background interpret and understand "the facts." It has further been eroded by the tendency to use narrow ideological considerations in the selection of judges.

in corporations. When these are accompanied by increasing polarization in the distribution of income and wealth it is little wonder that many in the middle and working classes are not only skeptical about big government, but also about big business and the justice and objectivity attributed to the market.

In short, paralleling the skepticism that has emerged among intellectuals concerning the possibility of developing objective truth is skepticism about the ability of democratic political institutions and capitalist markets to create a just social order. Of course, there is no clear separation of the intellectual and the economic-cum-political processes that I have discussed. In fact a central theme of postmodernism is the inseparability of intellectual life and politics. Hence, we should expect this to be the case not only for societal politics, but also for academic politics.

It is not accidental that university literature departments most enthusiastically embraced the rejection of objectivity and the move toward relativism. One aspect of this is the delegitmation of the narrator or the voice of the author and the reliance on the voices of the fictional characters to tell a story. The assertion that there can only be concrete multiple stories is the literary version of the rejection of abstraction, generalization, and transcendence.

It is literature departments that were most disadvantaged in an academia dominated by science. The social sciences, including history, may have been viewed as at best poor relations and often as pretenders, but they could at least claim to share science's search for objectivity and systematic knowledge. This avenue was largely closed to those who traditionally had evaluated and criticized literature and the arts. (There have been important technical developments in the study of texts, but these developments were often seen as secondary or even antithetical to the primary task of criticism.) While there have been theories of aesthetics that claimed to have a rational bases, few, if any, ever claimed that there were objective external criteria that could determine the relative value of literary and artistic work. Rather, it was a matter of taste and sensitivity. Moreover, rhetorical skills had always played an important part in these disciplines. Therefore, it is not surprising that it is they that were most open to attempts to radically question objectivity and to embrace pluralism and postmodernism. This included the less traditional members in these rather traditional disciplines developing a new, interdisciplinary perspective known as cultural studies. This perspective concentrated on showing the way that culture and ideas had been used as means of domination, especially of women and minorities.

This "elective affinity" (Weber, 1968) between literature departments and postmodernism is not, of course, proof that the arguments for postmodernism are false or that its supporters are only pursuing their academic self interest. It simply suggests that intellectual insights are influenced by social factors, and that this is true even of critical perspectives that claim to demystify the vested interest of past perspectives. Supposedly, this is an insight no postmodernist would deny in abstract. It is not, however, a point that they have tended to emphasize in their narratives about postmodernism.

Method, Objectivity, and Rationality

It is hardly surprising that the field that most embraced postmodernism, literary criticism, would provide the models for an intellectual methodology appropriate to a postmodern age. Hence, both philosophy (Rorty, 1989, 73–95, 1991: 78–92) and social science (Brown, 1987; Lemert, 1992; Seidman, 1991, 1994) are seen as closer to literary criticism than to mathematics or the natural sciences. The methodology is that of comparing texts and contrasting particular historical forms of life—rather than creating theorems of a universal logic or general theories that supposedly "represent" an external reality.

For theories to be powerful and useful it is necessary to be able to choose between alternative theoretical explanations. This usually assumes a more systematic form of comparison that takes the form of "testing" theories against "data." This, in turn, assumes the possibility of some type of objectivity. But the claim of objectivity is precisely what postmodernists are suspicious of. Or at the very least they reject the notion that there are external criteria such as "empirical reality" that can produce objectivity. More generally postmodernists deny that theories of knowledge or epistemologies (based on various kinds of foundational assumptions or theories of coherence) can resolve disputes; stated another way they cannot coerce a consensus by specifying what is objective knowledge and what is not. The attempts to rely on epistemologies to define truth and produce objectivity are seen as yet another misguided attempt to transcend historical experience and the limits of language.

The resort to epistemologies is seen as a way of disguising the inherent political nature of all social knowledge. Persuasive rhetoric in the form of new useful descriptions is the intellectual version of politics. Those who are committed to different fundamental values and perspectives, that is, to different "final vocabularies," can never prove to the satisfaction of the other person that they are wrong. The best that we can do is enter into ongoing conversations, and over time the pragmatic superiority of using one vocabulary rather than another may become apparent. But such disagreements cannot be resolved by reference to transcendent foundational principles. From a postmodernist perspective the resort to such measures leads to attempts at logical coercion. This all too easily lapses into more blatant forms of coercion and cruelty—in the name of truth. The common result of rejecting the politics of rhetoric is to substitute the politics of economic and political coercion. So, according to Rorty (1991: 21–34), what we should seek is solidarity not objectivity. This involves seeking intersubjectivity and consensus through conversation. Universalism is attained not by demonstrating some kind of externally validated objectivity, but by expanding the community of conversation and consensus.

Such skepticism about the possibilities of objectivity has not been limited to the social sciences or literary criticism. Increasingly the philosophical realism that has been implicitly held by virtually all of the sciences has been seriously called into question by philosophers of science (e.g., Fuller, 1988). Philosophers have extensively debated questions of realism and representationalism and their relevance to science.[4] The conventional view of the "scientific method" has been challenged. This conventional view sees changes in scientific knowledge as involving the rational evaluation of data according to agreed-upon standards leading to the slow but systematic improvement

---

[4] See Rorty (1979, 1991: 1–15) for an account of the debates from an anti-representationalist point of view. See Haack (1993) for a critique of Rorty's "crude pragmatism" and an attempt to reconstruct a "foundherenism" epistemology intended to avoid the limitations of both foundationalism and coherence theory.

in knowledge about an external objective reality. This view came to be seen as at best a gross over simplification spun into what Kitcher (1993) called a "legend." The revisionist view of science portrays it as a highly competitive conflict-ridden social institution in which new paradigms gain adherents through elaborate political coalitions that are based upon much more mundane and self-interested considerations than simply "the evidence" (Kuhn, 1970; Knorr-Cetina, 1983; Latour, 1987). Significant attempts have been made to show that variations for what passes for knowledge are related to the way that intellectual disciplines are structured (Fuchs, 1992). Stated in more general terms, the Enlightenment quest for objective knowledge and universalistic norms has been called into question. More accurately, what is called into question is any claim that there are extra historical criteria such as human nature or rationality that can resolve the question of what is objective, or justify a commitment to such universalism.

There are other attempts to criticize and refine the notion of objectivity that do not necessarily imply its abandonment.[5] Megill (1994) has usefully distinguished four different senses in which objectivity is used. The first is the absolute sense that is closely related to philosophical realism and attempts to represent things "as they really are." The second refers to the sense of objectivity that is derived from the consensus that exists within a given discipline at a given point in time. The third is the dialectical; objectivity is not the distancing of the observing subject from the observed object, but the careful specification of the relationship between subject and object. The fourth is the procedural that uses an impersonal method or procedure to define objectivity. Some examples might include a carefully specified experimental protocol, the training of telephone interviewers to ask the identical question in a neutral voice, standardized procedures for reviewing and accepting articles for publication, or committees of professional associations publishing the authoritative definitions of key concepts. I want to argue that to the degree that objectivity is abandoned—as contrasted to qualified and specified—there is a tendency for the last three types to collapse into one: proceduralism.

---

[5] See the essays in Megill (1994) for a sampling of the varieties of approaches and opinions on this issue.

From Value, Justice, and Truth to Proceduralism

Authority in the Postmodern World: As we have seen, Rorty (1989) has advocated that we abandon our concern with objectivity and seek, instead social solidarity. This solidarity is to be rooted in intersubjectivity arrived at through ongoing conversations with those who differ from us. The intent is to increase universality and agreement by widening the community of discourse. This is supposedly made easier by narrowing the areas about which consensus must be reached, and expanding the alternative modes of individual expression and self creation; in Rorty's terms we need a small final vocabulary for the public arena and a large one for private matters. But since an ironic attitude must be maintained about all human efforts, we must realize that any success at public consensus will, at best, be partial. Hence we must maintain openness and tolerance toward others, despite the inconclusiveness and even failure of our conversational efforts to create solidarity.

There have been various critiques of the attempt to substitute solidarity for external sources of authority, and, of course, other sociologists have responded to postmodernism.[6] Relatively little has been said, however, about the difficulties in creating solidarity.

The Sources of Social Solidarity

If the goal is solidarity rather than objectivity, it seems appropriate to ask what sociology tells us about the sources of solidarity. The classic sociological treatment of the sources of solidarity is, of course, Emile Durkheim's *Elementary Forms of Religious Life* (1965). Durkheim identifies two fundamental sources of solidarity. The first is sharing a common relationship to something that is totally other. More specifically, together people experience the sacred as something that is so totally "other" that it mutes the differences between them. Of course,

---

[6] Examples of those who are opposed to or skeptical of abandoning all attempts at developing cross-cultural and trans-historical sources of authority include Diggins (1994); MacIntyre (1984); Ryan (1995); Taylor (1991).

One of the most influential attempts of sociologists to respond to postmodernism is the set of essays edited by Seidman and Wagner (1992).

there is often a continuum between the sacred and the profane. Hence, a charismatic leader or a common enemy may be the "other" that produces solidarity. The second source is participating in common rituals. These are highly stereotyped patterns of action and interaction that give people a sense of shared experience. Out of such common experience social norms and a shared sense of morality often develop. Typically these two mechanisms—otherness and ritual—are used together and hence are mutually reinforcing: we participate in common rituals that affirm our sameness in relationship to the otherness of the sacred.[7]

When one of these mechanisms of solidarity tends to become too dominant over the other, well-known heresies or pathologies tend to develop. An overemphasis on the details and extensiveness of ceremony leads to activities that get bogged down in ritualism. Formal conformity to the rituals or the norms becomes an end-in-itself. This tendency is not restricted to religious groups, but is frequently found in businesses and government agencies and their "red tape"; it is what the older literature on formal organizations called "goal displacement."

The opposite tendency is to place so much emphasis on one's connection to the other that any sense of a common social life, and a related morality, disappears. Rituals and rules are seen as a sign of inadequate faith in, and connection to, the sacred other. The characteristic results are tendencies toward antinomianism or dogmatic fanaticism. Too strong a preoccupation with the other can also be found in more profane situations where one's connection to charismatic leaders or despots becomes the sole value, overruling any sense of common norms or morality—other than following the will of the leader. Nazism, Stalinism, and Mao's Red Guards approximate this ideal-type. In short, overemphasizing only one of these mechanisms usually produces unintended negative consequences.

---

[7] Of course, earlier, in *The Division of Labor in Society* (1933, 1984), Durkheim suggested that new forms of organic solidarity based largely on functional interdependence were replacing the supposedly older forms of mechanical solidarity. But even in this early optimistic work, the development of this new form of solidarity was seen as dependent upon a common collective consciousness that could be easily undermined by economic injustice deriving from the inheritance of private property and ascription in the occupational structure. It seems accurate to say that Durkheim himself and sociology in general became less sanguine about the easy substitution of organic for mechanical solidarity.

The Demystification of Life

For all of postmodernism's attacks on Enlightenment rationalism, it is still vitally concerned with the demystification of social and intellectual life. Not only must God be declared dead, so must philosophy or any attempt at universalistic categories or foundational assumptions. In the Durkheimian terms discussed above, solidarity through reference to a sacred other—even a secularized other—must be abandoned. No longer can we reach consensus and agreement by the commonality we share in some relationship to something "out there"—whether the "out there" is God or "empirical reality." For the foundational assumption of postmodernism is that there is nothing out there; nothing other than what particular groups and cultures have contingently and historically produced.

Hence a key programmatic feature of postmodernism is a search for new mechanisms to produce solidarity. This is most explicit in Habermas (1987: Chaps. 2 and 3), whose emphasis on undistorted communicative action is specifically referred to as "the linguistification of the sacred," that is, the production of consensus and solidarity by rational communication rather than ritual or reference to the sacred. While Rorty does not link his concern with solidarity to the Durkheimian model, his stress on conversation and tolerance is also a search for alternative sources of solidarity.

But abandoning old sources of solidarity and substituting new ones is not cost-free. Just as attempts at solidarity through ritual alone tend to lapse into ritualism, solidarity through communication and conversation tends to lapse into proceduralism. Since it is rare that even small groups can reach complete consensus, we agree to let the majority rule—or some other rule of procedure. When all forms of transcendence—sacred and secular—have been rejected, the only legitimate basis of authority—whether political, scientific, or whatever—becomes agreed upon social procedure.[8]

---

[8] There has been, of course, debate over how fair, just, and unbiased social decision-making procedures are and can be. Some have defended relatively traditional forms of democratic politics as the best alternative we have in the current historical circumstances (Rorty, 1989, esp. Chaps. 3 and 4 and 1991, 175–196), while others have suggested supposedly rational bases for notions of the just society (Rawls, 1971; Habermas, 1984, 1987; Sciulli, 1992).

That human understanding is necessarily limited by the contexts in which it develops, is, of course, a key assumption of much of postmodernism. Hence it seems appropriate to examine the move toward proceduralism as the basis of authority in its broad context.

The Rise of Proceduralism

The rejection of transcendent categories and the emphasis on historical concreteness must be seen in the context of long-term historical trends. Liberalism, in its historic sense, is at the core of these trends. A key assumption of liberalism is that procedure can be substituted for substantive agreement. Social processes can be established that produce checks and balances on partisan interest and insure that the exercise of power is publicly visible. The supposed result is a collective situation that is more tolerable for all concerned than are attempts to reach a general consensus or impose orthodoxy.

In the *economic realm* we have almost completely forsaken any notions of transcendent value or criteria. Natural law and the labor theory of value were abandoned long ago. "Value" is "price," which is determined by the complex of social procedures called "the market." In the context of the competitive market, value has no meaning other than the price resulting from the market's aggregation of the preferences of a set of historical actors in a particular time and place. Things or activities have no economic value outside of that process. If there is a truly competitive market operating, there is no economic basis for criticizing the values that are assigned commodities or the way these commodities are allocated among actors. The pursuit of self-interest, in aggregate, results in the common good. By definition we have the best of all possible economic worlds—at least at the given historical moment. Nonlibertarians would acknowledge that there are some activities that cannot be adequately provided by private entrepreneurs through the market: law and order (especially the protection of property), defense, and infrastructures such as roads are commonly mentioned examples. In a similar manner they recognize that the pursuit of private profit may require some regulation to reduce "externalities"—negative consequences for the broader community, as when factories dump pollution into rivers. The burden of proof, however, is always on those who claim that nonmarket procedures must be used, and there is the presumption that nonmarket production is inherently less efficient. The value of such activities is thought of largely in terms of "shadow prices" that estimate the market value of such activities. In sum, our very notion of value becomes identified with the outcome of particular economic procedures: exchanges in the market.

In the *political realm*, notions of constitutional democracy and procedural justice play a parallel role. Legal procedures produce checks and balances on power. These checks and balances supposedly result in compromises that are the best possible outcome under the given historical circumstances. "Justice" is being treated according to the prescribed procedures. The concept of law itself becomes detached from any notions of natural law or ethical principles, and becomes simply the rules that are formulated by means of legitimate procedures. There is no politically legitimate basis for resisting the outcome of decision-making processes if they were conducted according to the law. In the United States, if protest movements do not accept the outcome of the political process, they must be prepared to have the police powers of the state used against them—whether it is the Civil Rights Movement of the 1960s, the anti-Vietnam War protest of the 1970s, the anti-abortion protest of the 1980s, the militia movements of the 1990s, or the anti-globalization protestors of the 2000s. Even these protest groups sometimes implicitly accept the legitimacy of procedure.[9]

As we have seen in the *philosophical realm*, there has been a move toward historical concreteness and a rejection of transcendent categories, metaphysics, and all foundational assumptions. The aspect of this that is most directly relevant to sociology is the postmodernist critique of philosophical realism. Social processes and procedure are given a central role in defining "reality" and "truth." Just as economic and political values are socially constructed—through the market and democratic politics, respectively—so is our understanding of the empirical world. Hence, even scientific theories are largely self referential, determined as much by the traditions, assumptions, and procedures of a particular community of scientists as they are by an external reality;

[9] For example, anti-Vietnam war protesters did not reject the legitimacy of democracy—though many rejected capitalism. Rather they claimed that insofar as there was popular support for the war, it was because the U.S. government or the corporation-dominated news media controlled information and manipulated public opinion—making authentic democratic procedures impossible.

for the very observation of that reality is rooted in the socially con-structed categories of a particular community. Consequently, "truth," like "value" and "justice" has no independent basis, but is the product of a particular set of historical social processes. As in the economic and political realm there is a tendency to expand formal procedures as a means of collective decision-making.

The Limits and Costs of Historical Concreteness

Stated in other terms, a key thrust of postmodernism is to demystify reified concepts—such as value, justice and truth, time, space, God, etc.—and to forego attempts at generalized theories. Instead, the emphasis is on the need to re-describe human experience in relatively concrete, historically contextualized categories.

There is much to be said for the demystification postmodernism proposes. But, it also has its costs. In my opinion not the least of these is lulling us into the illusion that reification and alienation can be eliminated. This was a chief claim of the Marxian tradition. By forsaking idealism and embracing a thoroughgoing historical ma-terialism, humans were supposedly going to come to grips with the concrete historical forms of domination, which were the contingent source of reification and alienation. Most observers now think this was an illusion. Reified notions of human nature and the fetishism of commodities were replaced by reified notions of the proletariat and the fetishism of the party line. These led not only to new forms of domination and terror, but also to distorted forms of science and aesthetics such as Lysenkoism in genetics and socialist realism in art. Such surreptitious reification and alienation did not begin with and is not limited to the history of Communism.

As suggested above, similar processes have occurred many times in religious groups. The authority of a charismatic leader, proper ritual activity, or the processes of the collectivity become the sole definers of the sacred; deviant and eccentric understandings of the sacred are either defined as heresy or are ignored; in other words, the church and its ritual and governing procedures replace God as the de facto transcendent point of reference. Whether it is the Communist party or a religious group, when there is no basis of authority other than the concrete traditions of a particular historical community, and when all nonhistorical transcendent visions are declared as illusions or only a narrow, orthodox version is permitted, then resistance to authority in that community becomes even more problematic. The main thrust of George Orwell's work was to warn us of the dangers of self-contained social systems—and especially when social procedures become the arbiter of legitimate language.[10]

Of course, one response to this criticism is that the solution is to build into the very traditions of the community, the legitimacy of tolerance, criticism, and countervailing forms of power that check and limit domination, whether political or intellectual. Even more fundamental is taking an ironic position toward all human endeavors. But even where such traditions exist, they offer at best a limited basis for criticism. While relatively systematic idealized counterfactual models such as those proposed by Rawls (1971) and Habermas (1984) may be a useful beginning point for social and political criticism, they too seem closely wedded to proceduralism. Moreover, more thoroughgoing postmodernists such as Derrida, Lyotard, and Rorty would reject such models as yet another form of pseudo-universalism, transcendent naivete, foundationalism, and mystification. According to them the most we can do is continually re-describe our experience in concrete terms, in the tradition of Proust; according to this viewpoint, theories, even ironic theories, imply domination.

In my opinion, this strategy leaves us open to a dangerous outcome. What seems to actually happen when we reject transcendent bases of authority—whether sacred or secular—is that we resort to various forms of proceduralism to arrive at collective decisions. There can be many things good about such an outcome. The problem is when we deny the intellectual legitimacy of any attempt to create notions that might be used to criticize such procedures. There is no more reason to be confident that intellectual authority based upon the current consensus of even the most ideal intellectual community—not to speak of the National Academies of Science, the Modern Language Association, or the American Sociological Association—is safe from dogmatic provincialism, than to assume political democracy is immune

[10] See Rorty (1989: 169–188) for his attempt to deal with the issues that Orwell raises for his position.

from chauvinistic nationalism. Of course, transcendent categories and philosophical realism do not guarantee justice or truth, but they provide an ideological basis for resisting the outcomes of current social procedures. However great the dangers of reification, alienation, and mystification, and the persecution of others in the name of the sacred, the dangers of relativism and a provincial cultural hegemony seem at least as great.[11]

I do not mean to deny all legitimacy to capitalist markets, constitutional democracies, or perspectives that emphasize the social construction of reality and call into question any simple philosophical realism. I do want to argue that in all of these areas it is a mistake to reject the legitimacy of more abstract transcendent categories, including notions of objectivity and relatively general sociological theories. These will necessarily involve oversimplifications, historically contingent reifications, psychological projections, or ideological formulations that in turn call for critique and deconstruction. Nonetheless, we need to maintain the tension between attempts to deconstruct and demystify abstract concepts and the use of such concepts as a means of summarizing our knowledge and as a basis for calling into question the knowledge and values of the moment. To resolve the tension in either direction is likely to create more problems than it solves. Just as Durkheimian solidarity seems greatest when there is both a sacred referent (such as a god or totem) *and* ritual, I suspect that postmodern solidarity will also require analogues of each. We need both theory and concreteness; both transcendence and deconstruction. In the more specific matter concerning notions of truth, we are likely to need both a sense of how knowledge is socially and historically constructed and models and ideals of objectivity. There is a sense in which objectivity is rooted in social solidarity. But, there is also a sense in which social solidarity is

[11] Rorty's category of irony is intended as the ideological fulcrum or foundation from which to criticize any given consensus or perspective. In many respects it is parallel or functionally equivalent to the Christian concept of original sin: that is, it is a warning about the perpetual dangers of even the best and most informed of intentions producing tragic outcomes. But it seems unlikely that the doctrine of original sin would have had much power without a notion of a just and loving deity, that is a transcendent positive model. Likewise one has to be skeptical that a notion of irony, without transcendent notions with some positive content, is likely to be an effective check on provincialism and chauvinism.

rooted in transcendent notions such as objectivity. I am dubious that more mundane processes such as conversation will suffice.

Certainly all knowledge and truth is socially constructed in particular historical contexts. All are to some degree biased by asymmetries of power both during the social construction of the content of truth and in its applications in particular concrete instances. This does not mean, however, that all truth and knowledge is equally arbitrary and contingent. There are meaningful differences in different systems of determining what is true. In my opinion, there is a useful parallel between the "truth" created by legal institutions and academic/intellectual/scientific institutions. The knowledge that is created by all such institutions is, to some degree, biased by the interest of those who create and operate them and by the differences in power of those who are subject to them. There are, however, significant differences in the degree and content of such biases. Even relatively unsophisticated people who have had an opportunity to see systems of justice operate can make pretty sound judgments about which system they would rather be tried under if they are innocent and their life or freedom is at stake. In my opinion, much of the epistemological angst and rhetoric of recent years is not unlike the rhetoric of lawyers (in an adversarial system of justice) who are trying to discredit the arguments of their opponents rather than contribute what they can to clarifying matters. This parallel is not precise, of course. For one thing, most lawyers know and admit what they are up to and many academics do not.

In short, to answer the question posed in the subtitle of this chapter, as postmodernism suggests, it is a mistake to look to some abstract notion of objectivity as the sole source of solidarity and consensus—even in science. But, it is my strong suspicion that it is also a mistake to attempt to simply substitute solidarity for objectivity.

Irony is a favorite category of the postmodernist. Consequently, it is especially ironical that a thoroughgoing rejection of foundationalism (i.e., of generalizing theories and transcendent categories) attempts to accomplish exactly what poststructuralists and deconstructionists say cannot be done: create a system of ordered meaning with no remainder and no ambiguity. Of course, postmodernists acknowledge, and even glory in, the plurality of what they see as concrete cultural and historical meaning systems. But, any attempt to create categories that claim to transcend the concrete experiences of human historical experience (or, for some, even the experience of a particular culture) is intellectually illegitimate. For according to this perspective, there can be no legitimate reference to anything other than the socially constructed meanings of a given historical context. This certainly appears to be the privileging of one understanding of human experience and the attempted intellectual repression of all others. There is a humility shown toward pluralism, but there is a not-very-well-disguised arrogance toward any attempts at generalization, not to speak of an appreciation of mystery or transcendence. This unequivocal rejection of anything other than the particular, concrete, and historical is, ironically, one of the foundational assumption of anti-foundationalism.

In sum, it is my opinion that a useful and irresolvable tension between the particular and the general, the concrete and the abstract, the local and the universal, and the historical and the transcendent is more appealing than the elimination of either pole of these contrasts. Therefore, in my judgment, a constructive postmodernism will be less dogmatic about the illegitimacy of generalizations, objectivity, grand narratives, and transcendent categories.[12] In other words, it must take its exhortations to openness and pluralism more seriously than some of its advocates intend.

References

Althusser, Louis. 1969 [1965]. *For Marx*. London: Verso.

Barratt, Barnaby. B. 1993. *Psychoanalysis and the Postmodern Impulse*. Baltimore: Johns Hopkins.

Barthes, Roland. 1968. *Elements of Semiology*. New York: Hill and Wang.

Baudrillard, Jean. 1988. *Selected Writings. Edited and Introduced by Mark Poster*. Stanford CA: Stanford University Press.

Black, Donald. 1976. *The Behavior of Law*. New York: Academic Press.

———. 1993. *The Social Structure of Right and Wrong*. San Diego: Academic Press.

Blumer, Herbert. 1969. *Symbolic Interactionism: Perspective and Method*. Berkeley: University of California Press.

[12] In defending the legitimacy of what, for lack of a better name, I have called "transcendent categories," I have in mind religious notions of transcendence and various secularized versions of transcendental philosophy—though I would not necessarily exclude other notions of transcendence.

Brown, Richard Harvey. 1987. *Society as Text*. Chicago: University of Chicago Press.

Derrida, Jacques. 1976. *Of Grammatology*. Baltimore: Johns Hopkins University Press.

———. 1978. *Writing and Difference*. Chicago: University of Chicago Press.

Diggins, John Patrick. 1994. *The Promise of Pragmatism: Modernism and the Crisis of Knowledge and Authority*. Chicago: University of Chicago Press.

Dilthey, Wilhelm. 1976. *Wilhelm Dilthey: Selected Writings*. Ed. H. P. Rickman. Cambridge: Cambridge University Press.

Dirks, Nicholas B., Geoff Eley, and Sherry B. Ortner (eds). 1994. *Culture/Power/History: A Contemporary Reader in Social Theory*. Princeton: Princeton University Press.

Durkheim, Emile. 1933. *The Division of Labor in Society*. Trans. George Simpson. New York: Free Press.

———. 1984. *The Division of Labor in Society*. Trans. W.D. Halls. New York: Free Press.

———. [1915] 1965. *The Elementary Forms of Religious Life*. New York: Free Press.

Foucault, Michel. 1972. *The Archaeology of Knowledge*. New York: Harper Torchbooks.

———. 1973a. *Madness and Civilization*. New York: Vintage Books.

———. 1973b. *The Order of Things: An Archaeology of the Human Sciences*. New York: Vintage Books.

———. 1979. *Discipline and Punish: The Birth of the Prison*. Hammondsworth, England: Penguin Books.

———. 1980. *Power/Knowledge: Selected Interview and Other Writings 1972–1977*. New York: Pantheon Books.

Fuchs, Stephan. 1992. *The Professional Quest for Truth*. Albany: State University of New York Press.

Fuller, Steve. 1988. *Social Epistemology*. Bloomington: Indiana University Press.

Furfey, Paul Hanly. 1953. *The Scope and Method of Sociology*. New York: *Harper and Brothers*, Publishers.

Gadamer, Hans-Georg. 1992. *Truths and Method*. 2nd rev. ed. New York: Crossroad Publishers.

Geertz, Clifford. 1983. *Local Knowledge*. New York: Basic Books.

Gibbs, Jack. 1972. Sociological Theory Construction. Hinsdale IL: Dryden Press.

Guiraud, Pierre. 1975. *Semiology*. London: Routledge and Kegan, Paul.

Haack, Susan. 1993. *Evidence and Inquiry: Towards Reconstruction in Epistemology*. Oxford: Blackwell.

Habermas, Jurgen. 1984. *The Theory of Communicative Action*. Vol. I, Reason and the Rationalization of Society. Boston: Beacon Press.

———. 1987. *The Theory of Communicative Action*. Vol. II, Lifeworld and System: A Critique of Functionalist Reason. Boston: Beacon Press.

Heidegger, Martin. 1962. *Being and Time*. New York: Harpers.

Homans, George C. 1967. *The Nature of Social Science*. New York: Harcourt, Brace, World.

Jencks, Charles. 1986. *What Is Post-Modernism*. New York: St. Martin's Press.

Kitcher, Philip. 1993. *The Advancement of Science. Science without Legend, Objectivity without Illusions*. New York: Oxford University Press.

Knorr-Cetina, Karin. 1983. *Science Observed*. London: SAGE Publications.

Kuhn, Thomas. 1970. *Structure of Scientific Revolutions*. 2nd, enlarged ed. Chicago: University of Chicago Press.

Lacan, Jacques. 1977. *Ecrits: A Selection*. London: Tavistock Publications.

Latour, Bruno. 1987. *Science in Action*. Cambridge: Harvard University Press.

Lemert, Charles. 1992. "General Theory, Irony, and Postmodernism," *in Postmodernism and Social Theory*. Ed. Steven Seidman and David G. Wagner. Cambridge MA: Blackwell.

Levi-Strauss, Claude. 1969. *The Elementary Structures of Kinship*. Boston: Beacon Press.

———. 1975. *The Raw and the Cooked*. New York: Harper and Row.

Lundberg, George. 1975. *Can Science Save Us*. Westport CN: Greenwood Press.

Lyotard, Jean-Francois. 1984. *The Postmodern Condition: A Report on Knowledge*. Minneapolis: University of Minnesota Press.

MacIntyre, Alasdair. 1984. *After Virtue: A Study in Moral Theory*. 2nd ed. Notre Dame: University of Notre Dame Press.

MacIver, Robert. 1973. *Social Causation*. Glouchester MA: Peter Smith.

Megill, Allan (ed.). 1994. *Rethinking Objectivity*. Durham: Duke University Press.

Nietzsche, Friedrich Wilhelm. 1956. *The Birth of Tragedy and the Genealogy of Morals*. Garden City, NY: Doubleday.

Rawls, John. 1971. *A Theory of Justice*. Cambridge: Harvard University Press.

Ricoeur, Paul. 1981. *Hermeneutics and the Human Sciences*. Ed. John B. Thompson. Cambridge: Cambridge University Press.

Rorty, Richard. 1979. *Philosophy and the Mirror of Nature*. Princeton: Princeton University Press.

———. 1989. *Contingency, Irony, and Solidarity*. Cambridge: Cambridge University Press.

———. 1991. *Objectivity, Relativism, and Truth: Philosophical Papers*. Vol. 1. Cambridge: Cambridge University Press.

Ryan, Alan. 1995. "Pragmatism Rides Again," *The New York Review of Books*, 30–34, February 16.

Said, Edward W. 1979. *Orientalism*. New York: Vintage Books.

———. 1994. *Culture and Imperialism*. New York: Vintage Books.

Sarup, Madan. 1993. *An Introductory Guide to Post-Structuralism and Postmodernism*. 2nd ed. Athens: The University of Georgia Press.

Saussure, Ferdinand de. 1966. *Course in General Linguistics*. New York: McGraw-Hill.

Schleiermacher, Fredrich. 1986. *Hermeneutics: The Handwritten Manuscripts*. Atlanta: Scholars Press.

Sciulli, David. 1992. *Theory of Societal Constitutionalism*. Cambridge: Cambridge University Press.

Seidman, Steven. 1991. "The End of Sociological Theory: The Postmodern Hope," *Sociological Theory*, 9(2): 138–46.

———. 1994. *Contested Knowledge: Social Theory in the Postmodern Era*. Oxford: Blackwell.

Seidman, Steven and David G. Wagner. 1992. *Postmodernism and Social Theory*. Cambridge MA: Blackwell.

Taylor, Charles. 1991. *The Ethics of Authenticity*. Cambridge: Harvard University Press.

Weber, Max. 1949. *The Methodology of the Social Sciences*. New York: Free Press.

———. 1968. *Economy and Society*. New York: Bedminster Press.

Winch, Peter. 1970 [1958]. *The Idea of a Social Science and Its Relation to Philosophy*. London: Routledge and Kegan Paul.

Wittgenstein, Ludwig. 1968. *Philosophical Investigations*. 3rd ed. New York: Macmillian Publishing Co.

Wuthnow, Robert. 1987. *Meaning and the Moral Order: Explorations in Cultural Analysis*. Berkeley: University of California Press.

PART III

Many Faces of Postmodernism: Gender, Market Religions, Management Philosophy, and Culture

9

Feminism, Postmodern Contentions, and Emancipatory Politics

ROSALIND A. SYDIE

Postmodern theories have been both liberating and constraining for feminists as they attempt to theorise and implement feminist politics. In the early years when the buzz word—postmodern—became the fashionable perspective in the Western academy, feminists were understandably sceptical. Flax wondered why it was that postmodernism rejected fixed notions of self and subjectivity just when women had begun to "re-member their selves and to claim agnetic subjectivity" that was only available in the past to a "few privileged white men."[1] Hartsock (1990: 163) was blunter asking why, just as previously silenced populations began to speak for themselves and on behalf of their subjectivities, the concept of the "subject" becomes suspect and the possibility of discovering a liberating "truth" is declared impossible. In Hartsock's (1990: 164) view, this postmodern turn was neither an accident, nor was it a conspiracy; it was the "transcendental voice of the Enlightenment attempting to come to grips with the socialand historical changes of the middle-to-late twentieth century." Whilst it was clear that the voices of women had been left out of traditional scholarship, it was also clear that the voices raising the issue of postmodern exclusion were themselves a privileged minority of women—namely Western, and especially North American, largely white, middle-class feminists, most of whom were located in the academy.

The postmodern critique of abstract, totalizing, Western theory that had valorized the rational, autonomous individual (who was not specified because it was taken-for-granted that such an individual was

---

[1] Jane Flax (1990: 220) suggested that without a sense of self, action on behalf of self, as well as the collectivity with which the self is embedded, is impossible and no feminist can risk this sort of "repression again."

male) might be liberating for feminists in the long term (although as the discussion below indicates this is debatable), but it was constraining in the short term. The "death of the subject" was the death of the modernist, white Western male subject, but there was no necessary corresponding "death" of the "Other," especially the female other. It also became clear that non-Western women in particular remained Other to the extent that, well-meaning or not, it seemed that "*anything*" could be said "about women from other cultures as long as it appears to document their differences from 'us'" (Lazreg, 1990: 341). Consequently, a legacy of modernity remained in the understanding that women, whatever their nationality, race, or ethnicity, were (and are) always Other.

Sociology/Modernity/Postmodernity

Classical sociological theory was complicit in the project of modernity. The social sciences were the heirs of Enlightenment faith in Reason, embodied in science, as the path to a global utopian vision of social "Order and Progress."[2] From its inception, sociology was also conceptualized as a scientific and normative exercise critically engaged with the issues of the day. Harriet Martineau (1869, 2: 335) believed sociology was the "science or the knowledge of fact inducing the discovery of laws," as well as the "eternal basis of wisdom, and therefore of human morality and peace.", and Cooley (1930: 258) maintained that a "social science which is not also, in its central principles, an ethical science is unfaithful to its deepest responsibility, that of functioning in the aid of general progress."[3] There is, however, an inherent contradiction in

[2] Comte's positive sociology promised to reconcile order and progress under the guidance of scientists and industrialists who would act on behalf of all humanity. In his view, sociology's discovery of fundamental social laws meant that it would determine what is, what will be, and what should be and, as a result, put an end to the "revolutionary crisis which is tormenting the civilized nations of the world" (Comte, 1975: 37).

[3] Most of the classical sociologists, including Durkheim, Weber, Simmel, G.H. Mead, Spencer, Sumner, as well as Comte and Martineau, developed various conceptual frameworks designed to make sense of the social world *and* to suggest how that world might be improved.

the idea of sociology as a "science," based on modernist assumptions of the superiority of reason, independent of any social/historical context, as the means to provide objective knowledge of reality *and* the injunction that it should also provide the normative basis for the path to perfection in the social world. The contradiction was often dealt with by assuming that primary sources of contamination to a scientific sociology were the messy, emotional, irrational, passionate, feminine, and savage impulses.[4] The social sciences in general repudiated such impulses that they supposed animated traditional society, maintaining that modernity represented the triumph of the rational, male mind over the emotional female and savage heart.[5]

The postmodern challenge to the project of modernity was based on the observation that the emancipatory promise of universal reason was a myth. It was a powerful myth that had provided western nations with hegemonic global power. However, it became apparent that the rational, male mind suppressed the so-called feminine and "savage" at its peril. The modern, rational, autonomous individual who could use "his" freedom and power to advance human happiness through scientifically determined ethical conduct was now countered by the postmodern death of the subject, the grounded nature of theory, and the plurality of beliefs and values for which there is no necessary singular position to judge their efficacy or "truth." The modernist "view from nowhere" was replaced by a postmodern "view from everywhere." For sociology this meant that it could no longer, in Bauman's (1988: 228) words, "justify claims to universalistic authority or social management expertise on the basis of empirical 'truths'." The truth claims of the modern, rational subject were revealed as the privileged perspective of a minority of white males. But this normative vacuum did not necessarily alter the gender or racial configurations of knowledge production. As Bell Hooks (1990: 27) noted, "The overall impact of postmodernism

---

[4] Rattanzi (2011: 120) points out that 19th century discourses on class and race were "simultaneously gendered and sexualized" with "women and the 'lower races' ... regarded as being more child-like, impulsive and emotional, and lacking in the powers of abstract reasoning, which then folded into analyses of sexual deviance and criminality."

[5] The presumed impartiality of western social "science" essentially constructed the social and political "conceptual practices of power" that governed and controlled those defined as "others" (Smith, 1990).

is that many other groups now share with black folks a sense of deep alienation, despair, uncertainty, loss of a sense of grounding even if it is not informed by shared circumstances."

Difference, identity, and desire became the focus of postmodern feminist debates. Taking into account the intersections of gender, race, class, ethnicity, and sexual desire and practice was recognized as important in any feminist analysis if it was to respond to and counter the myriad forms of hegemonic masculinity. Focusing on differences also revealed the nature and problems with the taken-for-granted, all-encompassing, essentialist notion of "woman."[6] As Butler (1995: 50) pointed out, when the reified category of "woman" is deconstructed, then "multiple significations" can expand the possibilities of what it means to be a woman. Consequently, there can be no hegemonic feminist intellectual paradigm, and there will be considerable contestation within global feminist communities about the "best," or perhaps the most expedient approach to take theoretically and practically in addressing the multitude of issues facing women.

The resulting proliferation of feminist perspectives has been taken by some commentators as proof that feminism, like modernity, is either "irrelevant," "over," or "dead," and that we now exist in a postfeminist world. It is perhaps obvious to say that these claims are mostly advanced by critics in western, advanced nations, especially in neoliberal states. They are symptomatic of what Pels (2000: 176–177) calls a "discourse of nomadism." Pels claims that "it has become a cliché for connoisseurs of postmodern sensibility to say that we live in a world of flux, where mobility, experimentation, and transgression have turned into core signifiers of the daily management of life styles" and seeking adventure, living the "experimental life, to probe the limits of one's identity" are

---

[6] Lemert points out that when sociology takes women as "instances of a natural kind" and uses "gender as the sufficient variable unto a Sociology of Womankind," which involves essentializing (and dichotomizing) gender "as the covering concept for variations in the category of which women are proper members," then the probability that "gender is understood as continuous, probably contingent, certainly local (though not necessarily constructed), and surely not an essence" is then made immaterial, at least on "technical grounds." Sociology is not, of course, the only discipline guilty of essentialism, especially in regard to gender, Lemert's (2003: 77) point is that sociology's tendency to "an essentialism of practical reason" overestimates "central tendencies, at the expense of variance, thereby crippling its ability to generate empirically robust theories of social differences."

a "powerful motif in popular and elite culture alike." This discourse of nomadism is the "newest fad in self-stylization and self-celebration." But, if nomadism is characteristic of postmodern life, it is another Western conceit and a minority one even in western nations. It is a totally alien concept for third world lifestyles and identities, especially for women. In fact such a lifestyle is not only inconceivable to women of the third world, it is also insulting in that any "mobility, experimentation, and transgression" they undertake is not "play" but a vital necessity to ensure basic sustenance for themselves and their families.

Hawkesworth (2004: 965) suggests that there is a "clear moral" to such tales of feminism's demise, at least in North America, namely that "Modes of feminist activism that challenge boundaries fixed by the dominant culture in the United States must be banished from the land of the living." Woodhull's (2003: 76) examination of third wave feminist websites in the United States and other wealthy, western nations leads her to the conclusion that few third wave feminists seem to be concerned with social justice issues or with women's plight in the rest of the world. On the contrary, the new modalities of third wave feminism seem to fit the sort of nomadic lifestyles and identities outlined by Pels. Woodhull (2003: 78) finds this troubling, especially when mass communications technologies celebrated by third wave feminists are rightly seen as important means for addressing gender issues. She concedes that "Third wavers are right to claim that new modalities of feminism must be invented for the new millennium," but emphasises that it is essential that these new modalities be "conceived and enacted in global terms." But when the use of such technologies is confined to many Western third wave preoccupations, this is a missed opportunity. If the range and scope of new technologies offer opportunities to put "direct democracy into practice" by "gaining the attention of mainstream media, mobilizing and shaping public opinion, and putting pressure on governments to implement and enforce democratic policies to protect women's interests," they need to be employed globally in terms of on-the-ground preoccupations of all women (Woodhull, 2003: 77).

Feminists, of course, contest claims of irrelevance or "death" with evidence of the global necessity for continued feminist theory and practice. Most feminists also recognize that "feminist theorizing will always operate in a double register: it will both contest other ways of understanding the world (those theories that are often not seen as theories as they are assumed to be 'common sense'), as it will *contest itself,* as a way of interpreting the world (or of 'making sense' in a way which contests what is 'common')," (Ahmed, 2000: 101). The point for all feminists is that postmodernist assumptions make the demand for continuing debate and dissension a vital necessity in order to contest the continuing inequities and resulting subordination and disadvantages particular to "particular" women and in so doing produce a practical politics of social and cultural change.[7]

The necessity for continued debate that can hopefully lead to practical solutions is all the more significant in the context of an ever more tightly interconnected global world.[8] These inescapable interconnections mean that the theoretical analyses and, most importantly, the practical changes to eliminate gender inequities are difficult to effect because the subjected, marginalized, and often despised Other remains a critical divisive presence in relation to class, race, ethnicity, religion, and sexual desire and practice in global corporate/governmental institutions. For example, Bessis (2003: 641) points out that in the 1980's when the World Bank became aware of women as "dynamic economic actors and principle agents in the struggle against poverty," it developed a "sort of feminism that could best be defined as pragmatic." This pragmatic "feminism" took the form that "women should be assisted not because their rights are scandalously abused but because the abuse of their rights is an obstacle to the reproduction of dominant economic models in the countries of the South."[9]

A feminist postmodernism must embrace an ethical commitment to women's empowerment through realisable modes of participatory politics. This means that differences of class/race/ethnicity/religion/sexual desire and practice must be central to feminist theory and practice.

---

[7] "Particular" in terms of their racial, ethnic, religious, sexual, class, and positions/definitions, recognizing that these differences do not align neatly with national or State boundaries or correspond to the racial, ethnic, religious, sexual, class, and definitions of ruling powers.

[8] For women, globally, this is a critical issue given the UN estimate that 70 percent of the world's destitute are women and that over 8 million of their children are enslaved or trafficked.

[9] For example, the structural adjustment policies of the World Bank, and the International Monetary Fund, often made women and girl's situations worse in places such as India, Mexico, Asia, and the Caribbean (see, Goetz, 2001).

Conceptualizing *how* to incorporate these and other differences and distinctions is, however, difficult. The difficulties, especially in respect to race, are explored below and the possibilities of intersectionality and bricolage are examined as ways to approach the conceptual thickets of feminist theory and practice in a tightly connected, globalized world.

Feminisms and Postmodern Differences

Feminists can be found globally, but this does not mean that there is a global feminist sisterhood. Further, it does not mean that such a universal sisterhood is desirable and/or achievable.[10] From the beginnings of organized suffrage movements in North America and Europe, class and racial divisions among women were contested issues.[11] For example, when the ex-slave, Sojourner Truth rose and delivered her speech, "Ar'n't I a Woman?" to the women's convention in Akron, Ohio in 1851, some of the white women in attendance were against allowing her to speak. Sojourner Truth's speech reinforced their unease because she "exposed the class-bias and racism of the new women's movement" (Davis, 1983: 63).

Class and racial bias continued to have a divisive presence in the resurgence of feminist movements in the 20th century. In 1977, black feminists in the U.S.A expressed their dissatisfaction with the racism that persisted in many of the new feminist movements. The Combahee

---

[10] It should be noted that some males claim to be feminists so that the notion of a universal sisterhood as such is, at best, misleading. How men are feminists is an important issue that raises significant questions related to the sex/gender binaries that make, for example, contested, fluid, and alternative sexual identities an important consideration when attempting to definitively define the use of the term "feminist."

[11] In Britain, Emmeline Pankhurst, the leader of the militant Women's Social and Political Union, and her daughter Christabel were at odds with daughters Sylvia and Adela both of whose socialist efforts were seen to detract from what they believed should be the main focus—persuading Parliament to give women the vote. The split in the Pankhurst family was exacerbated by the advent of WW1 when Emmeline and Christabel became very vocal supporters of the war in contrast to Sylvia's pacifism (Adela was equally opposed to militancy, but was by then in Australia).

River Collective statement outlined their political commitment to "struggling against racial, sexual, heterosexual, and class oppression and see as our particular task the development of integrated analysis and practice based upon the fact that the major systems of oppression are interlocking."[12] This statement was a bedrock conviction for feminists, although often more honoured in the breech in subsequent theories and practices, especially among Western academics.

Feminists understand that the key issue for effecting any real changes in gender inequities has always been how to break the interlocking power/knowledge connections that define "difference," and thus maintain the marginalized, subordinated position of Others. They recognize the conceptual value of plurality and difference at the same time realising that there is nothing in any postmodern claims that prohibits or prevents reactionary interpretations. For example, good feminist intentions were often compromised by the fact that the voices of Western, generally academic, feminists have tended to dominate analyses of what constitutes "good" feminist theory and practice. Bell Hooks (1990) remarked,

> It is sadly ironic that the contemporary discourse that talks the most about heterogeneity, the decentred subject, declaring breakthroughs that allow recognition of Otherness, still finds it critical voice primarily in a specialized audience that shares a common language rooted in the very master narrative it claims to challenge.

Race and class continue to be central and contentious issues especially among feminist postcolonial writers and in subaltern studies programmes. Patricia Hill Collins challenged the sociological master narrative with the claim that gender, race, and class were inseparable. Collins claimed that the Black scholar's status of "outsider within" provided a unique standpoint that was missing in past research and that it was only by seeing the everyday world through the "both/and conceptual lens of the simultaneity of race, class, and gender oppression" that the "social relations of domination and oppression" could be clearly understood. She suggested that the former "additive models of oppression" had to be replaced with "interlocking ones" (1990:221, 225). In this way feminists (of any color) can recognize that there is

---

[12] Quoted by Barbara Ransby (2000).

a "matrix of domination" that governs social relations such that an individual may be "an oppressor, a member of an oppressed group, or simultaneously oppressor and oppressed" (1990: 229).[13]

In current postmodern explorations of "difference," race and class remain particularly salient in the current climate of global, national instabilities. Among feminists the question of oppressor/oppressed remains a difficult issue, particularly in relation to research involving so-called Third World women. As Mohanty (1984: 335) pointed out, the descriptor, "Third World", tends to produce a "reductive and ho-mogeneous notion of what I call the "Third World Difference"—that stable, ahistorical something that apparently oppresses most if not all the women in these countries." By using this term Western feminists again "appropriate and 'colonize' the fundamental complexities and conflicts which characterize the lives of women in different classes, religions, cultures, races and castes in these countries" (1984: 335). In the current political and ideological climate of fear that targets the racial other, the complexities surrounding the use of "race" and gender as significant social and political positions of "difference" need careful scrutiny from all feminists.[14]

The concept of race is particularly contentious because it has always been a critical part of Western master narratives and it is infinitely malleable, being "able to intertwine and interweave with, and fold itself around ideas of class, sexuality and, above all, that of 'nation'" (Rattansi, 2011: 119). During the 19th century, nation states endorsed various ideas about the "fixity of 'national character' always with racial undertones, and hardened the boundaries between those who belonged and those who were deemed to be outside the nation" (Rattansi, 2011: 121). Current evidence of the continuing significance of the nation/race connection is exemplified by the negative reactions to German "guest workers," in the fears raised by the migration of Others from

[13] The issue of women as "oppressors" is an important focus of feminist re-search on women's participation in right-wing movements. (see, Bacchetta and Power, 2002).

[14] In the concentration on race, I do not suggest that the other complex markers of "difference," outlined previously, are of less significance. On the contrary, the forthcoming discussion of intersectionality recognizes the range of differences that need to be taken into account in addressing women's interests, especially at the local level.

Eastern Europe and North African to Western European centers, and in the fear of the Islamic terrorist, all of whom are seen to represent threats to western safety and national "identities."[15]

The social sciences have been complicit in entrenching racial differences as unalterable "natural" fact. Ferreira da Silva (2011: 143) points out that it was "19th-century anthropology (the science of man)" that "manufactured the notion of 'racial types'," so that "racial difference" became the "formal key for identifying and distinguishing 'human collectives'." Visible markers of racial difference were understood not as "the effect of historical relations established between these collectives" but as "constants in nature that produced the human body independently of the determination of human will." As a result, colonialism and slavery were then rendered "irrelevant in the understanding of human collective's conditions of existence" (Ferreira da Silva, (2011: 143). Similarly, in "early 20th-century sociology … racial difference would acquire many other attributes, such as that of an index of moral (cultural) difference, a trigger for attitudes such as race prejudice, and behaviour such as racial discrimination" (Ferreira da Silva, 2011: 144).

This use of the concept of race has recently taken on a slightly modified but still heighted significance as a "natural," scientifically validated attribute. As Amin (2010: 3) points out, the "science that questions the validity of race as a reliable marker of human difference is now being used … to look for genetically validated differences between socially defined ethnic and racial groups, instead of questioning the given racial and ethnic categories in the first place." This form of "biological racism" is exemplified in the "genetic profiling of given racial and ethnic groups, to see if some of them are more open to heart disease, obesity, crime, educational under-achievement" (Amin, 2010: 3). Using race in this way as a differentiation for the Other usually depends on its (often unspoken) opposite – whiteness as a "human norm."[16] In many contexts "whiteness is invisible and unmarked," it is the "absent centre against which others appear only as deviants, or points of deviation" (Ahmed, 2007: 157). Being white is assumed to

---

[15] It should be noted that the rejection and fear of the "other" is not confined to Western states but is also a feature in, for example, Chinese reactions to "their" ethnic enclaves, religious and caste divisions in India, and the racial/class distinctions in many South American societies.

[16] Dyer, R. (1997: 2).

provide an "invisible 'raceless' identity" so that the "specific cultural mores and values" of white subjects are taken to be universal human mores and values (Thobani, 2007: 172).

Race and gender remain potent markers for "Othering" because they can still appear to provide a "natural" basis for differentiation and subsequent discrimination in terms of class, religious beliefs, ethnic identification, and sexual preferences. [17] As global political developments since 9/11 demonstrate, the equation of white/human is easily connected with specific actions against racial, ethnic, and religious others who are seen as "natural" threats to a "civilized" world. The "warnings from intellectuals, publics, and states of a calamitous war to come between the world of secular liberalism (conveniently traced to the skins and traditions of Europe/North America) and the world of religious society (conveniently traced to the skins and traditions of Islam and rarely those of Christian fundamentalism)" is a sign of the way in which "Bodily traits and 'ethnic' cultures are becoming that basis upon which peoples are allocated rights, identities, a place in the world ... at the expense of other modes of marking community and negotiating differences..." (Amin, 2010: 10). Western feminists have often been complicit, whether knowingly or not, in colonial/imperial racial Othering. Mohanty (1984: 353) remarks on the "latent ethnocentrism in particular feminist writings on women in the third world." And Thobani (2007: 183) suggests that the so-called War on Terror has reproduced the idea of "Western supremacy and white racial innocence" in current forms of colonial/imperial racial Othering against which, to date, feminist theory has offered little resistance.

An important part of such Othering is not taking seriously the demands and positions of Others which translates into a refusal to engage others in a mutually respectful open debate about difference. A closed mind provides fertile ground for unquestioned assumptions and the possible endorsement of negative attitudes and actions against any designated Other. In this context what is missing is what Modood (2008: 47) calls "a politics of recognition." Mohood bases his "politics of recognition" on the distinction Charles Taylor makes between two "different albeit related concepts—*equal dignity*, and *equal respect*" (2008: 47, emphasis in the original). Equal dignity refers to an appeal

---

[17] See, E. Said (1997).

to any person's humanity and "focuses on what people have in common and so is gender-blind, colour-blind and so on," and as such forms the basis for anti-discrimination policies. Equal respect is "based on an understanding that difference is also important in conceptualizing and institutionalizing equal relations between individuals" (2008: 48). In other words, acknowledging the Other cannot be a metaphorical "tipping of the hat" toward diversity or multiculturalism, it must be accompanied by listening to, taking account of, and seeking to understand the position, claims, and desires of the other and a willingness to adjust theory/practice as a result. Endorsing these two components of a politics of recognition is particularly important for any feminist researchers and activists who occupy privileged positions in the West and in the academy.[18]

Respectful feminist dialogues need to start with the recognition that white is also a color, and an uncertain one in any classificatory schema. For example, Modood and Ahmad (2007: 187) point out that Muslim has become a "prominent and charged communal category" in Britain (and elsewhere in the West and Europe) and although Muslims may "constitute more than a third of non-whites, this estimation is complicated by the fact that most Middle Easterners regard themselves as white, though it is doubtful that others unambiguously regard them as such." The so-called racial identity is multicolored and unstable but retains salience for any feminist proposals for change especially when race provides the basis for an undifferentiated general identity on the order of all Islamists are fundamentalist patriarchs and all Westerners are democratic modernists.[19]

In Ferreira da Silva's (2011: 146) view, racial difference along with cultural difference needs to be "de-naturalized" and feminists

---

[18] Woodhull (2003: 78) points out that despite the economic and political forces of globalization that shape economic, political, social, and cultural relations, new third wave feminist debates, "mainly address issues that pertain only to women *in* those contexts. At their best, they attend to issues of race and class as they shape the politics of gender and sexuality in the global North."

[19] Discussion of Muslims as an undifferentiated, monolithic, collective evidence in the mass media since 9/11 exemplifies this point. But long before 9/11, Mohanty (1984: 342–3) cautioned theorists against treating Islam as an ideology "separate from and outside social relations and practices" and taking "a specific version of Islam as *the* Islam."

must "refuse to re-deploy them as un-mediated descriptors of human beings." This recommendation is sometimes difficult because for many racial and ethnic communities their "difference" is often critical to the maintenance of their identity and, importantly, the justification for various claims to social, political, religious, and cultural rights and entitlements. In addition, adding gender and/or class complicates any homogeneous identity of racial Others in terms of those claims. For example, cultural markers such as the hijab may be used as an identification with Islam, but it may also have a more "complex and shifting situational" meaning for some women thus "pointing to different, and perhaps contradictory, social and institutional processes" (Werbner, 2007: 173). Werbner's research suggests that for some women the "adoption of a 'new' Islamic identity signalled by the veil/scarf" may be a "cunning solution invented by young people themselves to *appear* to honour their parents (and to defy others in positions of authority) while nevertheless demanding the right to decide their own destiny (2007: 179).

The multitude of meanings that may attach to various cultural markers is central to the difficulty of formulating accounts of difference and being attuned to the perspectives/positions of those designated as Other. As is clear from the above discussion, class interacts with race and other particular and variable differences in respect to life chances, life styles, and identities. Recognizing the complexity of these interconnections in a postmodern, globalized world poses difficulties for any feminist politics.[20] One response has been to call for a global feminism but Bergeron (2001: 1000) cautions that feminists "need to be wary of such images of transnational feminism within which varying local interpretations are collapsed into a homogeneous identity of 'women's interests' against global capitalism" most especially if those

---

[20] For some analysts an important characteristic of postmodernism is the formation of a "network society" made possible by global information and communication systems that challenge traditional and modern structures of power and authority. Such global communication structures could be useful tools for feminist networking. But Turner (2007: 117) cautions that the "central contradiction of the knowledge society is that governments and corporations embrace an ideology of the free flow of information while simultaneously trying to control information through patents and intellectual property laws, and by attempts to control spam, hackers and electronic viruses."

"interests" are "dictated by Western feminist concerns, which celebrate individuality and modernity and fail to recognize the diversity of women's experiences." It is also important to keep in mind that some claims, especially nationalist or religious claims, made on behalf of women can be the means of dividing, containing, or denying feminist claims.[21] For example, Narayan (2000: 1084) suggests that the "Packet Picture of Cultures" which represents cultures as "neatly wrapped packages, sealed off from each other, possessing sharply defined edges or contours, and having distinctive contents that differ from those of other cultural packages" can have quite negative consequences for women. The cultural content of these packages may change over time when elites willingly discard what were supposedly "important cultural practices," but those same elites will "resist and protest other cultural changes, often those pertaining to the welfare of women" and, when questioned, may well cast "feminist challenges to norms and practices affecting women as cultural betrayals."

In navigating the thickets of difference, identities, cultural practices, social relationships, and power structures, feminist theories and practices must ensure that the voices of Others are not silenced. This requires using a historically/socially informed contextual analysis that understands that difference (of whatever nature) is important but more significantly that there is *no difference* that is all encompassing or set in stone. Lately, intersectionality has been a method/theory/position that has been promoted as the way for feminists to ensure that the voices of Others are heard and taken into account and that their needs and interpretations of their situations are respected. Intersectionality insists that taking differences of any kind into account is central to the development of any theoretical explanation or methodological investigation especially in the light of the interlocking nature of global, transnational and transcultural issues and concerns. In the recognition that no group of women are necessarily a coherent, homogeneous group in all respects, that there is no ahistorical shared oppression, and that

[21] Bergeron (2001: 992) points out that "[i]n the name of national economic growth and stability, states have frequently collaborated with transnational capital's efforts to exploit women" and when feminists complain states claim that "their hands are 'tied' because globalization has decreased their ability to provide social services and protect workers from the negative effects of transnational capital."

women's needs and desires are never universally shared, it has been suggested that intersectional analysis can provide a basis for feminist strategic political actions.

Intersectionality and Bricolage

Although intersectionality promises to be an approach that breaks with the rigidity of modern disciplinary research boundaries and methods, feminist scholars are often confused about "what it actually is and how to use it" (Davis, 2008: 69). Davis sees intersectionality as generally referring to the "interaction between gender, race, and other categories of difference in individual lives, social practices, institutional arrangements, and cultural ideologies and the outcomes of these interactions in terms of power" (2008: 68). In her view the popularity of the term is accounted for by its "focus on a pervasive and fundamental concern in feminist theory, its provision of novelty, its appeal to the generalist as well as the specialists of the discipline, and its inherent ambiguity and open-endedness that beg for further critique and elaboration" (Davis, 2008: 70).

Intersectionality has its "origins in Black women's social theory and activism," and it has always been a "political strategy as much as it has been a theoretical lens" in its concern with the variety of political and cultural practices of discrimination and domination (Luft and Ward, 2009: 10). The term itself was coined by Kimberle Crenshaw (1991) in her article, "Mapping the Margins: Intersectionality, Identity Politics, and Violence against Women of Color." For Luft and Ward (2009: 13) the history of the term is important given the tendency to overlook the "racial habitus that produced the theoretical innovation" coupled with the fact that intersectional work by some white feminists still contains "little mention of race, racism, or racial justice, while overstating intersectionality's hegemony."

For feminist researchers intersectionality that studies the "relationships among multiple dimensions and modalities of social relations and subject formations" seems to answer the need for their research to be useful, inclusive, ethical, engaged, and "interdisciplinary" (McCall, 2005: 1771). It can provide "a platform for feminist theory as a shared enterprise" and one that fits "neatly into the postmodern project of conceptualizing multiple and shifting identities" (Davis, 2008: 72, 71). This optimistic view is, however, qualified by the observation that intersectionality cannot provide "written–in-stone guidelines for doing feminist inquiry," or "a kind of feminist methodology to fit all kinds of feminist research," and it certainly does not "produce a normative straitjacket for monitoring feminist inquiry in search of the 'correct line'" (Davis: 2008: 79).

If intersectionality seems to provide a framework for examining the multiple inter-relationships of gendered power and subordination the question remains—how to actually *do* such research—that is, what is the appropriate methodology for intersectional ethical research?[22] It is not, however, simply a question of appropriate methods, there is also the question of theoretical presuppositions that may, even unwittingly, re-inscribe Western hegemonic discourses. It is clear from past critiques, especially of Western feminist research, that the researcher's own cultural values and interests are difficult to detect even when the research proposals consciously attempt to take account of, and be accountable to, the research participants and their "difference(s)." This is why self-critique and a recognition of the provisional nature of theory, as opposed to hegemonic theory, is important.

Methodologically, case studies, personal narratives, fieldwork, participant observation, thick description, etc are some of the ways in which feminist researchers have attempted to be sensitive to social and cultural differences and have tried to minimize power relations between researcher and the participants. McCall (2005: 1795) suggests that adopting multiple approaches to intersectional studies is the way to overcome disciplinary boundaries, but she also recognizes that the methods and subject matter may be "shaped by the disciplines." However, using disciplinary-based methods does not mean that the "methodology as a whole is not a part of an interdisciplinary program," just that some methods may be more appropriate than others to the particular subject matter" (2005: 1795). Whatever the methodology utilized in the interests of intersectional research, it is important to keep the researcher/participant/subject power issues at the forefront

---

[22] See Sandra Harding and Kathryn Norberg (2005) on Methodologies, which presents a range of research work that attempts to use, come to grips with, and critique the idea of intersectionality.

of any enterprise, recognizing also that "such powers must always be negotiated within larger contexts of local, national, and global relations that are frequently themselves unstable" (Harding and Norberg, 2005: 2012). [23]

The instability of power relations at any level is, in some ways, an opportunity for feminist politics. Feminists recognized this at the outset in relation to postmodern identity claims. But they also cautioned that with these claims subjectivity as a definable state built on some core identity disappeared and the "I" seemingly became a discursive, unstable, even an imaginary state. The "I," however, soon re-emerged as the privileged, world-weary, male intellectual "possessed" by the seductions of a world of "virtual reality," but aware of the possibilities of recovery, of a politics that can resist and still hope for progress.[24] As a result feminists found that the promised politics of resistance and recovery turned out to be encased in the same old gendered conceptual structures of power and authority.

A postmodernism that cuts subjectivity loose from modern, bourgeois individualism needs to answer the question of cut loose for whom and to do what? It is in the doing and *who* does it, in a practical emancipatory politics, which is of concern to feminists. Tactically, for feminist politics, an intersectional approach might be usefully done as feminist bricolage. Levi-Strauss (1966: 17) defined the bricoleur as "someone who works with his hands and uses devious means" to get the job done. He contrasted the practical bricoleur with the scientist as someone whose "sensible intuition" inverts the abstract reasoning of the scientist (Levi-Strauss, 1966: 22). For Levi-Strauss, bricolage was a characteristic of primitive societies, but Turkle and Papert (1990: 130) find that often "objective" scientific discoveries are "made in concrete, ad hoc fashion and only later recast into canonically acceptable formalisms." In fact they suggest that the biographies of Nobel

---

[23] Harding and Norberg (2005: 2012–2013) suggest that standpoint methodologies that design projects that "can transform the conceptual framework of disciplines ... or projects in which they can directly affect social policy" are examples of the way in which "researchers can use their distinctive powers on behalf of disadvantaged groups."

[24] See, Arthur Kroker (1992), for a discussion of this move in western postmodern society, as exemplified in American technological society and decoded by various French theorists.

laureates reveal that they "relate to the their materials in the concrete and tactile style of Levi-Strauss's bricoleurs." [25]

The scientific ideal of objectivity is an important part of the conceptual practices of power that have traditionally been used to exclude Others. Turkle and Papert (1990: 150) contend, "From its very foundations, objectivity in science has been engaged with the language of power, not only over nature but over people and organizations as well." They point to the way in which standard notions of scientific objectivity have been used in the "social construction of gender: objectivity in the sense of distancing the self from the object of study is culturally constructed as male, just as male is culturally constructed as distanced and objective" (1990: 146). As a result they conclude that "epistemological pluralism" is a necessity to counter "cultural assumptions about formal logic as the 'law of thought'" and bricolage may be a viable approach in this regard (1990: 150–151).

The epistemological pluralism, which bricolage represents, has a subversive nature in the inclusion, in all aspects of the research process, of the Others/objects of canonical science. Levi-Strauss (1966: 21) characterized the bricoleur is a "sly handyman" who uses the stock at hand, whether material or mental, to produces new results. This "sly handyman" works not "only with things … but also through the medium of things: giving an account of his personality and life by the choices he makes between limited possibilities." In this sense, Weinstein and Weinstein (1991) see Georg Simmel as a perfect example of a sociological bricoleur who did not "interpret culture through a utopia," or "develop a special technical language to describe its deep structure or to explain its dynamics," he made do with what was at hand to construct "syntagmatic chains out of the stock" (1991: 162). Simmel pointed to the ruptures and oppositions that appear in cultural complexes and the "surprising connections" he made "disturb the taboos of hierarchy" and the "myths of identification" (Weinstein & Weinstein, 1991: 163).

Intersectional bricolage can be a tactical move for feminist strategies of emancipatory practice. By treating theory not as "Theory" but as a

---

[25] Turkle and Papert (1990: 146) point to Fox Keller's biography of Barbara McClintock. For McClintock, the "practice of science was essentially a conversation with her materials," which contradicts the objective, distanced stance that is assumed to be the scientific ideal. Methodologically she practised bricolage.

recipe for practice, modest in the claim for "applicability in contexts and for persons other than those who originate them," (Stanely, 1990: 41) feminists can, like Simmel, disturb taboos and challenge myths. Turkle and Papert (1990: 136) also suggest, bricolage is like cooking, "in the style of those who do not follow recipes and instead make a series of decisions according to taste." The results of this bricolage approach can be used "co-responsibly" as they may be "collected and not used, or used at some point, or used in changed or modified form, or scrapped as inapplicable" (1990: 136). Methodologically, feminists can act, not as "sly" but as honest handywomen, revealing themselves and their preconceptions as they work in tandem with others who will similarly reveal themselves and their needs.

Intersectional bricolage seems to be an opportunity for a postmodern feminist theory and practice that critiques any notion of stable identities, cultural essentialism, and the reality of theoretical abstractions. Central to any feminist theory and practice is the recognition of social and cultural specificities that produce complex constructions of identity. Thus, there is no generic bricoleur just as there is no generic "woman" (or generic "man") because gender is always a normative prescription that, being tied to a culturally constituted body, only *seems* to have a "natural" material reality independent of political use or abuse. Butler (1990: 148) maintains that there is no "ontology of gender on which we might construct a politics" because such ontologies are politically constructed "normative injunctions" that set out ways that "sexed or gendered bodies come into cultural intelligibility." But for any feminist emancipatory practice a feminist politics is a necessity. Feminism must always challenge power wherever it is found, they must demand rights, and call into account in the "interest of *striving for a future* that is less sexist, less oppressive, and less divisive" for women (Sydie, 2002: 384). As a result Gunnarson (2011: 32) suggests that the term "women" might be used without "assuming that 'women' is the only thing that these persons are, or that 'woman' is a fixed category," recognizing that any abstraction "presumes that the concrete totality from which one abstracts is not exhausted by the abstracted element." "Woman" is a position "from which a feminist politics can emerge" and when women take positions in the "moving historical context" they can "choose what to make of this position" and "how to alter the context" in emancipatory ways (Alcoff, 1988: 435). This is because, from the outset, "what feminists put their fingers on was that there was something quite disadvantageous about all women's lives and that this something had to do with their being women" (Gunnarson, 2011: 32). Feminist intersectional bricoleur practice seems particularly appropriate to a postmodern context, as a necessarily temporary political practice that cannot rely on any appeals to transcendental, abstract ideas, but must attend to the emancipatory needs and desires of concrete individuals who are, among other important identifiers of difference, women.

References

Alcoff, Linda. 1988. "Cultural Feminism versus Post-Structuralism: The Identity Crisis in Feminist Theory," *Signs*, 13(3): 405–436.

Ahmed S. 2000. "Whose Counting?" *Feminist Theory*, 1(1): 97–103.

———. 2007. "A Phenomenology of Whiteness," *Feminist Theory*, 8(2): 149–168.

Amin, Ash. 2010. "The Remainders of Race," *Theory, Culture and Society*, 27(1): 1–23.

Butler, Judith. 1990. *Gender Trouble: Feminism and the Subversion of Identity*. New York: Routledge.

———. 1995. "Contingent Foundations," in S. Benhabib et al. (eds), *Feminist Contentions*, pp. 35–57. London: Routledge.

Bauman Z. 1988. "Is There a Postmodern Sociology?" *Theory, Culture and Society*, 5(2–3): 217–237.

Bergeron, Suzanne. 2001. "Political Economy Discourses of Globalization and Feminist Politics," *Signs*, 26(4): 983–1006.

Bacchetta, P. and M. Power. 2002. *Right-Wing Women: From Conservative to Extremists Around the World*. New York: Routledge.

Bessis, S. 2003. "International Organizations and Gender: New Paradigms and Old Habits," *Signs*, 29(2): 633–647.

Cooley, Charles Horton. 1930. *Sociological Theory and Social Research*. Ed. Robert Cooley Angell. New York: Henry Holt.

Comte A. 1975. *Auguste Comte and Positivism: The Essential Writings*. Ed. Gertrude Lenzer. Chicago: University of Chicago Press.

Collins, Patricia Hill. 1990. *Black Feminist Thought*. Cambridge: Unwin Hyman.

———. 1992. "Transforming the Inner Circle: Dorothy Smith's Challenge to Sociological Theory," *Sociological Theory*, 10: 73–80.

Crenshaw, Kimberle. 1991. "Mapping the Margins: Intersectionality, Identity Politics, and Violence against Women of Color," *Stanford Law Review*, 43(6): 1241–1299.

Davis AY. 1983. *Women, Race, and Class*. New York: Vintage Books.

Dyer, R. 1997. *White*. London: Routledge.

Davis, Kathy. 2008. "Intersectionality as a Buzzword: A Sociology of Science Perspective on What Makes a Feminist Theory Successful," *Feminist Theory*, 9(1): 67–85.

Fox Keller, Evelyn. 1983. *A Feeling for the Organism: The Life and Work of Barbara McClintock*. San Francisco: W.H. Freeman.

Flax J. 1990. *Thinking Fragments: Psychoanalysis, Feminism, and Postmodernism in the Contemporary West*. Berkeley and Los Angeles: University of California Press.

Ferreira da Silva, Denise. 2011. "Notes for a Critique of the 'Metaphysics of Race'," *Theory, Culture and Society*, 28(1): 138–148.

Goetz AM. 2001. *Women Develop0ment Workers: Implementing Rural Credit Programmes in Bangladesh*. SAGE: Thousand Oaks, CA.

Gunnarson, Lena. 2011. "A Defence of the Category 'Women'," *Feminist Theory*, 12(1): 23–37.

Hooks B. 1990. *Yearning: Race, Gender, and Politics*. Toronto: Between the Lines.

Hartsock Nancy. 1990. "Foucault on Power: A Theory for Women?" in Linda J. Nicholson (ed.), *Feminism/Postmodernism*, pp. 157–175. New York: Routledge.

Hawkesworth M. 2004. "The Semiotics of Premature Burial: Feminism in a Postfeminist Age," *Signs*, 29(4): 961–985.

Harding, Sandra and Kathryn Norberg. 2005. "New Feminist Approaches to Social Science Methodologies: An Introduction," *Signs*, 30(4): 2009–2015.

Kroker, Arthur. 1992. *The Possessed Individual*. Montreal: New World Perspectives.

Lazreg M. 1990. "Feminism and Difference: The Perils of Writing as a Woman on Women in Algeria," in Marianne Hirsch and Evelyn Fox Keller (eds), *Conflicts in Feminism*, pp. 326–348. New York and London: Routledge.

Levi-Strauss, Claude. 1966. *The Savage Mind*. London: Weidenfeld and Nicholson.

Lemert C. 2003. "Against Capital-S Sociology," *Sociological Theory*, 21(1): 74–83.

Luft, Rachel E. and Jane Ward. 2009. "Toward an Intersectionality Just Out of Reach: Confronting Challenges to Intersectional Practice," in Vasilikie Demos and Marcia Texler Segal (eds), *Perceiving Gender Locally, Globally, and Intersectionally*, pp. 9–17. UK: Jai Press.

Martineau H. 1869/1983. *Autobiography*, 2 vols. London: Virago Press.

McCall, Leslie. 2005. "The Complexity of Intersectionality, Signs," *Journal of Women in Culture and Society*, 30(3): 1771–1800.

Mohanty Chandra Talpade. 1984. "Under Western Eyes: Feminist Scholarship and Colonial Discourses," *Boundary*, 2 (12.3/13.1): 333–358.

Modood, Tariq. 2008. "A Basis for and Two Obstacles in the Way of a Multiculturalist Coalition," *The British Journal of Sociology*, 59(1): 47–52.

Modood, Tariq and Fauzia Ahmad. 2007. "British Muslim Perspectives on Multiculturalism," *Theory, Culture and Society*. 24(2): 187–213.

Narayan, Una. 2000. "Undoing the 'Package Picture' of Cultures," *Signs*, 25(4): 1083–1086.

Ransby B. 2000. "Black Feminism at Twenty-One: Reflections on the Evolution of a National Community," *Signs*, 25(4): 1215–1221.

Rattansi, Ali. 2011. "Race's Recurrence: Reflections on Amin's 'The Remainders of Race'," *Theory, Culture, and Society*, 28(1): 112–128.

Smith, Dorothy. 1990. *The Conceptual Practices of Power: A Feminist Sociology of Knowledge*. Boston: Northeastern University Press.

Stanely, Liz. 1990. *Feminist Praxis*. London: Routledge.

Said, Edward. 1997. *Covering Islam: How the Media and the Experts Determine How We See the Rest of the World*. London: Vintage.

Sydie, R.A. 2002. "Feminist Sociology: Past and Present Challenges," in Nikolai Genov (ed.), *Advances in Sociological Knowledge*, pp. 372–395. Paris: CISS/ISSC.

Turkle, Sherry and Seymour Papert. 1990. "Epistemological Pluralism: Styles and Voices within the Computer Culture," *Signs*, 16(1): 128–157.

Thobani, Sunera. 2007. "White Wars: Western Feminisms and the War on Terror," *Feminist Theory*, 8(2): 169–185.

Turner, Bryan. 2007. "Religious Authority and the New Media," *Theory, Culture and Society*, 24(2): 117–134.

Weinstein, Deena and Michael A. Weinstein. 1991. "Georg Simmel: Sociological (*Flaneur) Bricoleur*," *Theory, Culture and Society*, 8(3): 151–168.

Woodhull, W. 2003. "Global Feminisms, Transnational Political Economies, Third World Cultural Production," *Journal of International Women's Studies*, 4(2): 76–90.

Werbner, Pnina. 2007. "Veiled Interventions in Pure Space: Honour, Shame and Embodied Struggles among Muslims in Britain and France," *Theory, Culture and Society*, 24(2): 161–186.

10

Julia Kristeva: Toward a Postmodern Philosophy of Feminism

MAHBUBA NASREEN

Introduction

Julia Kristeva, perhaps one of the most widely cited philosophers in contemporary times with diversified identities: "one of the most original and influential thinkers" (McAfee, 2004: 3); "most controversial" postmodern feminist (Tong, 1998: 204); "one of the most brilliant and versatile of the French intellectual figures of the last two decades" (Lodge, 1988: 224); "always destroys the latest preconception, the one we thought we could be comforted by, the one of which we could be proud" (Roland Barthes quoted in Lodge, 1988: 224); "...Kristeva's research has continually sought to formulate new modes of critical discourse in order to reflect logic and reality differently. Her principal objects for analysis are modern or modernist—especially avant-garde literary texts" (Volat, 1999). Kristeva, however, is mostly referred for her scholarly deliberations on psychoanalysis and postmodern feminism. Her contributions have also been acknowledged for analytical discussions on structuralism, linguistics, literature, and political theory.

The Algeria born French philosopher Julia Kristeva (migrated to France in 1960 to pursue her Doctor of Philosophy degree at the age of 23) was influenced by her contemporary philosophers Lucian Goldmann and Roland Barthes. Her own theories have been shaped through synthesizing elements from anthropologist Claude Levi-Strauss, psychoanalyst Jaques Lacan, postmodern philosopher Michel Foucault, and philosopher Mikhail Bakhtin. However, Julia Kristeva is continued to be discussed as one of the major French feminists along with Helene Cixous, Luce Irigaray, and Simone de Beauvoir. Her contemporary writings are identified more with feminine philosophy. This becomes prominent while in a recent lecture Kristeva declares that "humanism is a feminism. The liberation of desires could only lead to the emancipation of women. The battle for economic, legal and political parity, necessitate a new reflection on the choice and responsibility of motherhood. Secularization is until today the only civilization that lacks a discourse on motherhood. This passionate bond between mother and child, through which biology becomes meaning, alterity, and word, is a *'reliance'* that, different from the paternal function and from religiosity, completes the participation in full in the humanist ethic" (Kristeva, 2011).

Kristeva, however, is not keen to be indentified only with feminism and agrees that her work on feminism is not that intense. In her own point of view: "It is very difficult to trace back my interest in the "feminine." I suppose that at the very moment in which I started asking questions about myself, the question of the "feminine" had already been formulated in my mind, so one could say perhaps it started in the period of my adolescence when I became interested in literature which necessarily asks questions about the sexual differences.... in my theoretical work, this question is raised in a more succinct manner, perhaps also more discreet one, but which was nevertheless very intense" (Zivancevici, 2009). The present chapter is an attempt to portray Julia Kristeva through her feminine philosophy, which differs from those of "mainstream feminism" (especially in France), and is based on linguistics and psychoanalytic perspectives.

Feminism Visited Through Linguistics and Psychosymbolic Structure by Kristeva

In "The Ethics of Linguistics" (first published in 1974 and later reprinted as "Desire in Language: A Semiotic Approach to Literature and Art," 1980[1]) Julia Kristeva provides a systematic account of language. Kristeva argues that in the beginning of the 19th century Marx, Nietzsche, and Freud, with a primary goal of reformulating an ethic, contributed to the intellectual, political, and social ventures within the

[1] Translated by Thomas Gora, Alice Jardine, and Leon S. Roudiez and edited by Leon S. Roudiez.

Western society and discourse. She believes that ethics has shifted its orientation from coercive, customary manner of ensuring coerciveness through the repetition of a code of a particular group (mores, social contract) to the free play of negativity, need, desire, pleasure, and ecstasy. Since its inception linguistics has been systematic and continuing to discover the rules of fundamental social code, which is language. Kristeva pointed out that language is the system of signs or strategy of logical sequences. In her analysis she has added "poetic language" as the object of liguistics' attention in its pursuit of truth in language. However, Kristeva attempts to see linguistics is different in "Women's Time" in *New Maladies of the Soul* (1993), where focus is given more in context of social phenomena. Rejecting the predominant nature of language in postmodern society, which describes almost everything positively, Kristeva argues that it excludes politics of language and marginalization of people. To overcome such limitations, she prescribed that there is a need for: a) fracturing the interpretation and intellectual society into different parts; and b) multiplication of text, e.g., one language or word can be used for many senses through which difference in society can be identified.

Julia Kristeva is critical about both the capitalistic and Marxian ideologies. She is also critical about structuralist linguistics and suggests that to understand society one should be able to read the sign of contemporary society. For which she feels the need to develop a new sign to explain the changing trend or the contemporary problems of society. The sign, she named as "symanalyis," connects the body completely with its drive, life, and logic of the interpretation of world. It exists and can be linked with society. In analyzing the concepts Kristeva distinguishes the terms "semiotic" (the language itself which gives idea about text) from "semiotics" (provides idea of symbolic; exists with signifying process and explains beyond text). The semiotic is related to drives and articulations of the subject, whereas the semiotic can be expressed verbally. As opposed to symbolic, which is a way of signifying language as a sign system complete with its grammar and syntax, semiotic is not regular rules. Although semiotic and symbolic are not completely separate from each other, they are different. The semiotic could be seen as the modes of expression that originate in the unconscious; in contrast, the symbolic could be seen as the conscious way an individual tries to express using a stable sign system, eg, written, spoken, or gestured with sign language (McAfee, 2004: 17).

Daine Fuss (1992) made an effort to use Kristeva's notion of the homosexual-maternal facet to suggest the role of consumption by women of fashion ads as female homosexuality. According to Kristeva, female sexuality is fundamental to the daughter in her preoedipal identification with the mother. Borrowing Klien's (1963/1949) thought she suggested that the oceanic, chaotic indistinct moment/site before the splitting into subject/object, self/other, and mother/child still irrupts into the subject's daily life through semiotic *chora*. The semiotic is a perfect union, and it is sometimes reconstituted in the flow of poetry or images. She balances it against the "symbolic" (as used by Lacan for the realm of language and culture through which we become subjects) through using semiotic (Cranny-Francis, 2003: 157).

Julia Kristeva critically analyzes the Freudian interpretation of "Oedipus complex" in this context. She added a new phrase "ploymorphones," which is a preoedipus stage and argues that learning the language of a child actually happens in the preoedipus stage. This is the time when a child is born in the mother's womb and stays there till birth. Kristeva uses the word "abject" that is marginalized in society in the preoedipal stage and that is called semiotic. She argues that there is a need for women to make their own language to communicate feminine experience as well experiment with new ways of structuring that experience (Pilhcer, Jane and Imelda Whelehan, 2004: 123). Kristeva (1982) introduces the idea of "Other" at the heart of the "Subject" while discussing on abjection: "The concept of abjection derives from the disgusted fascination with products expelled from the body, which mark the boundaries of the body and the subject" (cited in Cranny-Francis et al., 2003: 65). According to Kristeva, abjection is the process by which an infant emerges from the undifferentiated union with her/his mother. At that time the infant does not have her/his clear or proper self, but the infant emergence is based on physical and mental expelling of the infant. Through this means a sense of a discrete "I" begins to be developed before s/he learns language.

Although in explaining semiotics Kristeva seems closer to psychoanalysis, it has a feminist perspective. Moreover, she prefers to analyze semiotics and her interest on the politics of marginality. This becomes prominent while Kristeva "describes the semiotic as 'feminine,' a phase dominated by the space of the mother's body" (Sarup, 1993: 124). Kristeva explains that while a baby is born in her mother's womb s/he becomes connected with the mother's emotions, her psychological stand,

and the nurturing and development of her body. At this stage she uses the term "semiotic chora" that defines the child's body, ego, and identity. Kristeva borrowed the term *Chora* from the Greek philosopher Plato, who uses the word in his *Timaeus*. Plato uses the term as the original space or receptacle of the universe, whereas Kristeva uses the term to identify with the mind, which belongs to each individual before she or he develops clear identity of her or his own. In this early psychic space, an infant experiences a wealth of drives, e.g., feelings, instincts, etc., that could be extremely disorienting and destructive if there was no relationship of the infant with her or his mother's body (McAfee, 2004: 19). In this context, the symbolic proposition acts within the domain of a woman's body. Kristeva argues that, therefore, feminine language is important to understand the society. She admits that "I am interested in language [langage], and in the other side of language which is filtered inevitably by language and yet is not language. I have named this heterogeneity variously. I have sought it out in the experience of love, of abjection, of horror. I have called it the semiotic in relation to the symbolic. But it is the doubling of language [la langue] that seems, at the moment, to be of more interest to women than to men" (O'Grady, 1998: 8–11).

She adds, it must be mentioned that "question (*of femininity*) is related to the notion of *chora*, which directs us back to the archaic state of language. This state is known to a child who is in a state of osmosis with his/her mother during which language manifests itself as co-lalia, a melodic alliteration that precedes the introduction of signs within a syntactic order" (Zivancevici, 2009).

Misplaced abjection has been cited as one of the causes of women's oppression by Kristeva. In *Tales of Love*, Kristeva (1983/1987: 374) argues that in "patriarchal cultures, women works have been reduced to reproductive activities, i.e., to the maternal functions." In *A New Type of Intellectual: The Dissident* (1977/1986: 298), she maintains that "real female innovation (in whatever field) will only come about when maternity, female creation, and the link between them are better understood."

As one of the most contributory postmodern feminists, Kristeva explains difference between women and men through psychosymbolic structure rather than emphasizing on biological differences.

...It is not biological differences that differentiate women from men. Even these differences have to be articulated to be meaningful. It is the symbolic realm that differentiates the sexes. Seeing the social order and the symbolic order as two dimensions of a large system (the psycho-symbolic structure), Kristeva argues that women's demands cannot be met by identifying with the system on by asking the system to identify with them. (McAfee, 2003: 96)

Kristeva notes that due to symbolic order in society women are taught the masculine language but not what she feels to express. Such psychosymbolic structure makes women feel frustrated and rejected from language and the social bond. In which women discover neither the affects nor the meanings of the relationships they enjoy with nature, their bodies, their children's bodies, another women, or a man. Kristeva (1993/1996: 213) points out that "the accompanying frustration, which is also experienced by some men, is the quintessence of the new feminist ideology. Consequently, it is difficult, if not impossible, for women to adhere to the sacrificial logic of separation and syntactic links upon which language and the social code are based."

In some ways her work can be seen as trying to adopt a psycho-analytic approach to the poststructuralist criticism. For example, her view of the subject and its construction shares similarities with Sigmund Freud and Jacques Lacan. It must be mentioned here that in general feminist thoughts in the 1970s were highly influenced by the psychoanalytic philosophies of Freud and Lacan. However, Kristeva rejects any understanding of the subject in a structuralist sense; instead she favors a subject always "in progress" or "in crisis." She discussed politics and marginality in context of semiotics and language, which makes her popular. Kristeva claims that "political discourses consistently fail to take account of individuals and subjectivity and this is why she advocates for political marginality and is critical of feminism as a collective movement" (Brooks, 1997: 82). Moreover, Kristeva uses singular "woman" in order to establish that there is no essential womanhood, not even a repressed woman. Her notion has some similarities and dissimilarities with her contemporary postmodern feminist Helene Cixous. Like Cixous, Kristeva identifies feminine forms of signification, which cannot be contained by the rational structure of the symbolic order and which threatened its sovereignty. Whereas, unlike Cixous, Kristeva does locate feminine aspects of language in women's female libido (Weedon, 1987: 69).

In "Women's Time" Kristeva also disagrees with already existing types of feminism. She specifically rejects the notion of first and second wave of feminism including the explanations of Simone de Beauvoir. One of the major differences between the thoughts of Kristeva and Beauvoir was that the former has been identified as literary theorist, cultural critic, as well as practicing psychoanalyst, whereas the latter has rejected the psychoanalyst perspective. Kristeva is identified as "essentialist"; Beauvoir, on the other hand, as existentialist. Simone de Beauvoir's "existential" explanation is claimed to be a totalizing or holistic explanation related to feminism. Beauvoir provides a two stage theory: the biological and genetic (historical) and a theory of social reproduction (Waters, 1994: 261–262). However, Kristeva's stands are often seems to be considered to reject feminism altogether including the one provided by Simone de Beauvoir. First wave feminism was connected with early socialist feminism in the late 19th and 29th centuries, and was concerned with access and equal opportunities of women. On the other hand, second wave feminism started in late 1960s and early 1970s, and was closely linked with radical views of women's empowerment and rights. Third wave feminism seeks to challenge and expand common definition of gender and sexuality. As opposed to the view of Simon de Beauvoir (1974), who argues that a society can only be understood through natural structure than biological structure, Kristeva mentions that multiple sexual identity can only be understood by unified feminine language, e.g., "mankind." Kristeva proposed the idea of multiple sexual identities rejecting the "unified feminine language."

She pointed out that new generation of feminists will be able to reconcile "maternal" time with linear time and will "no longer wishing to be excluded or no longer content with the function which has always been demanded of us (to maintain, arrange and perpetuate this symbolic contract...) how can we reveal our place, first as it is bequeathed to us by tradition and then as we want to transfer it." Kristeva argues that women must refuse to become a "him" to avoid supporting the patriarchal order, which marginalizes women. They must uphold the law and sexual difference. Therefore, women must not refuse to enter the symbolic order, but neither should they adopt a masculine model of femininity (Kristeva, 1977). She points out that "...it is not just biological differences that differentiate women from men. Even these differences have to be articulated to be meaningful. It is the symbolic realm that differentiates the sexes. Seeing the social order and the symbolic order as two dimensions of a large system (psychosymbolic structure), Kristeva argues that "women's demands cannot be met by identifying with the system on by asking the system to identify with them" (McAfee, 2003: 96). Kristeva identifies herself as third generation of feminists who challenge notions of the seamless identity, in general, and notion of women and men, in particular (Oliver, 1997: 299).

However, although Kristeva is concerned about the sexual difference between man and woman, it does not necessarily mean that she believes such identities are manifested in exactly the same way by each "female" or "male." She mentioned that the concept "woman" exists only at the political level and makes no sense at the ontological level. Women must use "we are women" for their demands such as freedom of abortion and contraception, daycare centers for children, equality on the job, etc. (Tong, 1998: 206).

Kristeva believes that feminism is one kind of ideology that excludes religion. She points out that feminism should be understood through individuality of women, as empowerment of women depends on individual's own writings, contributions, and socializations. She rejects the idea of seeing women from pluralism and suggests avoiding using the phrases such as "all women are exploited" or "women are exploited in all aspects." Kristeva argues that there is a counterbalance in society and it depends on uniformity and accessibility of individuals in all areas including information through language. She suggests that three matters are important for women's individual development, and these are: internalize, exploitative understanding, and acknowledgement.

Conclusions

The feminist perspective of Kristeva has been critically examined by the feminist critiques (Fraser, 1992; Butler, 1990; Grosz, 1989; Moi, 1986), especially for her view as an essentialist. The critiques were mainly around her as a practice of making false generalizations; as offering biological explanation for a psychological trait and as providing a substantive account of what it is to be certain kind of thing. (McAfee, 2004: 77). Ian Almond (2007: 132) is critical about Kristeva's "ethnocentrism" for the subject matter of her book *About Chinese Women (1977)*. He refers to Gayatri Spivak's comments on Kristeva that "the brief, expansive, often completely ungrounded way in which she writes about two thousand years of a culture she is unfamiliar with." Kristeva's remarks related to the Muslim world have also been seen negatively as she does not refer to anything other than the Rushdie fatwa in dismissing the entire Muslim faith as "reactionary and persecutory" (Almond, 2007: 154–55).

Julia Kristeva has often been highlighted as the most controversial amongst all the postmodern feminists, as she explicitly rejects (*French*[2]) feminism (Tong, 1998: 204). However, "…just because Kristeva disavowed feminism as it is understood in France does not mean that she has necessarily opposed the goals and strategies of feminism" (Tong, 1998: 204). Similar voice has been heard from Oliver (1993: 94) who points out that Kristeva's "rejection of (*French*) feminism can teach us some important lessons about feminism."

As a dynamic philosopher, Kristeva does not wish to level herself by one concept or to be "chained" or "confined" to her own thoughts and feel. According to her "I am very proud of the widespread use of my ideas and at the same time very much ashamed because they have become so fashionable. Everybody thinks and talks about 'intertextuality', everybody thinks and talks about 'abjection.' The ideas become politically correct everywhere in the world and I hate it because I think when people repeat what you have done and said, they can no longer recognise you yourself. You are denied. It's a kind of decay of this moment when the idea burst out of your mind. Now the idea is consumerised" (Sutherland, 2006).

It may be concluded that although Kristeva does not refer to her own works as feminist, many feminists synthesized her writings within the discourse of feminist theories and criticism (Oliver, 1998). Her feminism may differ from the mainstream, but it has a clear dimension for third generation feminists who view women and men based on their symbolic as well as biological existence. However, it can be predicted that Kristeva will continue to be highlighted as "logical" as well as "radical" for her grounding principles toward a postmodern philosophy of feminism.

[2] Although feminine philosophy of Julia Kristeva differs from the contemporary French feminists, she has been widely discussed in Europe, Asia, and some other parts of the world. She is the mostly referred postmodern feminist in contemporary sociology.

216   Mahbuba Nasreen

"Julia Kristeva's innovative explorations of questions on the intersection of language, culture, and literature have inspired research across the humanities and the social sciences throughout the world and have also had a significant impact on feminist theory. In her path breaking book La Révolution du langage poétique (1974; Revolution in Poetic Language, 1985) Julia Kristeva first advanced the theory that the process of signification in language is constituted by two different but interacting elements, the symbolic and the semiotic, thus bringing the living body back into language. Her trilogy Pouvoirs de l'horreur (1980; Powers of Horror, 1982), Histoires d'amour (1983; Tales of Love, 1987), and Soleil noir (1987; Black Sun, 1989) offers original and powerful theories of abjection, love, and depression. In Étrangersà nous-mêmes (1988; Strangers to Ourselves, 1991) her psychoanalytic approach provides crucial insights into the problems of migration, exile, and otherness. Julia Kristeva has published more than 20 books and continues to be remarkably productive. Recently she has been particularly interested in the lives of women writers and intellectuals." (Citation of the Academic Committee of the The Holberg International Memorial Prize established by the Norwegian Government for the purpose of annually awarding the outstanding scholarly work in the fields of the arts and humanities, social sciences, law, or theology was awarded for the first time on December 3, 2004, to Professor Julia Kristeva.)

References

Almond, Ian. 2007. *The New Orientalists: Postmodern Representations of Islam from Foucault to Baudrillard.* London: I.B. Tauris.

Beauvoir, Simon de. 1974. *The Second Sex.* Ed. H.M. Parshley. New York: Vintage Books.

Brooks, Ann. 1997. *Postfeminisms: Feminism, Cultural Theory and Cultural Forms.* London: Routledge.

Butler, Judith. 1990. *Gender Trouble: Feminism and Subversion of Identity.* New York and London: Routledge.

Citation of the Academic Committee of the Holberg International Memorial Prize (established by the Norwegian Government and was awarded for the first time on December 3, 2004 to Professor Julia Kristeva).

Cranny-Francis, Anna et al. 2003. *Gender Studies: Terms and Debates.* New York: Palgrave Macmillan.

Fraser, Nancy and Sandra Lee Bartkey (eds) 1992. *Revaluing French Feminism: Critical Essays on Difference, Agency and Culture.* Blumington: Indian University Press.

Fuss, Dianne. 1992. "Fashion and the Homospectatorial Look," *Critical Inquiry*, 18, 713–73, Summer.

Grosz, n Elizabeth. 1989. *Sexual Subversion: Three French Feminists*. London: Allen and Unwin.

Kelly, Oliver (ed.). 1997. *The Portable Kristeva*. New York: Columbia University Press.

Klein, Melanie. 1963/1949. *The Psychoanalysis of Children*. Ed. Alix Strachey. London: Hogarth Press.

Kristeva, Julia. 1977. *About Chinese Women*. London: Boyars.

———. 1982. *The Powers of Horror: An Essay on Abjection*. Ed. Leon Roudiez. New York: Columbia University Press.

———. 1983. *Tales of Love*. Ed. Leon Roudiez. New York: Columbia University Press, 1987.

———. 1993. *New Maladies of the Soul*. English Ed. Ross Guberman in 1995. New York: Columbia University Press.

———. 1994. *Time and Sense: Proust and the Experience of Literature*. Ed. Ross Guberman. New York: Columbia University Press, 1996.

———. 2011. Speech at the Day of reflection, dialogue and prayer for peace and justice in the world, that Benedict XVI convoked in Assisi, October 27, 2011.

Lodge, David. 1988. *Modern Criticism and Theory*. India: Pearson Education and Dorling Kindersley Publishing Inc.

Noëlle, McAfee. 2004. *Julia Kristeva*. New York and London: Routledge.

Moi, Toril (ed.). 1986. "A New Type of Intellectual: The Dissident" (originally published in 1977), in Toril Moi (ed.), *The Kristeva Reader*. New York: Columbia University Press.

———. 1985. *Sexual/Texual Politics: Feminst Literary Theory*. London and New York: Routledge.

O'Grady, Kathleen. 1998. Dialogue with Julia Kristeva, in "Parallax: Julia Kristeva 1966–96," *Aesthetics, Politics, Ethics*, 8(July–September): 5–16.

Oliver, Kelly. 1993. *Reading Kristeva: Unraveling the Double-bind*. Bloomington: Indiana University Press.

———. 1998. "Summary of Major Themes, Kristeva and Feminism." Available online at http://www.cddc.vt.edu/feminism/kristeva.html (downloaded on October 31, 2013).

Pilhcer, Jane and Imelda Whelehan. 2004. *50 Key Concepts in Gender Studies*. London: SAGE Publications Ltd.

Sarup, Madan. 1993. *An Introductory Guide to Post Strcuturalism and Post Modernism*. 2nd Ed. Athen: Georgia University Press.

Sutherland, John. 2006. "The Ideas Interview: Julia Kristeva," *The Guardian*, Tuesday, March 14, 2006.

Tong, Rosemarie Putnam. 1998. *Feminist Thought*. Colorado: Westview Press.

Volat, Hélène. 1999. "Julia Kristeva: A Bibliography. Stony Brook Library Homepage." Available online at http://ms.cc.sunysb.edu/~hvolat/kristeva/krist01.htm (last revised on October 30, 2011).

Waters, Malcolm. 1994. *Modern Sociological Theory*. New Delhi: SAGE Publications India Pvt Ltd.

Weedon, C. 1987. *Feminist Practice and Poststructuralist Theory*. Oxford: Blackwell.

Zivancevici, Nina. 2009. An Interview with Julia Kristeva, April 22.

11

"Market Religions" and Postmodern Globalization Theory

GABE IGNATOW AND LINDSEY A. JOHNSON

Introduction

The mass protests of the Arab Spring came as a shock to experienced Middle East analysts. The "new genre of revolution" (Allagui and Kuebler, 2011) represented by the Arab Spring, in which social networks and new media appeared to play central roles (Howard and Hussain, 2011; Khamis, 2011), has led to soul searching on the question of why virtually no analysts predicted the uprisings (Gause, 2011; Koehler and Warkotsch, 2011). While the Arab Spring has forced Middle East analysts to question their field's dominant theoretical frameworks and methodological tools, it has yet to merit much attention from comparative-historical social scientists or theorists of development and globalization. But the Arab Spring may prove to be at least as unsettling for these scholars as it has been for regional specialists (Schwarz and de Corral, 2011). The anti-authoritarian uprisings in Tunisia, Egypt, Libya, Yemen, Syria, Bahrain, and other Arab nations appear to be distinct from previous cycles of protest because they occurred nearly simultaneously in many countries, were led by educated urban youths (Khondker, 2011; Goldstone, 2011), were generally Islamic and nationalist, but not Islamist, in character (Feiler, 2011; Sayyid, 2011), and relied heavily on the Internet and social media (Allagui and Kuebler, 2011; Howard and Hussain, 2011; Khoury, 2011).

Those social scientists who have attempted to interpret or explain the Arab Spring thus far have done so mainly in terms of concepts and categories derived from modernist social theoretical frameworks— frameworks that presuppose a sharp distinction between modern and traditional institutions. Modernist theories provide several plausible interpretations of the Arab Spring (along with, among other movements, the Lebanese Cedar Revolution, the Iranian Green Movement, and, arguably, the Indian Anna Hazare movement). For instance, the uprisings can be interpreted through midcentury modernization theories (Lipset, 1963; Rostow, 1960) as a transitional phase for developing Middle Eastern countries on the road from premodern, authoritarian, and patriarchal systems of social relations to a universal global capitalist modernity (Khondker, 2011). In culturalist accounts these movements can be interpreted as manifestations of a rapidly expanding modern "world culture," Western in origin, which values individual rights and dignity over duty to the collective and preservation of sacred traditions (see Frank and Meyer, 2002; Lechner and Boli, 2005). In this scenario, the Arab Spring can be seen as a movement spearheaded by westernized, cosmopolitan elites whose privileged social positions insulate them from the poorer, more traditionalist, and devout majorities within their own countries. Such an interpretation dovetails with the modernist "civilizational analysis" of both Samuel Huntington (1996) and Peter Berger (1997). Huntington coined the term "Davos Culture" to refer to the culture of elite international business (see also Berger and Huntington, 2003), and Berger refers to a "faculty club culture" spread through educational and legal systems:

> While cultural globalization facilitates interaction between elites, it creates difficulties between these elites and the nonelite populations with whom they must deal. Many moral and ideological conflicts in contemporary societies pit an elite culture against a resentful mass of culturally accredited and economically underprivileged people. (Berger, 1997)

In arguing that such resentments may lead to the emergence of nationalist or religious counterelite groups, Huntington's analysis overlaps with aspects of dependency theories (e.g., Wallerstein, 1976) through which the Arab Spring can be interpreted as protests by actors in the heavily exploited peripheral regions of the global economy against the hegemony of core state actors (mainly the United States and EU). Although such theories were first developed in the 1970s as an alternative to the then-dominant modernization paradigm in development theory, dependency theories share many of modernization theories' methodological strategies and theoretical presuppositions, such as their "ideal type" method which "creates an opposition between a formalistic theoretical model of universal reference; on the one hand, and the particularities and 'accidents' of history on the other" (Skocpol, 1977: 1089), their consequent reliance on teleological assertions and *a posteriori* reasoning, their reduction of politics to economics, and their reliance on notions of social "systems," be they national or world systems (Skocpol, 1977). Working within a dependency theory paradigm, Chase-Dunn (2011) argues that the Arab Spring movements are part of a "new global left," a "contemporary network of global countermovements…seeking to transform the capitalist world-system into a more humane, sustainable, and egalitarian civilization." If these movements see themselves as opposed to the hegemony of core states over peripheral ones, then Wallerstein's framework would potentially help analysts to identify the goals, social origins, and demographic compositions of these movements (see Robinson, 2011). But in fact there is very little about the Arab Spring that conforms to the tenets of modernist social theories, whether in the guise of modernization theory, civilizational analysis, or dependency theory. The Arab Spring movements are not led by insular elites, but by educated, internet-savvy, but often unemployed or underemployed youths. The uprisings are not secularist, Kemalist, or otherwise anti-religious movements, but are rather heavily Islamic (Sayyid, 2011), as evidenced by the mass prayers in Cairo's Tahrir Square. But while they are Islamic, they have not been led by Islamists or religious fundamentalists. And contra dependency theories, they are not led by the poor or economically underprivileged but by the urban middle class, and were not directed at the states positioned in the core of the global economic system. Gauss (2011) notes that the "common enemy of the 2011 Arab Revolts is not colonialism, U.S. power, or Israel, but Arabs' own rulers," and even Chase-Dunn acknowledges that the revolts' targets "have been mainly authoritarian national regimes rather than global capitalism," and that the Arab Spring movements have therefore been "rather different from the global justice movements." They have been rather different indeed: with the Lebanese Cedar Revolution and Iranian Green Movement, the Arab Spring has mixed democratic idealism, Islamic and national identities, and aspirations for a fuller participation in the global economy. The protests are not modern in a way that rejects religious beliefs or traditional identities, nor are they reactionary, anti-modern, or anti-capitalist. In what terms, then, should the Arab Spring protests be analyzed?

A premise of our chapter is that to hope to understand the Arab Spring as well as a number of other contemporary movements and trends in politics, religion, and culture, what is most urgently needed is for social theorists and social scientists to give credence to the claims of scholars in developing and non-Western countries who argue, based not only on developments in postmodern theory but on a wide range of empirical studies, that under contemporary conditions of globalization, the modernist binary obscures at least as much as it reveals (e.g., on Turkey, see Adas, 2006; Aras and Caha, 2000; Hendrick, 2009; Kosebalaban, 2005). We propose that what is needed as an alternative to modernist theories are more thoroughly postmodernist theoretical frameworks, and that the most useful theoretical frameworks for understanding social change under conditions of intense globalization are likely to be postmodernist simply in the sense of not counterposing "modernity" and "tradition." One starting point for such postmodernist theories of globalization is the idea that hybridity is a basic feature of globalization, and thus of the contemporary era (Appadurai, 1990; Nederveen-Pieterse, 1993). Societies and cultures, if they can be envisioned as discrete entities in the first place, have been mixing, interpenetrating, and hybridizing throughout human history. But as the pace and intensity of this hybridization has increased dramatically due to global economic and technological interconnectedness, it may prove productive to interpret contemporary social and religious movements as instances of postmodern cultural hybridity driven by globalization (e.g., Ignatow, 2004, 2007, and 2008).

It is our contention that a globalization- and internet-driven refiguration of the world's religious traditions has been obscured since at least 9/11 by the wave of scholarly and popular interest in reactionary anti-modern religious movements (see Haenni, 2005; Turner, 2010: 164). Though this attention is perfectly understandable given the magnitude of 21st-century terrorist atrocities and the wars in Afghanistan and Iraq, the sheer number of people in the world participating firsthand in fundamentalist movements is minuscule in comparison to the numbers affected by globalization, urbanization, and the internet (Nasr, 2009).

It is unfortunate too, in our eyes, that over the same period academic discourses on development and globalization have been needlessly fragmented by a persistent, pernicious distinction between positivist and postpositivist research. While "quantitative" and "qualitative" researchers may appear to live in separate scholarly worlds (Büthe, 2002; Tilly, 2004), we see no necessary methodological implications that follow from setting aside the modernist binary in favor of postmodern notions of mixing, hybridity, and fusion. Quantitative and qualitative evidence can be brought to bear on postmodernist theories, as we use the term here, just as it can be for any theoretical framework that claims to offer insight into any social phenomenon. Such frameworks, be they modernist, postmodernist, or otherwise, can be tested rigorously and systematically using both qualitative and quantitative methods. We can be, and in practice most comparative-historical social scientists are, pragmatic and rigorous in building our arguments and testing their ability to explain social phenomena relative to other available theories (Büthe, 2002: 489).

The remainder of our chapter is divided into four parts. First, we briefly review recent developments in qualitative comparative-historical research methods from political science and sociology. Second, from several sources, including most prominently Haenni's (2005) concept of "market Islam" (*"l'Islam de marché"*) and Turner's exegesis of Weber's *Protestant Ethic* (Turner, 1974 and 2010), we develop the concept of "market religion," which we define as a religious movement that represents a response to pressures and opportunities set in motion by economic liberalization. We further define market religion by positing five main features as well as one intervening social mechanism that affects the relative success of market religions within particular national settings. We also discuss some limitations of the concept's application. Third, we analyze the post-1980 growth of the neo-Pentecostal movement in Guatemala *qua* market religion. We use qualitative, comparative-historical process tracing techniques to identify causal social mechanisms that have given rise to this movement, and find the market religion concept to be a useful tool for identifying systematic but undertheorized effects of economic liberalization on world religions. We conclude with a brief argument for a postmodernist sociological realism premised on the compatibility of postmodernist theory and rigorous social science research methods.

Social Mechanisms and Process Tracing

Recent developments in qualitative comparative-historical research methods in political science and sociology have provided researchers with new strategies and tools for constructing and testing theoretical models of historical processes (Bennett and Elman, 2006; Grzymala-Busse, 2011; Mayntz, 2004; McAdam, Tarrow, and Tilly, 2008). New methodological strategies such as "systematic process analysis" (Hall, 2003) are case-based rather than variable-based: rather than designating the explanandum as the "dependent variable" and its hypothesized causes as "independent variables" and then pursuing explanation based on statistical associations among variables (Mahoney, 2000), process analysis seeks to explain a given social phenomenon—a specific "case"—by identifying the processes through which it is generated. These processes are conceived as *causal* social mechanisms that are regularities of a less general scope than laws. They are "*recurrent processes* linking specified initial conditions and a specific outcome" (Mayntz, 2003: 241) that have a "finite number of links" (Elster, 1989: 7). The end result of a process analysis may be a historical narrative, but in its more theoretically ambitious versions, process analytic research strategies aim at generalizations involving historical processes. Process analyses generally include a number of related techniques and strategies.

The technique of *process tracing* (George and Bennett, 2005) is a hallmark of process analysis and causal reconstruction. The goal of process tracing is to achieve and refine causal inference. Causation is established by "uncovering traces of a hypothesized causal mechanism within the context of a historical case or cases" (Bennett and Elman, 2006: 459) through close engagement with cases and examining diagnostic pieces of evidence understood as parts of a temporal sequence of phenomena.

Because process analytic techniques start with circumscribed empirical fields and do not seek to uncover universal laws or to build general social theory, it is incumbent upon analysts to establish the *historical range* (or scope conditions) of hypothesized mechanisms and causal sequences (Mayntz, 2003: 253).

A challenge in process analysis is to define or *delineate historical sequences as distinct.* Processes analyzable as causal chains generally do not come as discernable units with a naturally given beginning or end. As analysts artificially pick out a part of the ongoing process and try to explain how it has come to the particular point that is the explanandum, the "clear specification of the explanandum is the only methodological justification for making choices about where to begin an analysis" (Büthe, 2002: 487–88).

Process analysis requires analysts to hypothesize both processes that occur in causal sequences and *intervening mechanisms*. Care must be taken not to equate intervening mechanisms with intervening variables as they are used in correlational analysis: while intervening variables are added in a multivariate analysis to increase the total variance explained, intervening mechanisms differ from intervening variables because the former must *explain why* a correlation exists between an independent and a dependent variable.

From *"l'Islam de marché"* to Market Religion

Regional specialists recognize that rapid capitalist development has coincided with a resurgence of religion in many parts of the world, and that there are a number of possible causal relationships between these two historical macro-trends (Csordas, 2009; Haddorff, 2000; Hefner, 2010; Juergensmeyer, 2005; Rudnyckyj, 2009 and 2010). While scholars often treat the global resurgence of religion as "a response to the retreat of the state in the face of a globally ascendant neoliberalism" and a "welcome expression of a civil society rising in the face of a long overbearing state" (Hefner, 2010: 1033), there has been little analysis of the relations between capitalist development and the specific forms new religious movements have taken.

A materialist strand in Weber's sociology of religion provides a useful starting point for analyzing the relations between contemporary capitalism and religious innovation. In his 1974 exegesis of the *Protestant Ethic*, Bryan Turner identified four distinct Weberian theses about the connection between religious beliefs and capitalism, theses that "cannot be successfully reconciled in one coherent Weberian theory about the secular significance of religious doctrines" (Turner, 2010: 230). In Turner's judgment only one of the theses, the "fourth Weber thesis," withstands close scrutiny. The fourth thesis asserts that "to explain actions we need to understand the subjective meaning of social actions, but the languages which are available for describing and explaining actions are determined by socioeconomic settings" (Turner, 2010: 234). This thesis "underlines the continuity between Marx and Weber by showing that Weber continuously draws attention to the ways in which beliefs are shaped by their socio-economic contexts" (Turner, 2010: 231). The fourth Weber thesis refutes the "facile notion that Weber was arguing with 'the ghost of Marx'" (Turner, 2010: 233) and is aligned with a "consistent Marxist undercurrent in Weber's sociology" (Turner, 2010: 233) as evidenced in Weber's (1896) public lectures on the decline of ancient civilization and his encyclopedia article *The Agrarian Sociology of Ancient Civilizations* (1909) (see Wiener, 1982). Turner cites with approval Walton's (1971: 391) suggestion that Weber's sociology enables scholars to study "the possession by particular actors or groups of vocabularies, phrases or outlooks, which, far from being rationalizations or mystifications of interests, act as motive forces for action itself." Turner also references C. Wright Mill's (1940) theory that groups "exercise social control, linguistically, by imputing good or bad motives to actions" (Turner, 1974: 234).

Haenni's recent analysis of *l'Islam de marché* ("market Islam") or *"religiosité* 'market-friendly'" (Haenni, 2005: 59) in the Middle East, Turkey, and Southeast Asia shares its theoretical stance on the relations of capitalism and religion with Mill (1940), Walton (1971), and the fourth Weber thesis. Because of its identification of changes in the global economy rather than Islamic doctrine or practice as the main cause of recent developments in Islam, there is no reason why Haenni's analysis of market Islam, which we condense to the following six points, should not be applicable within non-Islamic contexts.

Historical Timing: In keeping with the "fourth Weber thesis," Haenni claims that market Islam is a response to contemporary economic conditions. Specifically, it is an adaptation to free-market, neoliberal economic policies and practices. These policies have diminished the ability of states to manage their national economies, and concomitantly the prestige and legitimacy of states in the eyes of their publics (see Crook, Pakulski, and Waters, 1992). Therefore, by definition, market religions in developing countries experience sustained growth only during a period of trade liberalization and neoliberal economic and social reforms following a crisis of state-led development strategies.

Doctrine: As Calvinist doctrine provided a "vocabulary of motives" (Mill, 1940: 9–10) justifying capitalist acquisitiveness, market Islam's doctrines deemphasize sin, militarism, and "grand collective projects" in favor of an open, individualistic, economically oriented, "positive thinking" Islam (Haenni refers to *"Islam proactif"*). Market Islam, generalized to market religion, valorizes hedonism, consumption, and economic competitiveness rather than militancy or "ostentatious piety." It also promotes Weberian rationality (a distillation of elements of the Protestant ethic [Haenni, 2005: 10]) and a global cosmopolitan outlook.

Organizational and Communications Strategies: Market Islam makes use of modern corporate management ideology. Its organizations are relatively egalitarian and use modern techniques of human resource management and corporate strategy. They also make extensive use of global communications technology including satellite television (e.g., talk shows, religious stations) and the internet (sophisticated websites, Facebook, or Twitter), and publishing empires featuring self-help books.

Adherents: Haenni describes market Islam as a product of *embourgoisement*: its adherents are new bourgeoisie who do not wish to abandon their religion as they enter into global capitalist competition (Nasr, 2009).

Political Stance: For Haenni, market Islam's "new religious entrepreneurs" are less interested in "grand political designs" than are Islamists (p. 8). Representing the "neoliberal politicization of Islam" (p. 11), market Islam is not a prelude to the restoration of an Islamic state or the imposition of *Sharia* law, but rather a force for the privatization of the state. In this way, market Islam resembles the "faith-based inititiatives" and "compassionate conservatism" of the US conservatives.

Intervening Mechanism: In our reading, an implication of Haenni's analysis is that market Islam develops only where economic liberalization has been accompanied by media liberalization and globalization, and by at least limited officially sanctioned religious pluralism (Ignatow, 2011a and 2011b).

Guatemalan Neo-Pentecostalism

Although Haenni's generalizations about market Islam have yet to be subjected to systematic empirical scrutiny, assuming that his analysis of market Islam in the Middle East, Turkey (Adas, 2006 and 2008), and Southeast Asia (Rudnyckyj, 2009 and 2010) is at least partly correct, we can explore the social mechanisms that appear to have generated similar "market-friendly" religious movements in other regions. Beginning with a successful market-friendly religious movement, we should be able to trace the historical processes and events that preceded it using our formalizations of Haenni's arguments. Here, we choose one illustrative case that is not Islamic but is otherwise similar in many respects to the movements analyzed by Haenni: neo-Pentecostalism in Guatemala. Neo-Pentecostalism is a relatively new religious phenomenon (Meyer, 2010: 121) that is growing in popularity in Latin America, Africa, and parts of Asia. It is "one of the most influential theological-ecclesial movements today in Latin America" (Suazo, 2009a: 1).

In Guatemala neo-Pentecostalism is an offshoot of Pentecostalism, although some neo-Pentecostal churches originated in non-Pentecostal Protestant denominations (Schäfer, 1991; Suazo, 2009a). In 2005, Pentecostals represented about 73 percent of the Latin American Protestant population (World Christian Database) and at least 10 percent of the Guatemalan population (Pew, 2006). Neo-Pentecostalism's rate of growth is faster in Guatemala than in most other Latin American countries; there is evidence that the Catholic Church and many Protestant denominations have lost members to neo-Pentecostal churches (Evans, 1991; Suazo, 2009b).

In Guatemala, neo-Pentecostalism is a mainly urban and middle-class phenomenon (Smith, 2008) centered in the megachurches of Guatemala City. Four of the most prominent neo-Pentecostal mega-churches are the *Fraternidad Cristiana* (established in 1978 with a second church structure, popularly known as "*The Mega-Frater*," built in 1991), *El Shaddai* (1983), *La Familia de Dios* (1990), and *Casa de Dios* (1994). According to the *Fraternidad Cristiana's* website, its Mega Auditorium, which was finished in 2007, contains 12,200 seats (*Fraternidad Cristiana de Guatemala* 2011). *Casa de Dios* claims to reach 20,000 people on Sunday mornings through their on-site services and house groups (*Ministerios de Cash Luna*, 2010). *El Shaddai's* current building was built in 1995 and has 5,000 seats (*Iglesia Ministerios El Shaddai*, 2010).

Historical Timing: With other Latin American countries, in the 1970s and early 1980s Guatemala faced a crisis of its relatively inward-looking import-substitution economic model (Bulmer-Thomas, 2003;

Taylor, 1998). As a response to decades of slow growth, inflation, and recession, in the 1980s Guatemala instituted neoliberal policy reforms intended to open the country to foreign investment and competition (see Baer and Maloney, 1997). Guatemala returned to democratic rule in 1986 and in 1996 signed peace accords ending a 36-year civil war between guerrillas and the military. In 1995, the country joined the World Trade Organization and, in 2005, ratified the CAFTA-DR, which facilitated trade between Guatemala, the United States, and other Central American countries. The most rapid growth of neo-Pentecostalism in Guatemala occurred during the 1980s and 1990s, roughly simultaneous with the country's economic liberalization and democratization.

Doctrine: The "prosperity gospel" preached in neo-Pentecostal churches closely resembles the "market-friendly" Islamic sermons described by Haenni. Both religious ideologies have been directly influenced by American evangelicalism (see e.g., Sakr, 2007). The neo-Pentecostalism prosperity gospel, or the "health and wealth gospel" (Mora, 2008), "emphasizes a God who guarantees success" (Kim, 2006). Personal material wealth is interpreted as a sign of God's favor on the believer's life, and it is believed that people who give much to the church will be blessed with even more material prosperity (Cox, 2006; Smith, 2007). This is because "God has promised, in some way, the material prosperity of his children who are faithful, who have faith," and poverty is "a sign of sin" that a person has acted "against the will of God" (Suazo, 2009b: 3).

Neo-Pentecostals use the biblical passage *2 Corinthians 9:6* to justify the acquisition of material wealth: "Remember this: Whoever sows sparingly will also reap sparingly, and whoever sows generously will also reap generously." Pastors use this verse to encourage members to give money or material goods directly to the local neo-Pentecostal church with the promise that they will receive economic blessings (Robbins, 2004). For example, in a 2011 *Noches de Gloria* (Nights of Glory) event in Dallas, Texas, the Guatemalan neo-Pentecostal pastor Cash Luna cited this verse from Corinthians when asking those in attendance to donate at least $20 to defray the cost of the event. Prosperity gospel also teaches that as children of the King (God), Christians "have the right to inherit everything that belongs to the King" (Suazo, 2009b: 3). Prosperity gospel in the Guatemalan setting also includes self- and group-affirming messages. During his 2011 event in Dallas, Cash

Luna mentioned that the reason he decided to hold *Noches de Gloria* in the high-end American Airlines Center in downtown Dallas was because Latinos aren't "second-class people." Sermons preached in neo-Pentecostal megachurches generally do not focus on actions traditionally labeled as sinful (Smith, 2006).

While not making specific statements regarding gender roles, neo-Pentecostalism has elevated the role of women in places. Neo-Pentecostal pastors' wives are often referred to as *pastora* (the feminine of pastor). When speaking in public, Cash Luna refers to his wife as "Pastora Sonia." Pastora Cecilia de Caballeros rose to the main leadership position in *El Shaddai* after her husband stepped down to enter politics. And women serve as ushers and hold other leadership positions in many local neo-Pentecostal congregations (Smith, 2009; Drogus, 1998; Smith, 2007).

Organizational and Communications Strategies: Neo-Pentecostal churches generally follow modern, corporate-style management principles and practices throughout their organizational structures and in event planning. Senior pastors (or apostles) of the neo-Pentecostal megachurches in Guatemala City function much like corporate CEOs: each church is led by a charismatic pastor who is believed to have received unique spiritual authority directly from God—an "'anointed' leader who fulfills the will of God" (Freston, 2001: 277). Power and authority are centralized in the churches (Levine, 2009), and senior pastors are generally not accessible to regular church attendees.

Neo-Pentecostal churches often use a franchise business model (Smith, 2008: 4). Many of the neo-Pentecostal megachurches in Guatemala City have satellite churches in rural parts of the country and have even established churches outside Latin America, and many of these churches include bookstores that feature books written by their own pastors along with other Christian-themed merchandise.

Credentialism is pronounced in Guatemalan neo-Pentecostalism. Apostles and senior pastors often advertise their many degrees, including honorary degrees, which were obtained mainly from higher education institutions in the U.S. Harold Caballeros; former pastor of *El Shaddai*, holds a masters in International Relations from Tufts University, a masters in Business from Miami University, a doctorate in Theology, and a graduate degree in Sociology from the Weatherhead Center for International Affairs at Harvard (*Partido VIVA: Visión con Valores*, 2011). Cash Luna holds a bachelors degree in Systems Management and a doctorate in Pastoral Ministry from California Christian University (*Ministerios Cash Luna* 2010). Jorge H. López, pastor of *Fraternidad Cristiana*, earned a Masters of Divinity from Logos Graduate School and an honorary doctorate in Humane Letters from the Institute of International Studies in Virginia (*Fraternidad Cristiana* 2011).

The Guatemala City neo-Pentecostal megachurches all use high-tech media in the form of television stations (*Canal 27*, *Enlace*), radio (*Stereo Visión*, *Radio Exclusiva*), and websites. During Cash Luna's *Noches de Gloria* event in Dallas, electronic signs throughout the stadium flashed Cash Luna's Facebook and Twitter addresses. As of 2011 Luna had approximately 70,000 Twitter followers, over a million Facebook fans, and a YouTube profile that made videos of his sermons and teachings available free of charge. Harold Caballeros, Jorge H. López, and Cecilia de Caballeros also have popular web sites and Twitter and Facebook pages.

Adherents: While in Guatemala traditional Pentecostalism is popular among the poor and working classes, in Guatemala City and other urban areas neo-Pentecostalism attracts mainly the middle and upper classes (Freston, 2001; Evans, 1991; Smith, 2009; Robbins, 2004). Steigenga refers to Guatemalan neo-Pentecostals as a "unique group among Protestants" who are generally "more educated, score higher on a self-anchored scale rating social position, and report lower levels of perceived religious discrimination and religious conflict in their communities" (Steigenga, 1999: 173). Freston (2001: 279–280) notes that neo-Pentecostalism is attractive to "better-off Protestants" who are "elite and middle-class professionals." Neo-Pentecostal megachurches in Guatemala City are almost always located in wealthy areas of the city or on the outskirts of the city at a remove from poor areas.

Political Stance: Neo-Pentecostals appear to be more politically active than are adherents of the new market-friendly forms of Islam. Neo-Pentecostals' political activities are guided by what is known as "dominion theology," a theological system claiming that "believers are destined to rule the world in the name of God" (Mathews Samson, 2008: 83). Though there have been few studies of neo-Pentecostals' political activity, there is evidence of a growing influence of neo-Pentecostalism on Guatemalan national politics. Presidents Efraín

Ríos Montt (1982–1983) and Jorge Serrano Elías (1991–1993) were both members of the neo-Pentecostal church *El Verbo*, and both appointed church leaders to high government positions (Mathews Samson, 2008).

During Ríos Montt's presidency, one of his secretaries, Francisco Bianchi, who had ties to *El Verbo* and to Guatemala's business elite, unsuccessfully ran for president in 1999 for the ARDE (Democratic Reconciling Action) Party. While the ARDE did not identify itself as an evangelical party, it was a self-described "party of biblical principles" (Mathews Samson, 2008: 74). Bianchi was also a member of *Asociación LIDER*, a Christian political association that encourages businessmen and religious leaders to become involved in politics.

In 2007 former senior pastor Harold Caballeros left the *El Shaddai* pastorate to found the *Visión Con Valores* (Vision with Values) political party, and attempted to run for president in that same year, but was disqualified due to his registering late. In the presidential election in September 2011, Caballeros finished fifth. His platform promoted capitalism and free trade as solutions to Guatemala's economic problems.

Steigenga (1999: 174) argues that neo-Pentecostals have the "background, resources, and the motivation to take advantage of the democratic openings occurring in the Guatemalan political system." Furthermore, as the neo-Pentecostal population grows and as Guatemalans grow increasingly weary of violence and corruption, neo-Pentecostal politicians who promote social and moral values are positioned to continue to grow in popularity.

Religious Pluralism As an Intervening Mechanism: Though the country has been predominantly Catholic since the Spanish Conquest, Guatemala is characterized by relative religious pluralism among Latin American countries (Steigenga, 1999: 174). Religious pluralism increased in 1873 when, in an effort to weaken Catholic hegemony, President Justo Barrios invited Protestant missionaries to settle in the country. In 1976, devastation from a major earthquake brought many independent aid charismatic groups from the United States, including from Gospel Outreach, which founded the neo-Pentecostal church *El Verbo* in that same year (Stoll, 1990; *Iglesia Cristiana Verbo Zona 16*, 2009). Levine (2009) identifies religious pluralism and democratization as the major contributing factors to the growth of neo-Pentecostal Protestantism in Guatemala.

Conclusions

We have argued that the Arab Spring protests and other recent urban social movements confound contemporary theories of development and globalization, that scholars would do well to develop alternatives to theoretical frameworks premised on a the modernist binary of "tradition" versus "modernity," and that postmodernist theories of globalization-as-hybridization can be subjected to rigorous methods of qualitative comparative analysis. We developed the concept of *market religion* as a prototypical postmodernist concept in order to suggest that contemporary non-Islamic religious movements may share central features and social mechanisms with market Islam, and used process tracing methods to explore the applicability of the market religion concept to the neo-Pentecostal movement in Guatemala. We found that market-friendly Islamic movements and Guatemalan neo-Pentecostalism resembled each other closely in terms of their historical timing, organizational and communications strategies, doctrines, and the demographic compositions of their followers. We also found differences in terms of the level of political involvement of adherents of market Islam versus neo-Pentecostalism, but despite these differences, market religion may prove a useful conceptual tool for identifying systematic but undertheorized effects of economic liberalization on world religions. Though at this stage our analysis has at best *prima facie* validity, we hope it demonstrates the compatibility of postmodernist theories of development and globalization with rigorous techniques of comparative-historical research, and that we have contributed to the conceptual resources with which scholars of development and globalization can trace causal chains within increasingly globalized, hybridized financescapes, ideoscapes, and faithscapes (Edensor, 2002: 61).

References

Adas, Emin Baki. 2006. "The Making of Entrepreneurial Islam and the Islamic Spirit of Capitalism," *Journal for Cultural Research*, 10(2): 113–137.
———. 2008. "Culturalizing Economies, 'Economizing' Cultures: Religion and Entrepreneurship in Turkey," *University of Gaziantep Journal of Social Sciences*, 7(1): 165–171.

Allagui, Ilhem and Johanne Kuebler. 2011. "The Arab Spring and the Role of ICTs," *International Journal of Communication*, 5: 1435–1442.

Appadurai, Arjun. 1990. "Disjuncture and Difference in the Global Cultural Economy," *Public Culture*, 2(2): 1–24.

Aras, Bulent and Omer Caha. 2000. "Fethullah Gulen and His Liberal 'Turkish Islam' Movement," *Middle East Review of International Affairs*, 4(4): 30–42.

Baer, Werner and William Maloney. 1997. "Neoliberalism and Income Distribution in Latin America," *World Development*, 25(3): 311–327.

Bennett, Andrew and Colin Elman. 2006. "Qualitative Research: Recent Developments in Case Study Methods," *Annual Review of Political Science*, 9: 455–476.

Berger, Peter. 1997. "The Four Faces of Global Culture." Available online at http://nationalinterest.org/article/four-faces-of-global-culture-711

Berger, Peter and Samuel P. Huntington. 2003. *Many Globalizations: Cultural Diversity in the Contemporary World*. Oxford: Oxford University Press.

Bulmer-Thomas, Victor. 2003. *The Economic History of Latin America since Independence*. Cambridge: Cambridge University Press.

Büthe, Tim. 2002. "Taking Temporality Seriously: Modelling History and the Use of Narrative as Evidence," *American Political Science Review*, 96(3): 481–493.

Chase-Dunn, Christopher. 2011. Continuities and transformations in the evolution of world-systems: Terminal crisis or a new systemic cycle of accumulation? Keynote address to be presented at the Vth Brazilian Colloquium of PEWS, State University of Campinas (UNICAMP), August 8–9, 2011. Conference theme: "The Contemporary Capitalist World-Economy: Terminal Crisis or Hegemonic Transition?" Available online at http://irows.ucr.edu/papers/irows70/irows70.htm (accessed on December 18, 2013).

Cox, Harvey. (2006). "Spirits of Globalization: Pentecostalism and Experiential Spiritualities in a Global Era," in Sturla J. Stalsett (ed.), *Spirits of globalization: The Growth of Pentecostalism and Experiential Spiritualities in a Global Age*, pp. 11–22. London: SCM Press.

Crook, Pakulski, and Waters. 1992. *Postmodernization: Change in Advanced Society*. London: SAGE Publications.

Csordas, Thomas J. (ed.). 2009. *Transnational Transcendence: Essays on Religion and Globalization*. Berkeley: University of California Press.

Drogus, Carol Ann. (1998). "Private Power or Public Power: Pentecostalism, Base Communities, and Gender," in Edward L. Cleary and Hannah W. Stewart-Gambino (eds), *Power, politics and Pentecostals in Latin America*, pp. 55–76. Boulder, CO: Westview.

Edensor, Tim. 2002. *National Identity, Popular Culture, and Everyday Life.* Oxford: Berg.

Evans, Timothy E. 1991. "Percentage of Non-Catholics in a Representative Sample of the Guatemalan Population." Paper presented to the Latin American Studies Association, 4–6 Apr., Crystal City, Virginia. Washington, D.C.

Elster, Jon. 1989. *Nuts and Bolts for the Social Sciences.* Cambridge: Cambridge University Press.

Feiler, Bruce. 2011. *Generation Freedom: The Middle East Uprisings and the Remaking of the Modern World.* New York: Harper Perennial.

Foltz, Richard. 2007. "The Religion of the Market: Reflections on a Decade of Discussion," *Worldviews*, 11(2): 135–154.

Frank, David J. and John W. Meyer. 2002. "The Profusion of Individual Roles and Identities in the Postwar Period," *Sociological Theory*, 20(1): 86–105.

Fraternidad Cristiana de Guatemala. (n.d.) *Nuestra historia.* Available Online at http://frater.org/es/acerca-de/nuestra-historia/ (accessed on December 18, 2013).

———. (n.d.) *Vida ministerial en Guatemala.* Available Online at http://frater. org/es/pastores/dr-jorge-h-lopez/biografia-completa/vida-ministerial-en-guatemala/ (accessed on December 18, 2013).

Freston, P. 2001. *Evangelicals and Politics in Asia, Africa and Latin America.* Cambridge: Cambridge University Press.

Gause III, F. Gregory. 2011. "Why Middle East Studies Missed the Arab Spring," *Foreign Affairs*, 90(4): 81–90.

George, Alexander L. and Andrew Bennett. 2005. *Case Studies and Theory Development in the Social Sciences.* Cambridge, MA: MIT Press.

Goldstone, Jack A. 2011. "Understanding the Revolutions of 2011," *Foreign Affairs*, 90(3): 8–16.

Grzymala-Busse, Anna. 2011. "Time Will Tell? Temporality and the Analysis of Causal Mechanisms and Processes," *Comparative Political Studies*, 44(9): 1267–1297.

Haddorff, David W. 2000. "Religion and the Market: Opposition, Absorption, or Ambiguity?" *Review of Social Economy*, 58(4): 483–504.

Haenni, Patrick. 2005. *L'Islam de Marché: L'Autre Révolution Conservatrice.* Paris: Seuil.

Hall, Peter A. 2003."Aligning Ontology and Methodology in Comparative Research," in James Mahoney and Dietrich Rueschemeyer (eds), *Comparative Historical Research in the Social Sciences*, pp. 373–407. New York: Cambridge University Press.

Hefner, Robert W. 2010. "Religious Resurgence in Contemporary Asia: Southeast Asian Perspectives on Capitalism, the State, and the New Piety," *The Journal of Asian Studies*, 69(4): 1031–1047.

Hendrick, Joshua D. 2009. "Globalization, Islamic Activism, and Passive Revolution in Turkey: The Case of Fethullah Gülen," *Journal of Political Power*, 2(3): 343–368.

———. 2009. "Globalization and Marketized Islam in Turkey: The Case of Fethullah Gulen." Working Paper, University of California, Santa Cruz.

Howard, Philip N. and Muzammil M. Hussain. 2011. "The Role of Digital Media," *Journal of Democracy*, 22(3): 35–48.

Huntington, Samuel. 1996. *The Clash of Civilizations and the Remaking of World Order*. New York: Simon and Schuster.

Huntington, Samuel P. 1999. "125th Anniversary Symposium, Cultures in the 21st Century: Conflicts and Convergences." Keynote Address, Colorado College. Colorado, February 4. Available online at http://www.colora-docollege.edu/academics/anniversary/Transcripts/HuntingtonTXT.htm (last accessed on December 18, 2013).

Iglesia Cristiana Verbo Zona 16. 2009. *Historia de Ministerios Verbo en Guatemala*. Retrieved from http://www.verboz16.com/2009/02/historia-de-ministerios-verbo-en-guatemala/

Iglesia Ministerios El Shaddai. 2010. *Historia*. Available online at http://www.elshaddai.net/iglesia/iglesia-el-shaddai/historia-iglesia (accessed on December 18, 2013).

Ignatow, Gabriel. 2004. "From Science to Multiculturalism: Postmodern Trends in Environmental Organizations," *Global Environmental Politics*, 5(2): 88–113.

———. 2007. *Transnational Identity Politics and the Environment*. Lanham, MD: Lexington Books.

———. 2008. "Transnational Environmentalism at Europe's Boundaries: Identity Movements in Lithuania and Turkey," *Current Sociology*, 56(6): 845–864.

———. 2011a. What has Globalization Done to Developing Countries' Public Libraries? International Sociology, 26(6): 746–768.

———. 2011b. "National Identity and the Informational Welfare State: Turkey and Malaysia Compared," *The Information Society*, 27(3): 158–171.

Juergensmeyer, Mark. 2003. *Terror in the Mind of God. The Global Rise of Religious Violence*. Berkeley: University of California Press.

——— (ed.). 2005. *Religion in Global Civil Society*. Oxford: Oxford University Press.

Keskin, Tugrul. 2009. "A Comparative Analysis of Islamist Movements in the Neoliberalization Process: Jama'at-e-Islami in Pakistan and the Fethullah Gulen Movement in Turkey—Reactions to Capitalism, Modernity and · Secularism." Faculty Working Paper, Department of Sociology, Virginia Tech University.

Khamis, Sahar. 2011. "The Transformative Egyptian Media Landscape: Changes, Challenges and Comparative Perspectives," *International Journal of Communication*, 5: 1159–1177.

Khondker, Habibul H. 2011. "Many Roads to Modernization in the Middle East," *Society*, 48(4): 304–306.

Khoury, Doreen. 2011. "Social Media and the Revolutions," *Perspectives: Political Analysis and Commentary from the Middle East*, 2: 80–85.

Kim, Sung-Gun. 2006. "Pentecostalism, Shamanism and Capitalism within Contemporary Korean Society," in Sturla J. Stalsett (ed.), *Spirits of Globalization: The Growth of Pentecostalism and Experiential Spiritualities in a Global Age*, pp. 23–28. London: SCM Press.

Koehler, Kevin and Jana Warkotsch. 2011. "Putting Institutions into Perspective: Two Waves of Authoritarianism Studies and the Arab Spring." Paper presented at the Panel Conceptualizing Autocracy at the 2011 General Conference of the European Consortium for Political Research, Reykjavik.

Kosebalaban, Hasan. 2005. "The Impact of Globalization on Islamic Political Identity: The Case of Turkey," *World Affairs*, 168(1): 27–37.

Lechner, Frank J. and John Boli. 2005. *World Culture: Origins and Consequences*. Malden, MA: Blackwell.

Levine, Daniel H. 2009. "The Future of Christianity in Latin America," *Journal of Latin American Studies*, 41(1): 121–145.

Lipset, Seymour M. 1963. *Political Man: The Social Bases of Politics*. New York: Anchor Books.

Mahoney, James. 2000. "Strategies of Causal Inference in Small-N Analysis," *Sociological Methods and Research*, 28(4): 387–424.

Maigre, Marie-Elisabeth. 2007. "The Influence of the Gülen Movement in the Emergence of a Turkish Cultural Third Way." Paper presented at the Gulen Conference, London, UK, October 26, 2007. Available online at http://gulenconference.org.uk/userfiles/file/Bios/Bio%20-%20 Maigre,%20ME.pdf (accessed June 16, 2011).

Mathews Samson, C. 2008. "From War to Reconciliation: Guatemalan Evangelicals and the Transition to Democracy, 1982–2001," in Paul Freston (ed.), *Evangelical Christianity and Democracy in Latin America*, pp. 63–95. New York: Oxford University Press.

Mayntz, Renate. 2004. "Mechanisms in the Analysis of Social Macro-Phenomena," *Philosophy of the Social Sciences*, 34(2): 237–259.

McAdam, Doug, Tarrow, Sidney, and Charles Tilly. 2008. "Methods for Measuring Mechanisms of Contention," *Qualitative Sociology*, 31(4): 307–331.

Meyer, Birgit. 2010. "Pentecostalism and Globalization," in Allan Anderson, Michael Bergunder, André Droogers, and Cornelis van der Laan (eds),

Studying Global Pentecostalism: Theories and Methods, pp. 113–130. California: University of California Press.

Mills, C. Wright. 1940."Situated Actions and Vocabularies of Motive," *American Sociological Review*, 5(6): 904–913.

Ministerios Cash Luna. 2010. *Casa de Dios*. Retrieved from http://cashluna. org/index.cfm/page/conocenos/view/Ministerios-Cash-Luna (accessed on December 18, 2013).

———. 2010. *Pastor Carlos Luna (Cash)*. Retrieved from http://cashluna. org/index.cfm/page/conocenos/show/208/Pastor-Cash-Luna (accessed on December 18, 2013).

Mora, G. Cristina. 2008. "Marketing the 'Health and Wealth Gospel' Across National Borders: Evidence from Brazil and the United States," *Poetics*, 36(5–6): 404–420.

Nasr, Vali. 2009. *Forces of Fortune: The Rise of the New Muslim Middle Class and What It Will Mean for Our World*. New York: Free Press.

Nederveen-Pieterse. 1993. "Globalization as Hybridization." *International Sociology*, 9(2): 161–184.

Partido VIVA. 2011. *Harold Caballeros*. Retrieved from http://www.vision-convalores.com/harold_caballeros.php (accessed on December 18, 2013).

———. 2011. *Identidad*. Retrieved from http://www.visionconvalores.com/ identidad.php (accessed on December 18, 2013).

Pew Forum on Religious and Public Life. 2006, October 5. "Historical Overview of Pentecostalism in Guatemala.". Retrieved from http:// pewforum.org/Christian/Evangelical-Protestant-Churches/Historical-Overview-of-Pentecostalism-in-Guatemala.aspx (accessed on December 18, 2013).

Robbins, Joel. 2004. "The Globalization of Pentecostal and Charismatic Christianity," *Annual Review of Anthropology*, 33: 117–143.

Robinson, W. 1998. "Beyond Nation-State Paradigms: Globalization, Sociology, and the Challenge of Transnational Studies," *Sociological Forum*, 13(4): 561–594.

Robinson, William I. 2011. "Globalization and the Sociology of Immanuel Wallerstein: A Critical Appraisal," *International Sociology*, 26(6): 723–745.

Rostow, Walt W. 1960. *The Stages of Economic Growth: A Non-Communist Manifesto*. Cambridge: Cambridge University Press.

Rudnyckyj, Daromir. 2009. "Market Islam in Indonesia," *Journal of the Royal Anthropological Institute*, 15(s1): S183–S201.

———. 2010. *Spiritual Economies*. Ithaca: Cornell University Press.

Rudolph, Susanne Hoeber and James Piscatori (eds). 1997. *Transnational Religion & Fading States*. Boulder, CO: Westview Press.

Sakr, Naomi. 2007. *Arab Television Today*. London: I.B. Tauris.

Sayyid, S. 2011. "Dis-Orienting Clusters of Civility," *Third World Quarterly*, 32(5): 981–987.

Schäfer, Heinrich. 1991. *Church identity between Repression and Liberation: The Presbyterian Church in Guatemala*. Geneva: World Alliance of Reformed Churches.

Schwarz, Rolf and Miguel de Corral. 2011. "States Do Not Just Fail and Collapse: Rethinking States in the Middle East," *Democracy and Security*, 7(3): 209–226.

Smith, Calvin L. 2009. "Pentecostal Power, Presence and Politics in Latin America," *Journal of Beliefs & Values*, 30(3): 219–229. DOI: 10.1080/13617670903371530.

Smith, Dennis A. 2006. *Los teleapóstoles guatemaltecos: Apuntes históricos y propuestas para la investigación*. Contribution to the panel for the Latin American Studies Association. San Juan, Puerto Rico.

———. 2007. *Communication, Politics and Religious Fundamentalism in Latin America*. Contribution to the panel for the Latin American Studies Association. Montreal, Quebec.

———. 2008. *Una tipología de las iglesias evangélicas en Guatemala*. Unpublished manuscript.

Stoll, D. 1990. *Is Latin America Turning Protestant?* Berkley: University of California Press.

Suazo, David. 2009a. "Movimiento Neo-Pentecostal: Origen y desarrollo," Class notes, Ed. Lindsey A. Johnson. Central American Theological Seminary, Guatemala City.

———. 2009b. Movimiento Neo-Pentecostal: Ideas Principales (Class notes). Ed. Lindsey A. Johnson. Central American Theological Seminary, Guatemala City.

Skocpol, Theda. 1977. "Wallerstein's World Capitalist System: A Theoretical and Historical Critique," *American Journal of Sociology*, 82(5): 1075–1090.

Steigenga, Tim. 1999. "Guatemala," in Paul E. Sigmund (ed.), *Religious Freedom and Evangelization in Latin America*, pp. 150–174. Maryknoll, New York: Orbis Books.

Taylor, Alan M. 1998. "On the Costs of Inward-Looking Development: Price Distortions, Growth, and Divergence in Latin America," *The Journal of Economic History*, 58(1): 1–28.

Tilly, Charles. 2004. "Observations of Social Processes and Their Formal Representations," *Sociological Theory*, 22(4): 595–602.

Turner, Bryan S. 1974. "Islam, Capitalism and the Weber Thesis," *British Journal of Sociology*, 25(2): 230–43.

———. 2010. "Revisiting Weber and Islam," *The British Journal of Sociology*, 61(s1): 161–166.

Wagner, Peter C. 1999. *Churchquake: How the New Apostolic Reformation Is Shaking Up the Church As We Know It*. Ventura, California: Regal Books.

Weber, M. 1947. *The Theory of Social and Economic Organization*. Eds. A.M. Henderson and Talcott Parsons. New York: Oxford University Press.

Wallerstein, Immanuel. 1976. *The Modern World-System: Capitalist Agriculture and the Origins of the European World-Economy in the Sixteenth Century*. New York: Academic Press.

Walton, Paul. 1971. "Ideology and the Middle Class in Marx and Weber," *Sociology*, 5(1): 391.

Wiener, Jonathan M. 1982. "Max Weber's Marxism: Theory and Method in *The Agrarian Sociology of Ancient Civilizations*," *Theory and Society*, 11(3): 389–401.

12

Critical Management Studies and Postmodernist Movements

ANANDA DAS GUPTA

Introduction

With a view to radically transform management practice, the common core is deep skepticism regarding the moral defensibility and the social and ecological sustainability of the prevailing forms of management and organization. Critical Management Studies' (CMS's) motivating concern is neither the personal failures of individual managers, nor the poor management of specific organizations, but the social injustice and environmental destructiveness of the broader social and economic systems that these managers and organizations serve and reproduce. This chapter reviews CMS's premises, practices, problems, and prospects, with the aim of providing an accessible overview of a growing movement in management studies.

To begin, it might be useful to illustrate what we mean by "critical." We take teamwork as a mundane example. In a large body of mainstream research, teamwork is presented as a means by which managers can more effectively mobilize employees to improve business performance. By reorganizing work so as to better accommodate task interdependencies, and by leaving team members a margin of autonomy in deciding how to handle these interdependencies, teamwork is often presented as a "win-win" policy, making work simultaneously more satisfying for employees and more effective for the business. Issues such as workforce diversity are studied as factors that can facilitate or impede effective teamwork, and if they impede it, research addresses how the problem can be mitigated.

Postmodernism

During the 1990s, new streams of theory emerged in CMS, many of them collected under the umbrella headings of "postmodernism" and "poststructuralism." As noted earlier, these streams problematize the credibility of Burrell and Morgan's dimensions and the comprehensives of their framework.

The terms postmodernism and poststructuralism are used in various ways. Broadly speaking, however, postmodernism has sought to theorize the broad shift in Western societies beyond the limits of a modernist Weltanschaung toward greater flexibility and hybridity (see e.g., Lyotard, 1984; on postmodernism in management research, see Hassasrd and Parker, 1993; Calás and Smircich, 1997, 1999; Kilduff amd Mehra, 1997). It reflects and theorizes a growing disillusionment with established authorities, whether it be the authority of managers, of government, of science, or even of the figurative aesthetic in art. For postmodernists, modernity is exemplified by bureaucracy and suffers from an excess of instrumentalism: modernity is premised on a generalized repression of spontaneity and creative imagination. In this sense, postmodernism is a new romanticism. Poststructuralism can be seen as part of a (postmodern) movement critiquing the rigidities of structuralist thinking that accord insufficient attention to contingency and undecidability. Where Marxists draw on the Enlightenment tradition of reason as a force that can enable social progress, postmodernism and poststructuralism more often draw inspiration from Nietzsche's critique of the use of reason as a mask of power. Following Nietzsche, they regard as problematic and potentially dangerous the Enlightenment's claim to secure universally valid knowledge. In their radical skepticism, these new streams of thought are responsive to, as well as reflective of, the historical demise of the Left over the last two or three decades of the 20th century. We discuss postmodernism here, and leave the discussion of poststructuralism to the following section on critical epistemologies.

Postmodernism can be seen as an intensification of the modernist rejection of the confines of tradition: it is indeed more postmodern than anti-modern. Postmodernism brings to our attention the limits of modernist ambitions to control every contingency. Such ambition is exemplified in both classical and progressive forms of management theory—such as in the claims of Peters and Waterman (1982) to manage and even exploit irrationality through the medium of "strong culture" and their advocacy of "empowering" teamwork. Postmodernism is about releasing us from myths of modernity by celebrating serendipity and diversity—not as a hypermodern instruments of "best employment practice," but as a basis for valuing all kinds of beliefs and activities that are currently marginalized and devalued, if not denigrated, by modernist values and associated agendas.

The postmodernists' intent is not to abandon the project of emancipation, but to reconstitute it in the light of dark historical and creative intellectual developments of the 20th century.

Feminism

Feminism and environmentalism are broad intellectual movements that draw on and develop a variety of critical theories, including those discussed above, and have developed since Burrell and Morgan constructed their framework in the mid-1970s. The literatures in these two areas prioritize the concerns of two of the most vibrant political movements in the contemporary world. As such, feminist theory and environmental studies are particularly significant to critical management studies scholars. In both cases, there has been productive tension between liberal-reformist and more critical views.

Environmentalism

The recently released Millennium Ecosystem Assessment (2005), a massive technical report that reflects the opinions of 1,300 distinguished scientists from 95 countries, calls attention to the alarming fact that 60 percent of the earth's ecosystems studied have been degraded significantly as a result of human activity. Not everyone agrees that natural systems have reached a crisis state; but the mounting evidence is increasingly convincing experts, the general public, and the media that a global environmental crisis is looming.

This global environmental degradation is attributed to a variety of causes. Many analysts point to increases in human population (Brown, 2000; Kearns, 1997; National Academy of Science, 1994). Critical scholars, however, are skeptical of such apolitical explanations (see Foster, 1998 for a review). They do not see the root cause lying in population growth as much as in the way people exploit the environment for private gain with its attendant (obscenely) asymmetrical distribution of wealth and life chances. Marxist critics point to the destructive effects of decision-making under the profit imperative (e.g., Foster, 2000). Other radical critics focus on the role of corporate interests in encouraging high-consumption lifestyles, anthropocentric worldviews, exploitative-patriarchal culture, and other forms of domination (e.g., Hawken, 1993; Devall & Sessions, 1985; Warren, 1997). As with feminist theories, critical environmentalism draws on a wide variety of perspectives, and has developed several variants, notably deep ecology, social ecology, and eco-feminism (Zimmerman, 1994). Of particular interest to management scholars is the rise of corporate environmentalism and the assertion that effective leadership in addressing the phenomena of environmental degradation should come from the corporate sector (e.g., Hart, 1997). Long blamed for despoiling the environment, corporations and their leaders have recently launched initiatives not only to conserve resources and curb the damage, but also to restore and replenish the environment. They increasingly argue that they alone have the resources, access, and expertise necessary to promote practically effective environmentalism. Mainstream scholars have drawn on a wide variety of frameworks to make sense of these corporate practices (Sharma, 2002; Jermier et al., 2006 for a review). To date, however, the vast bulk of the scholarship on corporate environmentalism lacks the critical edge necessary to distinguish between incremental, reformist improvements and more radical innovations that come closer to matching the seriousness of the rapidly developing environmental crisis.

Taken together, several recent studies are beginning to form the foundation for comprehensive critique of corporate environmentalism. Welford (1997) developed an early critique of the "hijacking" of the broader environmental movement by corporate capitalism. He raised questions about whether any form of corporate environmentalism can be compatible with the interests of government regulators, environmental NGOs, the broader citizenry, and the natural harmonies of the earth itself. A key orienting concept in the critical analysis of corporate environmentalism is greenwashing—constructing green symbolism without taking the radical steps required to deliver a full measure of green substance. Greenwashing is a central phenomenon in an era in which organizations face social pressure to address concerns about environmental degradation and resulting declines in human health. Studies on greenwashing have focused attention on the distortion of environmental performance and initiation, the mix of corporate and related institutions whose role is to undercut genuine environmentalism through obfuscation and misrepresentation of facts while promoting weak reformist programs, green marketing, and other image management techniques and the development of theoretical perspectives on greenwashing behavior (Lyon and Maxwell, 2004; Forbes and Jermier, 2002). Other noteworthy critical resources include: Seager's (1993) ecofeminist explanation of business as usual and the ecological establishment, Newton and Harte's critique of environmentalist evangelical rhetoric, regulatory reinforcment, and Castro's (2004) radical reformulation of the concept of sustainable development.

Tasks ahead for CMS environmentalists include the critique of green imposters and the further development of green critical theory. Another challenge lies in overcoming the tendency of environmentalists, even radically critical ones, to narrow the focus on the natural environment in a way that decouples it from the broader context of capitalism, patriarchy, racism, and imperialism.

Critical Epistemologies

While some empirically oriented critical scholarship proceeds from positivist epistemological premises common in mainstream research, the drive to critique mainstream theory often prompts CMS proponents to engage with debates on epistemology that were a hallmark of Frankfurt School analysis (see earlier) and that have been heated within the philosophy of the social sciences. Within the CMS movement, there are a number of partly competing and partly overlapping epistemologies at work. We discuss here the three main families of views—standpoint theory, poststructuralism, and critical realism.

CMS researchers reject this logic, contesting as an ideological fantasy the neoclassical economic theory that enshrines shareholder value as the socially (Pareto-) optimal goal, and challenging the normalized role of management scholars as servants of power.

Increasingly, mainstream scholars are paying attention to this critique of the narrowness of much management theory, of the blind spots in understanding that result from reliance on elite standpoints (e.g., Van de Ven and Johnson, 2006); but they generally remain wedded to a managerial standpoint, albeit now somewhat pluralized. From a CMS perspective, these concerns about "blind spots" cannot be effectively addressed without turning to more radical forms of analysis, which are dedicated to remedying this blindness.

Poststructuralism

Poststructuralism can be approached—and has garnered some of its support—via its critique of standpoint theory. Standpoint theory assumes that actors who occupy a given position in the social structure have common, objective interests that will provide them with a shared perspective. Standpoint feminist research, for example, assumes the existence of a single, coherent, feminist identity that could serve as the foundation for a feminist standpoint. This assumption was challenged by black feminists, third-world feminists, and others who asserted their own identities and points of view, and who thereby questioned what they saw as the hegemony of middle-class white women in the feminist movement. This challenge was theorized by poststructuralists as demonstrating the problem of attributing essential interests to women—or to social classes, or indeed to any structurally defined social category. Standpoint theorists respond that a common identity and awareness of common interests are not automatic consequences of a common structural position: the latter simply afford the opportunity to forge common identities and interests (see e.g., Jameson, 1988). However the poststructuralists challenge even this more modest causal claim, arguing that such common interests cannot be determined by analytical fiat.

On this understanding, organizations can be studied as objects possessing distinctive characteristics that can be stated as variables. This is a deeply institutionalized understanding of organization. Upon it are based diverse forms of functionalist and structuralist analyses that provide knowledge based upon what Chia (1996) has termed "being-realism." In contrast, *proximal* thinking conceives of organizations as comprising diverse ongoing and open-ended activities. Whatever boundaries or variables are identified by researchers—or indeed by participants themselves—are constructed and unstable, rather than more or less adequate reflections of the world "out there." Whereas distal thinking encourages an understanding of knowledge as something like a map of a comparatively well-defined objective reality, knowledge generated by proximal thinking articulates and promotes an appreciation of the precarious and incomplete processes that constitute our taken-for-granted sense of the "out there." In Chia's (1996) terminology, proximal thinking is an articulation of "becoming-realism."

In terms of its contribution to critical analysis, poststructuralist thinking is important for two reasons. First, the acknowledgement of proximal thinking provides for the possibility and legitimacy of deconstructing the claims of distal thinking, encouraging us to appreciate the dependence of the latter upon available, commonsense meanings that are idealized as "method." Second, it invites us to reflect upon the role of power in fixing, or institutionalizing, a particular way of making sense, as if this way of making sense of things had universal, observer-independent truth-value and authority. Needless to say, the attribution of self-evidence to a specific, orthodox way of representing the world (e.g., as organizations with structures and goals) is a powerful means of reproducing the status quo; but poststructuralists point out that the dominance of this institutionalized form of understanding can never become total, not least because any exercise of power provokes resistance (as discussed earlier). What counts as "deviant behavior" is therefore a consequence, and not simply a condition, of control. Any attempt to control or fix the meaning of any word—including words like "management" or "organization"—is inherently precarious since reality is always in excess of what is signified by any particular set of signifiers. Poststructuralists in CMS celebrate this excess and strive to widen and deepen its (potentially subversive) scope and influence.

Critical Realism

Critical realism is appealing to those who are critical of the mainstream's positivism, but are unpersuaded or disturbed by what they see as the excessive value-dependence of standpoint theory and the illogical relativism of poststructuralist epistemology. Critical realist epistemology is compatible with a broad range of political viewpoints; but, a growing number of CMS researchers (as well as scholars in other disciplines such as economics) have found critical realism to be a fruitful way to conceptualize the challenges facing the social sciences, as positivism loses its plausibility and as poststructuralism challenges the established, positivist basis of differentiating science from other forms of knowledge.

Critical realism today is most commonly associated with the work of Roy Bhaskar (1978). Bhaskar argues that what differentiates the practice of scientific investigation is the assumption that the object of its investigation has a real existence independent of the observer that, in principle, is available to objective knowledge. Where empiricism and positivism see science as finding patterns among observable facts, critical realism strives to identify the real structures that generate these facts and patterns—structures that are typically not visible to the naked eye. When scientists conduct experiments, they aim to trigger events that are attributed to the operation of these structures, and thus test their hypotheses concerning them. Critical realists understand reality to be layered: beneath the *empirical* layer (observable by human beings), there is the *actual* (existing in time and space); and given that mechanisms may or may not be actualized, beneath the actualized lies the *real*. The real is, therefore, a set of structures that have causal powers from which observable events emerge.

Such a layered ontology is congenial to a critical structuralist perspective on management, where the observed regularities of organizational behavior are understood to hide as much as they reveal about the underlying social and psychological causes of domination. In effect, the critical realism aims to provide a basis for challenging the scientific standing of accounts that naturalize the social world by reporting its manifestations without regard for the underlying structures.

Poststructuralist critics contest the assertion that there are real mechanisms that science can detect. They argue that a disinclination to recognize critical realism as a *particular* kind of discourse that makes universalizing claims results in an authoritarian view of science as the font of objective, impartial knowledge. Critical realists reply that science does not claim to possess objective knowledge, only that it has developed procedures that offer reasonable hope of progressing toward it. On the critical realist view, the danger of authoritarianism is forestalled by the openness of science to rational refutation and debate, thereby affirming a benign, rather than potentially malevolent, conception of rationality.

Prospects

CMS has an ambitious objective of contributing to a progressive transformation of management theory and practice. Our survey suggests four recommendations for strengthening CMS.

First, the development of CMS will benefit from a continued diversity of forms of critique. We can take the epistemology debate as illustration: it is likely that all these families of epistemology will continue to co-exist in CMS. Perhaps standpoint epistemology will appeal more strongly to those who are committed to a particular cause, and who are intent on generating knowledge that supports its cause. Perhaps critical realism will appeal more strongly to those who believe that social science should aim to deliver objective truth. And perhaps poststructuralism will appeal more strongly to those who value more reflexive and playful forms of understanding in which alternative ways of knowing are opened up rather than closed off, perhaps prematurely. But, the overall field of CMS will benefit from continued pluralism.

Second, CMS should foster vigorous debate among its different approaches. In CMS as in any other community of research, debate inhibits the atrophying of positions and thereby acts as a potentially progressive force. At its best, debate enhances mutual understanding and respect; it challenges the parties to articulate and offer some justification of their position that may then be subjected to critical scrutiny, resulting in greater clarity for all the participants. Such debate, however, requires norms that are only partially and patchily honored in academe, in general, and in the CMS movement, in particular.

Third, CMS should promote dialog and debate with the mainstream. To date, such engagement has been largely one way, with conspicuously few mainstream academics being sufficiently interested or prepared to subject constituent elements of CMS to serious or sustained examination. CMS scholarship is, however, likely to benefit from sustained efforts to engage mainstream research in dialog. "Ghettoization" would be debilitating for the intellectual vitality of CMS.

Finally, even though these debates within CMS and with the mainstream are important, engagement with the world outside academia is, we submit, even more crucial. Those committed to advancing critical studies of management will doubtlessly continue to refine their theories and to debate the merits of their different approaches; the bigger challenge, however, and the one that provides the warrant for this internal debate, is to contribute more forcefully to shaping public agendas. The mainstream of the US Academy of Management has become increasingly cognizant of the importance of engaging public and private policy under which we argue that, following a distinctively radical path, CMS should broaden the audience to include social movements of resistance.

In this, CMS can take inspiration from the recent call by Michael Burawoy (2004) for critical sociologists to develop a "public sociology." Burawoy distinguishes mainstream and critical sociology, and their respective academic and nonacademic audiences. Mainstream "policy sociology" reorients "professional sociology" (mainstream academic research) toward actionable knowledge that can support the technocratic efforts ofpolicy makers. Likewise, Burawoy argues, "public sociology" reorients "critical sociology" away from internal debates within the field and toward pubic dialog in support of struggles for emancipation. Such public dialog can take more traditional forms (books that stimulate pubic reflection and opinion columns that address current issues) or more "organic" forms that engage directly with specific communities and social movements.

References

Bhaskar, R. 1978. *A Realist Theory of Science*. New York: Harvester Press.

Brown, L.R. 2000. "Challenge of the New Century," in L. Starke (ed.), *State of the World 2000: A Worldwatch Institute Report on Progress Toward a Sustainable Society*. pp. 145–167. New York: WW Norton.

Burawoy, M. 2004. "Public Sociologies: Contradictions, Dilemmas, and Possibilities," *Social Forces*, 82(4): 1603–1618.

Calás, M.B. and L. Smircich (eds). 1997. *Postmodern Management Theory*. Aldershot: Ashgate.

———. 1999. "Past Postmodernism? Reflections and Tentative Directions," *Academy of Management Review*, 24(4): 649–671.

Castro, C.J. 2004. "Sustainable Development: Mainstream and Critical Perspectives," *Organization and Environment*, 17(2): 195–225.

Chia, R. 1996. *Organizational Analysis as Deconstructive Practice*. Berlin: de Gruyter.

Devall, B. and G. Sessions. 1985. *Deep Ecology: Living as if Nature Mattered*. Layton, Utah: Gibbs M. Smith, Inc.

Forbes, L.C. and J.M Jermier. 2002. "The Institutionalization of Voluntary Organizational Greening and the Ideals of Environmentalism: Lessons About Official Culture from Symbolic Organization Theory," in A. Hoffman and M. Ventresca (eds), *Organizations, Policy and the Natural Environment: Institutional and Strategic Perspectives*, pp. 194–213. Stanford: Stanford University Press.

Foster, J.B. 2000. *Marx's Ecology: Materialism and Nature*. New York: Monthly Review Press.

Foster, John Bellamy. 1998. "The Scale of Our Ecological Crisis,"*Monthly Review Volume*, 49(11).

Hart, S.L. 1997. "Beyond Greening: Strategies for a Sustainable World," *Harvard Business Review*, 66–76, January–February.

Hassard, J. and M. Parker (eds). 1993. *Postmodernism and Organizations*. London: SAGE Publications.

Hawken, P. 1993. *The Ecology of Commerce: A Declaration Of Sustainability*. New York: Harper Business.

Jermier, J.M., L.C. Forbes, S. Benn, and R.J. Orsato. 2006. "The New Corporate Environmentalism and Green Politics," in S.R. Clegg, C. Hardy, T.B. Lawrence, and W.R. Nord (eds), *The SAGE Handbook of Organization Studies*, pp. 618–650. 2nd ed. London: SAGE Publications.

Kearns, F. 1997. "Human Population and Consumption: What Are the Ecological Limits?" *Bulletin of the Ecological Society of America*, 78(2): 161–163.

Kilduff, M. and A. Mehra. 1997. "Postmodernism and Organizational Research," *Academy of Management Review*, 22(2): 453–481.

Lyon, T.P. and J.W. Maxwell. 2004. *Corporate Environmentalism and Public Policy*. Cambridge: Cambridge University Press.

Lyotard, J. 1984. *The Postmodern Condition: A Report on Knowledge*. Minneapolis: University of Minnesota Press.

National Academy of Science. 1994. *Population Summit of the World's Scientific Academies*. Washington, DC: National Academy of Sciences Press.

Peters, T.J. and R.H. Watermann. 1982. *In Search of Excellence: Lessons from America's Best-run Companies*. New York: Harper and Row.

Sharma, S. 2002. "Research in Corporate Sustainability: What Really Matters?" in S. Sharma and M. Starik (eds), *Research in Corporate Sustainability: The*

Evolving Practice of Organizations in the Natural Environment, pp. 1–29. Cheltenham, UK: Edward Elgar.

Warren, K.J. (ed.). 1997. *Ecofeminism: Women, Culture, Nature.* Bloomington: Indiana UP.

Welford, R. 1997. *Hijacking Environmentalism: Corporate Responses to Sustainable Development.* London: Earthscan Publications.

Zimmerman, M.E. 1994. *Contesting Earth's Future: Radical Ecology and Postmodernity.* Berkeley: Berkeley UP.

Further Note

Critical Management Studies: Premises, Practices, Problems, and Prospects: Paul S. Adler (University of Southern California); Linda C. Forbes (Franklin and Marshall College);

Hugh Willmott (University of Cardiff); draft for Annals of the Academy of Management version: November 2, 2006.

13

Globalization, Postmodernism, and Literary Criticism

IMRE SZEMAN

One can refute Hegel (perhaps even St. Paul) but not the *Song of Sixpence.*

—Northrop Frye, Conclusion to the *Literary History of Canada*

Globalization and Literary Studies

What possibilities does globalization open up for literary studies, and more specifically, for our understanding of the politics of the literary today? To put this another way: is it possible to still imagine a social function for literary studies in an era dominated by visual spectacle, the triumph of the private and the apparent dissolution of the public sphere? Is there anything like a position of (relative) autonomy from which critics might reflect on the circumstances we have the misfortunate to inhabit?

To speak of the opening up of new possibilities and even new political functions for literature and literary criticism today might seem quixotic at best: a tilting against the windmills of a radically transformed society that no longer has much use for the written word—or for culture more generally, for that matter. But, if we attend carefully to globalization and consider how the practices of literature and literary criticism figure into the contemporary social and political landscape, it seems to me that some unexpected political possibilities emerge. While globalization signals the beginning of many new processes, those of us concerned with language, culture, and politics have often come to take it only as the name for the end of things: the end of democracy, of unmediated experience, of the public sphere, of the experiment (warts and all) called the Enlightenment, and, effectively, of poetry and literature, too. I want to argue that both literature and literary criticism have an essential political role to play in the era of globalization, even if they do so in transformed and difficult circumstances.

Integral to literary studies is the view that the "real" is always metaphorical in nature. All of our epistemologies, however secure and self-satisfied they might be in their ultimate veracity, are constituted by the appearance of the "real" in language: it is only by passing through metaphor that what is "outside" of language can become linguistic and thus intelligible at all. What better practice to challenge the self-certainties of the narratives of globalization—which function in part by denying their core metaphoricity—than literary theory and criticism? To grasp how and why the literary might provide the conditions for mutinous metaphors against the dominant ones articulated in the discourse of globalization, it is necessary first to describe (yet again) what globalization is (and is not) and how literature and the study of culture fits (or does not fit) into it; and so, it is here that I begin.

Globalization is Not Postmodernism

At the core of Karl Marx's investigation of the operations of capitalism is a sometimes forgotten critique of scholarly methodology. The political economists of his time mistook the *dramatis personae* of the modern economy—owners and workers—as *a priori* ontological categories, rather than as social positions that come into existence only as the result of a specific course of historical development. This methodological "failure" describes, of course, a more general process of reification that takes place throughout much of contemporary social reality and at many levels: our own creations take on the character of "natural," preordained reality in a way that obscures the quotidian character of their invention. Marx's point goes beyond simply criticizing method. For one of the singular inventions of capitalism is the commodity form, which itself ceaselessly, on an ongoing and daily basis, *re-reifies* existing social relations. "The commodity," Marx writes, "reflects the social characteristics of men's own labour as objective characteristics of the products themselves, as the socio-natural properties of these things" (Marx, 1976: 165). The commodity, one might say, acts as an objective reifying force that extends beyond the ideologies of capitalists and capitalism: we *live* this reification, whether we believe the larger social script in which it is embedded or not.

It should come as no surprise that "globalization" plays an important role in this ongoing narrative of capitalist reification. Just as surely as political economy for Marx, globalization hides reality from us even as it proposes to explain it. Just how does it do so? At first blush, the promise of the term "globalization" is that it offers us a way to comprehend a set of massive changes (clustered around the economic and social impact of new communications technologies and the almost unfettered reign of capital across the earth) that have radically redefined contemporary experience. These changes cut across spheres of social experience *and* areas of scholarly analysis, which were imagined previously to be separate (i.e., the economic, the cultural, the social, the political, and so on). And, confusingly, "globalization" names at one and the same time both the empirical and theoretical novelty of the processes most commonly associated with it. It names both a new reality and the new concept (or set of concepts) needed to make some sense of this reality. It is not surprising that this double role has made it an inherently unstable and amorphous concept, "used in so many different contexts, by so many different people, for so many different purposes that it is difficult to ascertain what is at stake in… globalization, what function the term serves, and what effects it has for contemporary theory and politics" (Kellner, 2006: 1). The immense debates that have ranged over what globalization "is" and what phenomena should (and should not) be included within it, the question of what the "time" of globalization might be (is it post-1989? the arrival of Columbus in the New World? the explosion of cross-regional trading in the 11th century?), the issue of the politics of globalization, and the possibilities of alternate globalizations to this one—all draw attention to the fact that the empirical realities that the term is meant to capture can potentially be arranged and re-arranged in very different and even contradictory ways. In other words, although globalization is at one level "real" and has "real" effects, it is also decisively and importantly rhetorical, metaphoric, and even fictional; it is a reality given a narrative shape and logic, and in a number of different and irreconcilable ways. But right away, one can also see that as soon as the idea of concept as metaphor—concept as not the thing itself (how could it be otherwise?) but as necessarily a substitution meant to produce an identity—is introduced, the real begins to fade away. What we take as the "real" of globalization necessarily comes mediated by the apparatus of numerous concepts strung together in an effort to grasp the fundamental character of the contemporary.

This characterization of globalization—as an amorphous term for the present, as an analytically suggestive and yet confusing concept that binds epistemology and ontology together, as an impossible yet compelling idea that names the logic organizing all experience, as a term that is potentially all things to all people and can be bent to multiple purposes—makes it sound like the successor to another concept that was intended to do similar kinds of work: postmodernism. Indeed, it is hard to avoid the idea that "globalization" carries out the periodizing task once assigned to postmodernism, naming the character and dynamics of the contemporary moment, if with far more attention paid to the material realities, struggles, and conflicts of contemporary reality on a worldwide scale. Globalization can thus appear to be a new and improved version of postmodernism, but one for which the issues of (for instance) the legacies of imperialisms, past and present, play a constitutive (instead of ancillary) role.

But as soon as this connection is ventured, it is clear that globalization is far from a replacement term for postmodernism. The differences between the two terms are instructive, especially with respect to the situation of literature and criticism at the present time. The postmodern was first and foremost an aesthetic category, used to describe architectural styles, artistic movements, and literary strategies (Anderson, 1998), before ever becoming the name for the general epistemic or ontological condition of Western societies—the "postmodern condition" that Jean-Francois Lyotard detected in his review of Quebec's educational system (Lyotard, 1985). Criticisms of postmodernism focused on the adequacy of the term as an aesthetic descriptor (was postmodern fiction not really just more modernist fiction?), on its overreaching ambition at global applicability (was the "post" in "postmodernism" really the same as the one in "postcolonialism?"), or on the fact that there was far too little attention paid to the historical "conditions of possibility" of the emergence of the aesthetic and experiential facets of the postmodern. In short, this lack of attention hid the fact that postmodern style represented something more primary: the cultural logic of late capitalism (Jameson, 1991).

Whatever else one might want to say about globalization, it is clear that the term has little relation to aesthetics or, indeed, even to culture in the way that postmodernism does. It is meaningless to insist on a global style or global form in architecture, art, or literature. There is no "globalist" literature in the way that one could have argued that there was a postmodernist one, nor a globalist architecture as there was (and still is) a postmodern one, even if there are global architects (such as Rem Koolhaas, Frank Gehry, or Zaha Hadid) and a global corporate vernacular in (say) airport or office tower design. This lack of relation to culture can be seen in the fact that we lack even the adjective for such a category—"global" literature being something very different from postmodern writing, without the immediate implications for form or style raised by the latter category. "World cinema" similarly names a moment rather than a style, though here perhaps one could argue that there has been a broad bifurcation of film into the cinema of the culture, industry, and the products of a new, globally-dispersed avant-garde (Hou Hsiao-hsien, Emir Kusturica, Agnès Varda, etc); both can claim the title of "world cinema," if for wildly different reasons. "World poetry" names not even a moment in this sense, but simply the poetry of the whole world, samples of which we might expect to find collected in an anthology or reader of the kind that is constructed to be attentive to the differences of nation, region, and locality. The aesthetic may not have disappeared. But the category "global" as a periodizing marker doesn't address it, as if the ideological struggles and claims once named by the aesthetic and pursued by various avant-gardes have for some reason been rendered moot and beside the point.

If postmodernism comes to our attention through various formal innovations that prompt us to consider symptomatically what is going on in the world to generate these forms, globalization seems to invert this relationship. It places emphasis on the restructuring of relations of politics and power, the re-scaling of economic production from the national to the transnational, on the lightspeed operations of finance capital, and the societal impacts of the explosive spread of information technologies. With globalization, we thus seem to have suspended what was central to debates and discussions of postmodernism—the category of representation. Indeed, the contemporary reality named by globalization is meant to be immediately legible in the forces and relationships that are always already understood to be primary to it and to fundamentally constitute it (e.g., transnational economics, bolstered by the changing character of the state, and so on). What the comparison between postmodernism and globalization highlights is that there is not only no unique formal relationship between contemporary cultural production and the cultural-political-social-economic dominant named by globalization. In addition, there is apparently less reason to look to culture to make sense of the shape and character of this dominant, which apparently can explain itself, and which views culture as little more than name for just one of the many aspects of commodity production and exchange today. Put another way, globalization seems to have transformed culture, on the one hand, into mere entertainment whose significance lies only in its exchangeability. On the other, it shifts it to refer to a set of archaic cultural practices that of necessity have little to say about the skylines of Shanghai's Pudong district or the favelas of Rio, other than to render an increasingly mute complaint about a world that has passed it by. If globalization is postmodern come to self-recognition, it appears in the process to have transformed culture into mere epiphenomenon and to have rendered cultural criticism in turn into a practice now in search of an object. This state is evident especially as one of its older political functions—making visible the signs and symptoms of the social as expressed in cultural forms—has been eclipsed by history itself.

This analysis might suggest that anxieties about the decline of (a certain vision of) culture in the era of globalization are, in fact, justified. But, there is also another crucial difference between globalization and postmodernism that needs to be pointed to first, which will begin to turn us back to the question of the activity of literature and literary criticism in relation to globalization—and to the productive of metaphor in relation to globalization as well. Postmodernism was never a public concept in the way that globalization has turned out to be. The postmodern never made anything more than a tentative leap from universities to the pages of broadsheets, appearing only occasionally in an article on the design of a new skyscraper or in sweeping dismissals of the perceived decadence of the contemporary humanities. It is a concept in decline, used these days mainly as a term for strange and incoherent phenomena or forms of social instability. By contrast, globalization is argued for by the World Bank, named in the business plans of Fortune 500 companies, and on the lips of politicians across the globe; it constitutes official state policy and is the object of activist dissent: the Zapatistas did not rise up against postmodernism, nor was it the preponderance of self-reflective, ironic literature in bookstores that brought anarchists into the streets of Genoa. There is clearly more at stake in the concept of globalization than there ever was with postmodernism. There is a politics that extends far beyond the establishment of aesthetic categories to the determination of the shape of the present and the future—including the role played by culture in this future. Even if both concepts function as periodizing terms for the present, globalization is about blood, soil, life, and death in ways that postmodernism could only ever pretend to be.

The public ambition of the concept of globalization makes it clear that there are two broad uses of this concept that need to be separated. Significantly, the confusions over the exact meaning and significance of globalization that has characterized much academic discussion have *not* in fact cropped up in the constitution of globalization's public persona. Far from it, the wide-ranging debate in the academy over the precise meaning of globalization might point to the fact that it is a concept open to re-narration and re-metaphorization, thereby keeping focus, too, on the unstable relationship between the realities the term names and its heuristic role in grappling with this reality. Like any concept, it is not equivalent to reality, but a way of producing some meaningful interpretive order out of the chaos of experience. Against this status, however, one must consider the function of the widespread public consensus that has developed on what globalization means. This is globalization in its most familiar garb: the name for a process that (in the last instance) is understood as economic at its core. Globalization here is about accelerated trade and finance on a global scale, with everything else measured in reference to these dimensions. Although one can have normative disagreements about the outcome and impact of these economic forces (does it "lift all boats," bringing prosperity to everyone? does it merely restore the power of economic elites after a brief interval of Keynesianism?), what the public discourse on globalization insists on is, first, the basic, immutable objectivity of these economic processes, and second, that these processes now lie at the core of human experience, whether one likes it or not.

It is in this way that the discourse of globalization carries out what has to be seen as its major function: to transform contingent social relations into immutable facts of history. It carries out this reifying function in a novel way. Unlike the categories of the political economists of Marx's time, globalization insists not on the permanence of social classes, but on the coming into being of *new* social relations, technologies, and economic relationships. The overall effect is the same, however. Old-style political economy reified capitalism by insisting that existing social relations would extend indefinitely and unalterably into the future, based on their origins in the very nature of things. New-style globalization also makes a claim on the inevitability of capitalism and the persistence of the present into the future. However, its necessary imbrication with the "new"—globalization always being the name for something distinctly different than what came before it—means that it cannot so easily appeal to nature or ontology to insist on the unchanging character of the future. Rather, borrowing a page from Marxism, globalization offers a narrative of the historical development of social forces over time, the slow (now accelerating) transformation of individuals and societies from the inchoate mess of competing and warring nationalisms to a full-fledged global-liberal-capitalist civilization. Thus, famously does Francis Fukuyama (1993) appropriate the movement of the Hegelian dialectic to capitalist ends. He argues that the lack of alternatives to capitalism, signalled by the collapse of communism, coincides with the "end of history" as such: there will only be capitalism from now on, and, of course, it will be everywhere, on a global scale. The erasure of the distinction between globalization as a conceptual apparatus and the name for contemporary reality as such is hardly an accident—or at least no more so than the categories of classical political economy. It is, rather, a political project through and through, meant (in the terms that I have outlined here) to deliberately confuse the potential analytic functions of the concept of "globalization" with an affirmation of unchanging reality of global capitalism as both "what is" and "what will be." In changing circumstances that *have* opened up new realities and political possibilities, the public face of globalization aims not only to keep capitalism at the center of things, but to clear the field of all possible challenges and objections.

Some clarification is in order here. I have claimed that globalization is a political project, which suggests some organizing force or set of actors or agents behind the scenes pulling the levers of state and economy in order to shape the world into a desired state. This claim would make globalization a strictly ideological concept, a knowing sleight of hand by which the Grand Inquisitors of Davos pull the wool over the world's eyes. It would be naïve as well as empirically incorrect to deny that actors in industry and the state have actively participated in the reconstitution of relations between state and capital on a global scale for their own benefit, with consequences ranging from the release of public assets to the market at fire sale rates, to the increasingly precarious state of global labor markets (Arrighi, 2005; Comaroff and Comaroff, 2000; Harvey, 2005a; Harvey, 2005b). At the same time, there is a tendency by many critics to ascribe too much insight and control over the system of neoliberal globalization to specific individuals (CEOs, government leaders, etc) or institutional elements (government agencies, WTO, IMF, etc.). It is as if to suggest that these actors view globalization from the outside and with a clarity that allows for the perfect decision to be made in every case.

The politics of our global era do not permit an easy reliance on a vision of the social order in which change can be achieved by cutting off the head of the king. Globalization as an ideological discourse (in the way I have described it) appears within an already entrenched social and political system, which is the product of the dynamics and techniques of modernity's structuring of the social order and the production of subjectivities. This modernity is one whose logics, it has to be added, extended across the ideological divide of the Cold War: modernization and Taylorization represented the future for the Soviets and the West alike. The fundamental drive of the system as a whole continues to lie in the core imperative of capitalism: the unlimited accumulation of capital by formally peaceful means (Budgen, 2000: 151). As Michael Hardt and Antonio Negri argue, the tension that exists within this social fantasy—endless accumulation without strife—has been dissipated historically through the availability of an "outside" to the system of capital where surpluses can be actualized, thus avoiding the potential social trauma of overproduction (Hardt and Negri, 2000: 221–239). The moment when capital finally finds itself victoriously spread across the globe—its extensivity confirming its supposed superiority as a social as well as economic system—is also a moment when its contradictions, inhumanity, and fundamental absurdity become increasingly evident, especially as processes of "accumulation by dispossession" (Harvey, 2005b: 137–182) accelerate. As the collective Retort (2006: 8) points out, "insofar as the spectacle of social order presents itself now as a constant image-flow of contentment, obedience, enterprise, and uniformity, it is, equally constantly, guaranteed by the exercise of state power. Necessarily so, since contentment, obedience, enterprise, and uniformity involve the suppression of their opposites, which the actual structure and texture of everyday life reproduce—and intensify—just as fast as the spectacle assures us they are things of the past."

In this context, both ideology and state intervention reappear as necessary to maintain order and stability. The public discourse of globalization engages in the effort to secure the existing social order at all costs, but not only because of the obvious benefits it provides to some. There is a systemic effect at work, which comes out of deep, intensive social commitments to order, expertise, technology, progress, consumption, and capital. Margaret Thatcher's turn to the ideas of von Hayek, Milton Friedman, and others, originates not as a strictly ideological move; it is one occasioned by the need to resolve seemingly intractable economic problems within the existing framework of liberal democracy. Although the championing of markets, private property, and entrepreneurial energies may have pushed the state toward the market away from social welfare, commitments to these ideals were hardly external to the modern state to begin with. All power here is on the side of modernity. In the absence of compelling or convincing alternative political narratives, the social chaos engendered by neoliberalism all the more powerfully confirms its necessity. Existing systems alone appear to have the capacity to manage the radical economic and social change that has produced the economic instability and social precariousness in which we all live.

Globalization and Literary Criticism

How does this account of globalization open up new possibilities for literature and literary criticism? Perhaps the major response to globalization within literary studies has been to redefine its practices in light of a world of transnational connections and communications. Globalization has often been interpreted as signalling the end of the nation-state and of the parochialisms of national culture. Waking up to the limits of its own reliance on the nation as a key organizing principle, literary studies and poetics have thus come to insist on the need to take into account the global character of literary production, influence, and dissemination. Much of contemporary literary studies have focused correspondingly on the transfer and movement of culture: its shift from one place to another, its newfound mobility, and the challenges of its extraction, de-contextualization, and re-contextualization at new sites. At one level, this encounter of criticism with "globalization" has simply required the extension or elaboration of existing discourses and concepts, such as diaspora, cosmopolitanism, the politics and poetics of the "Other," and the language of postcolonial studies in general. For many critics, literary criticism was already moving toward globalization in any case, or was even there in advance, as suggested by accounts stressing the existence of global literary relations long before the present moment (Greenblatt, 2001).

There have been other developments as well. There has once again been serious attention to the politics of translation and renewed focus on the institutional politics of criticism, especially the global dominance of theory and cultural criticism by Western discourses (Spivak, 2003; Kumar, 2003). There have also been new sociologically-inspired "mapping" projects that have sought to explore how literary and cultural forms have developed and spread across the space of the globe (Casanova, 2005; Moretti, 1996). Finally, criticism has taken up an investigation of new literary works whose content, at least, criticizes and explores the tensions and traumas produced by globalization—a potentially huge set of works given the fact that globalization is often taken to be coincident with contemporary geo-politics as such. There have been rich critical discoveries in every one of these attempts to take up in literature and criticism the challenges—real or imagined—posed by globalization.

However productive and interesting such analyses are, there is nevertheless a way in which they are all too willing to take globalization at face value. They acquiesce to the character and priority of capital's own transnational logics and movements, instead of questioning and assessing more carefully the narrative that underlies them. The critical agenda is thus set by the operations of globalization *qua* global capital. The need for criticism to concentrate its own energies on movement and border-crossings, while not entirely misplaced, comes across as rearguard manoeuvres to catch up with phenomena that have already taken place at some other more meaningful or important level. In this anxious attempt to claim the terrain of the global and the transnational for culture and criticism, the minimized role of culture within the narrative of globalization that emerges out of the comparison of globalization with postmodernism is troublingly reaffirmed, even if this affirmation is not the intent of these various and varied new approaches to culture in the era of globalization.

This is not to say that the approaches to globalization described above are without impact or value. It is simply to call attention to the fact that the project called globalization demands other responses that address directly its rhetorical and fictional character, and in particular, the ideological attempt to seal off the future through the assertion of a present that cannot be gainsaid. At one level, such a response would simply be to remind us insistently of the fiction that is the public face of globalization. It calls attention to and exposes the endless employment of rhetoric in the struggle over the public's perception of the significance and meaning of the actions of businesses and governments, people, and publics in shaping the present for the future, and indeed, in shaping what constitutes "possibility" itself. What better practice to do this than literary criticism, which is characterized by nothing other than its attention to the powerful uses (and abuses) of language in shaping and mediating our encounter with the world? The consistent anthropomorphisms applied to globalization, which make globalization into a beast that penetrates markets, speeds up time, breaks boundaries, and changes the world seemingly independently of human involvement is one of the key issues that criticism can bring to the fore.

This is just one possibility, and one which still seems to leave the literary in the dust of globalization by turning literature and literary criticism into a broader form of cultural criticism; its continued utility is justified only by its usefulness as a tool against ideology. The object of literary studies in this case would be the tropes and turns of language used explicitly to shape public perception: "axis of evil," "weapons of mass destruction," "democracy," "progress," and even "development," "empowerment," and the like (Cornwall and Brock, 2005). The political possibilities of literature and criticism today are in any case larger and more general than these terms, if also perhaps less satisfactorily and explicitly definable, and, unfortunately, more troubled and difficult as well. I have introduced two senses of globalization: one which remains open to debate and re-narrativization, even about so fundamental an issue as "when" globalization might be; and another, which seems to know definitively when (now) and what (global trade) globalization is. The second globalization aims to undo and even to eliminate the contradictions and confusions opened up by the first, in order to reassert capitalism's ontological legitimacy. The political possibilities that globalization opens up for the literary can be grasped only by asking the question of why capitalism needs the new rhetoric of "globalization" at this time. Why does the lumbering beast of capital have to be re-described and given perhaps even greater autonomy than it possesses in its most metaphorically potent guise as the "invisible hand"? Do not the old categories of political economy continue to assert their mystificatory role in the ways that they have for so long?

The negative answer to this last question is pointed to in the very instability of the concept of globalization. Its claim to articulate uniquely the new and the future leaves it open to endless doubts and questions that require its ideological dimensions to be affirmed anew over and over again (for two recent examples, see Tierney, 2005; "The New World," 2005)—not least as a result of the "suppression of opposites" described above by Retort. Globalization is breathlessly confident, a master narrative that demands that all other concepts, ideas, and practices be redefined in relation to it. And yet, the insistence of globalization narratives on the absolute priority of the economic also interrupts its legitimacy at the moment it imagines itself as most forcefully asserting it.

Critical Imaginings

In the colonization of the globe by capital, and the simultaneously geographic spread of communication technologies and cultural forms of all kinds, we might imagine that the reign of commodity fetishism, for instance, is affirmed as never before. But as capital reaches the limits of the globe, there is another story emerging which shakes its hold over the future. If the globalization of production has necessitated new narratives of the "good" of trade liberalization—the "good" of capital—it is because the complex, dispersed modes of contemporary production have not hidden away the social realities of production in the absent corners of the globe, but has rather drawn ever more attention to the social relations embedded in commodities. In *Capital,* Marx famously writes that "so soon as [a table] steps forth as a commodity, it is changed into something transcendent. It not only stands with its feet on the ground, but, in relation to all other commodities, it stands on its head, and evolves out of its wooden brain grotesque ideas" (Marx, 1976: 165). But what tables today dare to evolve out of their wooden brains' grotesque ideas or dance of their own free will? They must instead give an account of their productive parentage: from where did they come? How and by whom were they made? (By child laborers? By well-paid unionized workers?) For what purpose? Under what conditions? (In sweat shops? On industrial farms? In third-world tax havens?), and, at what cost to that ultimate social limit, the environment? Though no less part of the system of exchange, the commodity today can no longer be depended on to buttress capitalism by shielding from view the social relations that create it. The response offered by the narrative of globalization is not to hide these social relations, but to claim first their inevitability, and then to provide a utopic future-oriented claim about a coming global community in which the traumas of the present will be resolved in the fluid shuttling of freely traded goods around the world.

The utopia offered by the dominant narrative of globalization is one that has to be rejected, perhaps along with the concept itself, which has become so deeply associated with the current drive and desire of capital as to make it now almost impossible to wrest anything conceptually productive from it. The focus should instead be on the production of new concept-metaphors that might open up politically efficacious re-narrativizations of the present with the aim of creating new visions of the future. For all its ubiquity and hegemonic thrust, the instability of the concept of globalization presents an opportunity to do so; and so, far from being sidelined in globalization, there is an opening for creative critical thinking of all kinds to intervene and generate alternatives. It is here that literary and cultural production and literary criticism have roles to play: not only to shock us into recognition of reality through ideological critique, but also to spark the imagination so that we can see possibility in a world with apparently few escape hatches.

Why concept-*metaphor*? At its most basic level, metaphor involves the production of identity through substitution in a manner that opens up new and unexpected relationships and ideas. Metaphor is fundamental to literary language; it is what distinguishes it from mere reportage, nonfiction, or journalism. The phenomenological chaos that those concepts which are circulated between state and institutional social science are meant to tame or foreclose is the very medium of literary and cultural narrative—what they puzzle over and tarry with. While elements of the discourse of globalization may employ metaphor, globalization as such is *anti*-metaphoric. Even as it appeals to innovation and creativity for its increasingly immaterial, informational economy, it nonetheless demands a resolution or adjournment of time in order to control and manage the newness thus brought into life. This is no doubt why, as I have argued earlier, the aesthetic has disappeared from globalization; if "culture" shows up at all, it is in the guise of a commodity that contributes to economic vitality (as in Richard Florida's "creative class") or as a form whose main purpose is to ameliorate social problems through state cultural programs and national cultural policy (Yúdice, 2003). Through metaphor, on the country, temporality is subjected to interrogation and dead objects and concepts are brought back to life through the evocation of impossible identifications. It is in this way that newness comes into the world and the presence is not all that remains.

For what is genuinely lacking today is the imaginative vocabulary and narrative resources through which it might not only be possible to challenge the dominant narrative of globalization, but to articulate alternative modes of understanding those processes that have come to shape the present—and the future. This need is often narrowly imagined as a political lack, the absence of a big idea to take the place of state socialism after the collapse of the Soviet Union and the colonization of the Western left by disastrous "third way" political approaches. The imaginative resources that are needed to shape a new future are, however, necessarily broader—or at least, a new political vision is impossible without a revived poetics of social and cultural experience as well. This evocation of imagination in relation to poetics and the politics of globalization can be read in the wrong way: at best, as an appeal to Arjun Appadurai's (1996) still shaky use of "imagination" in his influential *Modernity at Large*; at worst, as a Romantic, idealist faith in the autonomous origin of ideas and their power to shape reality. What I have in mind is neither of these, rather Peter Hitchcock's use of "imagination as process" in his account of the promise of a theoretical manoeuvre that would be able to seize upon the conceptual openings that "globalization" has generated within capital itself. He writes that

> [w]hile there are many ways to think of the globe there is yet no convincing sense of imagining difference globally. The question of persuasiveness is vital, because at this time the globalism most prevalent and the one that is busily being the most persuasive is global capitalism. To pose culture alone as a decisive blow to global modes of economic exploitation is idealist in the extreme... Yet, because such exploitation depends upon a rationale, a rhetoric of globalism if you will, so culture may intervene in the codes of that imaginary, deploying imagination itself as a positive force for alternative modes of Being and being conscious in the world. (Hitchcock, 2003: 1)

There is a great deal that can be said here about the possibilities and limits of literature and literary criticism in reference to the imagination and persuasiveness. On the one hand, it is meaningless to assert that literature in general produces, through narrative and through metaphor, social visions other than the ones we work through in daily life. The kind of genre literature that comprises most the market for literary texts reinforces the dynamics and logics of capitalism. Or does it? Even in such cases, the need to reproduce the entire world in fictional form recreates, whether implicitly or explicitly, the tensions and contradictions between the experience of the world and the discourses meant to describe this experience. In other cases, from Jamaica Kincaid's *A Small World* to Mahasweta Devi's *Imaginary Maps*, or from Paulo Lins' *City of God* to the Peter Watts' Rifters trilogy (which explores a capitalism that persists into the future despite its intense contradictions), the aim is precisely to give flesh to the abstractions of globalization and to highlight the contradictions of neoliberalism. The point here is to insist on the importance of these imaginings, drenched in the metaphoric, as a counterweight to those discourses of globalization that claim to have already put everything in its place, including literature and culture more generally. What is more difficult to assert and to argue for is the significance or importance of this or that specific text, their persuasiveness, or their impact on imagination and the generation of "alternative modes of Being." In his exploration of the increasing use of "culture as resource" today, George Yúdice (2003: 9) writes that "the role of culture has expanded in an unprecedented way into the political and economic at the same time that conventional notions of culture largely have been emptied out." If literary texts and critical approaches to them do not constitute a program to up end or overcome the deprivations and limits of globalization, at a minimum they engage in a refusal of the contemporary prohibition on metaphor and its imaginative possibilities.

Rather than give a determinate account of the how and why of the ways in which culture can intervene into the imaginary, I want to leave this sense of imagination open and suggestive, and end by discussing briefly one more shift for aesthetics, in general, and literature, in particular, in relation to globalization. If we are to speak about the imaginary and its powers in the way Hitchcock does, we can do so today only in reference to an aesthetic that is very different than is normally conceptualized. This is an aesthetic that no longer claims its potential political effect by being transcendent to the social, but by being fully immanent to it. A half-century or more of literary and cultural criticism has insisted that culture be viewed as part of the social whole—generated out of and in response to its contradictions, its certainties as well as its uncertainties, an exemplar of its division of labor and its use of symbolic forms to perpetuate class differences through the game of "distinction." For those invested in a literary or cultural politics premised on a vision of the autonomy of art and culture from social life, the demand to take into account the social character of the literary comes as a loss, as does the more general massification of culture, which seems to announce the draining of the energies of the poem, the novel, the art work. Insofar as globalization has also been seen as announcing a "prodigious expansion of culture throughout the social real, to the point at which everything in our social life… can be said to have become 'cultural'" (Jameson, 1998: 48), it, too, seems to suggest the general decline of the politics of culture. This is no doubt why globalization is construed as a threat to poetics: it is nothing less than mass culture writ large over the face of the globe.

But this is the wrong lesson to draw from the folding of the aesthetic into the social, or of the expansion of culture to encapsulate everything. In his assessment of the politics of avant-garde, Peter Bürger identifies the contradictory function of the concept of "autonomy" in the consti-tution of the aesthetic: it identifies the real separation of art from life, but covers over the social and historical origins of this separation in capitalist society. The aim of the historical avant-garde—and perhaps I could venture to say all artistic movements since Kant—is to reject the deadened rationality of capitalist society through the creation of "a new life praxis from a basis in art" (Bürger, 1985: 49). Bürger suggests that this had already happened by the middle of the 20th century. Art had been integrated into life, but through the "false sublation" of the culture industry rather than through the avant-garde. In the process, he claims that what has been lost is the "free space within which alternatives to what exists become conceivable" (54). Yet to see the sublation of art into life through mass culture as "false" or as a "loss" requires the affirmation of the problematic autonomy of art from life produced by social divisions that we should be glad to see dissolved. That these divisions have not been dissolved by the culture industry, but have taken new forms, is clear; equally clear, however, should be the fact that the ability of culture to conceive alternatives, far from lost, has been diffused across the spectrum of cultural forms, which is why the imaginative capacity I am pointing to above can potentially come from anywhere. What an immanent aesthetic lacks that a transcendent one possessed in spades is that revolutionary spirit that animated 19th- and 20th-century politics and culture, in which the right moment or perfect cultural object could—all on its own—shatter the ossified face of social reality. The writer or artist as vanguardist guardian of the good and the true is definitively over. But to this we can only say: good riddance. Welcome in instead a politics and poetics that proceeds uncertainly, through half-measures and missteps, through intention and accident, through the dead nightmare of the residual and the conservative drag of hitherto existing reality on all change, in full view of the fact that nothing is accomplished easily or all-at-once, or in absence of the collective energies of all of humanity, and through the imaginative possibilities of literature, yes, but other cultural forms, too.

A Final Word

Repudiation of the present cultural morass presupposes sufficient involvement in it to feel itching in one's finger tips, so to speak, but at the same time the strength, drawn from this involvement, to dismiss it.

Theodor Adorno, *Minima Moralia*

So much for the function of culture at the present moment. But I cannot end without asking directly: what of the autonomy of the critic? The question of autonomy—the precise relationship of structure to agency (if, indeed, agency exists at all) in the field of culture—has been perhaps the central theme of literary and cultural criticism since 1968. Every major critic and theorist of the period, from Louis Althusser to Slavoj Zizek, has struggled to formulate how individual and/or collective agency functions in a period in which—for reasons of global scale as well as technological "advance"—human social life seems shaped and controlled in ever more extreme, invasive, and unstoppable ways. Thus, we have the development of ideas such as Michel Foucault's biopower, Pierre Bourdieu's *habitus,* and numerous others, which offer narratives of a structure that generate the very forms of (imagined) agency that might then want to resist the system. It is a classic chicken-and-egg problem, if one encumbered with more abstruse vocabulary and the weight of the whole history of philosophy.

If individual subjects are produced by the structures in which they live (and how could it be otherwise?), the very ability of critical thought to grasp these structures—to paint a picture of the circumstances in which we find ourselves, clearly and explicitly as if from the "outside"—must necessarily come into question. At the end of *Dialectic of Enlightenment* (1944), their savage and hugely influential account of the dead end of the Enlightenment in the parking lot of the cultural industries, Max Horkheimer and Theodor Adorno pause to reflect on the conditions that make possible their own critical vantage point. They claim that their critique can emerge only because they occupy an unusual position: the interstices between the end of classical German philosophy and the burgeoning of American mass culture. It is only because the former is radically incommensurate with the latter that Horkheimer and Adorno could "hate [both of them] properly" (Adorno, 1974: 52) and in so doing introduce the mode of criticism that has come generally to be referred to as critical theory.

This is a very specific location, a critical vantage point created only as result of the trauma of World War II, which saw members of the Frankfurt School relocated to Los Angeles. But this structural misfit is perhaps more general than this example might suggest, extending to *all* literary and cultural criticism. Antonio Gramsci (1971, 5) made a useful distinction between two kinds of intellectuals: traditional and organic. Organic intellectuals are those who work with ideas and thus give capital "homogeneity and an awareness of its function not only in the economic but also in the social and political fields." For Gramsci, the exemplary organic intellectual for the contemporary age was the engineer; in our moment of finance capitalism and dreams of the "creative class," academics and cultural workers—all those who might be referred to as "content providers" (O'Brien and Szeman, 2003)—are if not examples of model intellectuals, then certainly part of the mix of the "idea men" necessary for the functioning of the present.

At the same time, what distinguishes intellectuals in the humanities from their brethren in some other parts of the university (research scientists, engineers) is that they also occupy a position that is decidedly out-of-step with the times—a "residual" position which makes them both connected to, and yet separate from, the dominant ideas of the moment (Bourdieu's memorable phrase for this class was "the dominated fraction of the dominant class"). To put this point in Gramscian terms, literary and cultural critics are also "traditional" intellectuals—traditional understood here not as an evaluative term but as the name for a *structural* category that does not depend on the subject of analysis (Manet or multimedia; Flaubert or film). For Gramsci (1971: 7), traditional intellectuals are connected to one another across time. Since "traditional intellectuals experience through an '*esprit de corps*' their uninterrupted historical continuity and their special qualification, they put themselves forward as autonomous and independent of the dominant social group"; the lack of synchrony with the present, sometimes experienced by intellectuals as a frustration, is in fact a source of their analytic strength. It is this simultaneous connection to the present and filiation to the past that creates a position in which a degree of autonomous thought—a critical vantage-point on the present—is made possible.

And it is perhaps at the moment of globalization that this vantage point emerges with special force. As I suggested above, culture in globalization is simultaneously imagined to be everywhere and yet treated as inconsequential as a result of this very ubiquity. The attempt by the narrative of globalization to write cultural criticism out of the picture is a sign of the force and importance of this practice. Slavoj Zizek (1994: 5) asks: "Does not the critique of ideology involve a privileged place, somehow exempted from the turmoils of social life, which enables some subject-agent to perceive the very hidden mechanism that regulates social visibility and non-visibility? Is not the claim that we can accede to this place the most obvious case of ideology?" Put this way, it is essential to be vigilant about the simple belief that the critic stands above and outside of social life in a way that allows her to understand the mechanisms that produce reality. But it would be equally ideological to acquiesce to a global narrative that has tried ceaselessly to transform this genuine and necessary critical suspicion of a pure critical autonomy into a belief that literary and cultural critics cannot do anything at all.

References

Adorno, Theodor. 1974. *Minima Moralia: Reflections from Damaged Life*. Ed. E.F.N. Jephcott. London: New Left Books.

Appadurai, Arjun. 1996. *Modernity at Large*. Minneapolis: University of Minnesota Press.

Anderson, Perry. 1998. *The Origins of Postmodernity*. New York: Verso.

Arrighi, Gionvanni. 2005. "Hegemony Unravelling–I," *New Left Review*, 32: 23–80.

Bürger, Peter. 1985. *Theory of the Avant-Garde*. Ed. Michael Shaw. Minneapolis: University of Minnesota Press.

Budgen, Sebastian. 2000. "A New 'Spirit of Capitalism'," *New Left Review*, 1: 149–156.

Comaroff, Jean and John L. Comaroff. 2000. "Millennial Capitalism: First Thoughts on a Second Coming," *Public Culture*, 12(2): 291–343.

Cornwall, Andrea and Karen Brock. 2005. "What Do Buzzwords Do for Development Policy? A Critical Look at 'Participation,' 'Empowerment' and 'Poverty Reduction'," *Third World Quarterly*, 26(7): 1043–1060.

Casanova, Pascale. 2005. *The World Republic of Letters*. Cambridge: Harvard University Press.

Der Spiegel. 2005. "The New World." *Der Spiegel*, Special International Edition 7:3.

Fukuyama, Francis. 1993. *The End of History and the Last Man*. Toronto: HarperCollins Canada.

Gramsci, Antonio. 1971. *Selections from the Prison Notebooks*. Ed. Quintin Hoare and Geoffrey Nowell Smith. New York: International Publishers.

Greenblatt, Stephen. 2001. "Racial Memory and Literary History," *PMLA*, 116(1): 48–63.

Hardt, Michael and Antonio Negri. 2000. *Empire*. Cambridge: Harvard University Press.

Horkheimer, Max and Theodor Adorno. 1988. *Dialectic of Enlightenment*. Ed. John Cumming. New York: Continuum.

Hitchcock, Peter. 2003. *Imaginary States: Studies in Cultural Transnationalism*. Chicago: University of Illinois Press.

Harvey, David. 2005a. *A Brief History of Neoliberalism*. New York: Oxford University Press.

———. 2005b. *The New Imperialism*. New York: Oxford University Press.

Jameson, Fredric. 1991. *Postmodernism, or, the Cultural Logic of Late Capitalism*. Durham, NC: Duke University Press.

———. 1998. *The Cultural Turn: Selected Writings on the Postmodern, 1993–1998*. New York: Verso.

Kumar, Amitava (ed.). 2003. *World Bank Literature*. Minneapolis: University of Minnesota Press.

Kellner, Douglas. 2006. *Globalization and the Postmodern Turn*. UCLA Graduate School of Education and Information Studies' ED 253A course web page. Available at www.gseis.ucla.edu/courses/ed253a/dk/GLOBPM.htm.

Lyotard, Jean-Francois. 1985. *The Postmodern Condition: A Report on Knowledge*. Ed. Brian Massumi. Minneapolis: University of Minnesota Press.

Marx, Karl. 1976. *Capital*. vol. 1. Ed. Ben Fowkes. New York: Penguin.

Moretti, Franco. 1996. *Modern Epic: The World-System from Goethe to García Márquez*. Ed. Quintin Hoare. New York: Verso.

O'Brien, Susie and Imre Szeman. 2003. Content providers of the world unite! The cultural politics of globalization. Working Paper GHC 03/3, Hamilton, ON: Institute on Globalization and the Human Condition Working Paper Series, McMaster University.

Retort. "An Exchange on *Afflicted Powers: Capital and Spectacle in a New Age of War*." *October* 115 (2006): 3–12.

Spivak, Gayatri Chakravorty. 2003. *Death of a Discipline*. New York: Columbia University Press.

Tierney, John. 2005. "The Idiots Abroad," *NY Times*, A27, November 8.

Yúdice, George. 2003. *The Expediency of Culture*. Durham, NC: Duke University Press.

Zizek, Slavoj. 1994. "Introduction: The Spectre of Ideology," in S. Zizek (ed.), *Mapping Ideology*, pp. 1–33. New York: Verso.

About the Editors and Contributors

Editors

Samir Dasgupta is a Professor of Sociology at the University of Kalyani, West Bengal, India. He is the Former Director of College Development Council, Kalyani University, Former Visiting Faculty, Department of Agriculture and Rural Development in West Bengal State University, and Advisory Committee Member of the Centre for the Study of Social Exclusion and Inclusive Policy, University of Calcutta. His research interests lie on Applied Sociology, Development Studies and Sociology of Globalization, Urban Sociology, Economic Sociology, Environment Studies, and Peace Studies. He has received an award from the University of Kalyani for his contribution to the promotion of culture.

He is the author of more than fifty research papers and twenty two book chapters. His publications include: *The Changing Face of Globalization* (edited volume, 2004); *Globalization and After* (co-edited with Ray Kiely, 2006); *Discourse on Applied Sociology: Theoretical Perspectives* (co-edited with Robyn Driskell, 2007); *Discourse on Applied Sociology: Practicing Perspectives* (co-edited with Robyn Driskell, 2007); *Politics of Globalization* with Jan Nederveen Pieterse (2009); *Understanding the Global Environment* (2010); *Arthanaitik Samajtatwa* (2011); and *Globalization and Humanity* (Authored, 2011).

He serves as an editorial board member of the international journal *Nature and Culture*, U.S.A and Leipzeig, Germany, and *International Journal of Business Ethics in Developing Economies*.

Peter Kivisto is Richard A. Swanson Professor of Social Thought and Chair of Sociology, Anthropology and Social Welfare at Augustana College and Finland Distinguished Professor at the University of Turku. His current research involves a collaborative project on multiculturalism with colleagues in Finland. His interests include immigration, social integration, citizenship, and religion. Among his recent books are *Key Ideas in Sociology* (2011), *Illuminating Social Life* (2011); *Beyond a Border: The Causes and Consequences of Contemporary Immigration* (2010, with Thomas Faist); *Citizenship: Discourse, Theory and Transnational Prospects* (2007, with Thomas Faist); and *Intersecting Inequalities* (2007, with Elizabeth Hartung). He serves on the editorial boards of *Contexts, Ethnic and Racial Studies, Journal of Intercultural Studies*, and on the Publication Committee for *Sociology of Religion*.

Contributors

Ananda Das Gupta has been engaged in teaching and research for more than eighteen years. Currently he is Head (HRD-Area). His core areas of teaching and research include Organizational Development, Strategic Human Resources Management, Corporate Social Responsibility, and Business Ethics at Indian Institute of Plantation Management, Bangalore. Ananda Das Gupta's books include the following: *Human Values in Management*, 2004; *Ethics in Business*, 2005; *Corporate Citizenship: Perspectives in the New Century*, 2008; and *Ethics, Business and Society* (ed.), 2010.

Gabe Ignatow is an Associate Professor of Sociology at the University of North Texas. He is a sociological theorist with research interests in cultural theory (with a focus on individual-society and mind-body interactions, text analysis methods, new media, and the sociology of morality), and globalization theory (focusing on the effects of globalization on developing countries in the areas of information policy, environmental politics, religious change, and philanthropy). He is a faculty fellow at the Center for Cultural Sociology at Yale University. His major publications include *Traditional Identity Politics and the Government*, 2007.

Lindsey A. Johnson is a doctoral student in Sociology at the University of North Texas. Her research interests include globalization, development, inequality, and religion.

Douglas Kellner is George Kneller Chair in the Philosophy of Education at UCLA and is the author of many books on social theory, politics, history, and culture, including *Camera Politica: The Politics and Ideology of Contemporary Hollywood Film*, co-authored with Michael Ryan (1988), and an Emile de Antonio Reader co-edited with Dan Streible (2000). Other works include: *Critical Theory, Marxism, and Modernity* (1989); *Jean Baudrillard: From Marxism to Postmodernism and Beyond* (1989); works in cultural studies such as *Media Culture* (1995) and *Media Spectacle* (2003); a trilogy of books on postmodern theory with Steve Best in 2010; he published in 2010 *Cinema Wars: Hollywood Film and Politics in the Bush/Cheney Era* and *Media Spectacle and Insurrection, 2011: From the Arab Uprisings to Occupy Everywhere* in 2012.

Jason L. Mast was a visiting fellow at the Yale University's Center for Cultural Sociology. Since then he has been a postdoctoral fellow at the Karl Mannheim Chair for Cultural Studies at Zeppelin University in Germany. Mast writes on culture, politics, knowledge, and innovation, is the author of *The Performative Presidency* (2012) and the co-editor of *Social Performance* (2006).

Murray Milner, Jr., is Professor Emeritus of Sociology at the University of Virginia and is currently a fellow at the Institute for Advanced Studies in Culture. Much of his work applies his theory of status relations to an array of different status systems such as the Indian caste system, American teenagers, contemporary celebrities, and human rights. He is the author of four books: *The Illusion of Equality: The Effects of Educational Opportunity on Inequality and Conflict* (1972); *Unequal Care: A Case Study of Interorganizational Relations in Health Care* (1980); *Status and Sacredness: A General Theory of Status Relations and an Analysis of Indian Culture* (1994); *Freaks, Geeks, and Cool Kids: American Teenagers, Schools; and the Culture of Consumption* (2004).

Mahbuba Nasreen is the Director of the Institute of Disaster Management and Vulnerability Studies (IDMVS), University of Dhaka. She has been involved in research in the areas of Gender, Environment, Disasters, Education, Disadvantaged groups such as women, poor, Indigenous community, and other areas of Social Development since 1988. She joined as a Lecturer in the Department of Sociology and became Professor at the same department in 2005, University of Dhaka.

Jan Nederveen Pieterse is Mellichamp Professor of Global Studies and Sociology at University of California, Santa Barbara and specializes in globalization, development studies, and cultural studies. He is honorary Professor of Globalization at Maastricht University. He has been serving as a Visiting Professor in Argentina, Brazil, China, Germany, India, Indonesia, Japan, Pakistan, South Africa, Sri Lanka, Sweden, and Thailand. He edits book series on *Emerging Societies* (Routledge) and *Frontiers of Globalization* (Palgrave Macmillan), is the co-editor of *e-Journal of Global Studies*. He has written numerous books including:

- *Is There Hope for Uncle Sam? Beyond the American Bubble* (2008)
- *Ethnicities and Global Multiculture: Pants for an Octopus* (2007)
- *Globalization or Empire?* (2004)
- *Global Mélange: Globalization and Culture* (2003)
- *Development Theory: Deconstructions/Reconstructions* (2001)
- *Politics of Globalization* (co-edited, 2008)

Andy Scerri is Assistant Professor in Environmental Politics, Policy and Ethics at Virginia Polytechnic Institute and State University, Blacksburg, USA. His research and teaching center on two areas: environmental political and social theory and comparative studies of debates over urban sustainable development policies. He is author of *Greening Citizenship: Sustainable Development, the State and Ideology* (2012).

Nico Stehr is Karl Mannheim Professor of Cultural Studies at the Zeppelin University, Friedrichshafen, Germany. His research interests center on the transformation of modern societies into knowledge societies and developments associated with this transformation in different major social institutions of modern society. Among his recent book publications are: *Biotechnology: Between Commerce and Civil Society* (2004); *Knowledge* (with Reiner Grundmann, 2005); *Experts: The Knowledge and Power of Expertise* (with Reiner Grundmann, 2011); and the monograph, *The Power of Knowledge* (with Reiner Grundmann, 2012).

Rosalind A. Sydie is a Professor Emeritus, University of Alberta, Edmonton, Alberta, Canada. Her areas of interests are sociological theory, postmodern theory, gender, and art and culture, and she is currently researching gender configurations of urban spaces from a historical perspective. Her major publications include: *Sociological Theory* (co-authored, 2001) and "Beatrice Webb and Charlotte Perkins Gilman: Feminist Debates and Contradictions" in *Sociological Origins* (co-authored, 2000).

Imre Szeman is Canada Research Chair of Cultural Studies and Professor of English and Film Studies at the University of Alberta. His recent books include *Cultural Theory: An Anthology* (2010, co-ed); *After Globalization* (2011, with Eric Cazdyn); and *Contemporary Literary and Cultural Theory* (2012, co-ed). He is currently working on a book on the cultural politics of oil.

Immanuel Wallerstein is a Senior Research Scholar at Yale University. He was associated with Binghamton University as the Emeritus Professor of Sociology. A renowned Sociologist, he was the Director, Fernand Braudel for the study of Economies, Historical Systems, and Civilizations. He was also associated as the Professor of Sociology at McGill University and Columbia University. Professor Wallerstein was the President, International Sociological Association (1994–98). His major publications include:

- *World-Systems Analysis: Theory and Methodology* (1982)
- *Questioning Nineteenth-Century Assumptions about Knowledge: Reductionism* (2010)
- *Questioning Nineteenth-Century Assumptions about Knowledge: Determinism* (2010)
- *Questioning Nineteenth-Century Assumptions about Knowledge: Dualism* (2010)

Index